# COLUMBIA RIVER BASKETRY

*Gift of the Ancestors, Gift of the Earth*

# COLUMBIA RIVER BASKETRY

*Gift of the Ancestors, Gift of the Earth*

MARY DODDS SCHLICK

A SAMUEL AND ALTHEA STROUM BOOK
*University of Washington Press*
*Seattle and London*

This book is published with the assistance of a grant from the Stroum Book Fund, established through the generosity of Samuel and Althea Stroum.

Library of Congress Cataloging-in-Publication Data
Schlick, Mary Dodds.
   Columbia River basketry : gift of the ancestors, gift of the earth
/ Mary Dodds Schlick.
      p.  cm.
   "A Samuel and Althea Stroum book."
   Includes bibliographical references and index.
    1. Indians of North America—Columbia River Valley—Basket making. 2.
Basket making—Columbia River Valley—Classification. 3. Basket making—
Columbia River Valley—Themes, motives.  I. Title.
   E78.C64S35  1994
   746.41'2'089974–dc20            93-30658
   ISBN 0-295-97249-1 cl.; 0-295-97289-0 pbk.      CIP

Front matter illustrations:

p. ii: *The Reverend W. C. Curtis's collection of baskets arrayed in his study in the First Congregational Church at The Dalles, c. 1890. Photographer unknown. Maryhill Museum of Art cat. no. 1951.01.186.*

p. iii: *Varied rib patterning and tiny human figures as "filler" distinguish this unusual Wasco-style bag collected near Lyle, Washington, c. 1900. Private collection. Photo by Joseph Schlick.*

p. vi: *"Trunk" with Wasco-style figures collected by Mrs. Thomas Burke between 1900 and 1920. H11 in., W20 in. Photo by Joseph Schlick. Thomas Burke Memorial Washington State Museum cat. no. 2.2311.*

p. x: *Sally Buck, Yakima, uses cotton twine to weave a round twined bag. The design is in false embroidery. Photo by W. T. Schlick.*

*In memory of Na'iłas, Julia Pimms Sohappy,*
*my first teacher,*
*and to all the others who allowed me to learn*

# Contents

# Color Illustrations

# Foreword

The native people of the Mid-Columbia area inherited an art of basketry. This art is expressed in various forms that are created from materials gathered from the Mother Earth. Basketry is an important part of the native peoples' daily lives. When the basketry is shared with other cultures, there is an opportunity to increase understanding of the native people and their cultures. Thus, the accurate portrayal of historical and cultural information regarding native people is vitally important.

Information on Mid-Columbia basketry is either nonexistent or scattered in various places, which makes it extremely difficult to access needed information. This book fills that gap. It can be used as a handbook for collectors, museum curators, and librarians. The lay person interested in learning more about Mid-Columbia basketry and the people who make baskets will have an excellent resource.

The most qualified person to present this information is Mary Schlick. Mary is a respected friend of the native people in the Mid-Columbia area where she lives. She has gained many long-lasting friendships, particularly among the women, and was honored with the name Anipashnmí Latít (meaning "wild potato's blossom").

Mary researched Mid-Columbia basketry in libraries and museums. She learned how to create the various basketry forms and has gained an understanding of how the natural materials used to create the baskets were and are prepared. Importantly, her interpersonal skills enabled her to communicate with and learn from the native women who love and cherish the art of basketry. The native women willingly share their teachings with Mary.

Mary Schlick is a person who is willing to help bridge cultural gaps in a sensitive and positive manner. Her ability to communicate across cultures is one of many gifts that the Creator has given to her.

This book, *Columbia River Basketry: Gift of the Ancestors, Gift of the Earth,* is Mary's expression of her special gift.

MARTHA B. YALLUP, ED.D
*Deputy Director*
*Department of Human Services*
*Yakima Indian Nation*

# *Preface*

*"One can learn about a people from their arts."*

Nearly thirty years ago Blanche Tohet lifted the lid on a tin suitcase to show the extension agent and me the family treasures she was sending from her home on the Warm Springs Reservation in north central Oregon to the Wasco County Fair for the Indian exhibit. The wondrous sight of heirloom art and handwork stimulated in me an interest that has never waned.

That glimpse awakened me to the beauty of the basketry in all its forms created by the native people of the Mid-Columbia River. I had thought of baskets as the most fragile of all textiles, but here were ancient root storage bags that appeared to be new. These works of art that were at the same time utilitarian household objects linked my neighbors to their ancestors.

From that time I began to watch for the twined hats, round "sally" bags, flat twined "cornhusk" bags, coiled berry baskets, and folded bark baskets used and treasured by the people whose families came from the Mid-Columbia River, its tributaries, and the plateau above. I saw this work in museums, in private collections, and, of course, in the homes and gathering places of the people themselves. But I could find little about it to read. Much of what I did find had sketchy or inaccurate information about the materials or techniques, and especially about basketry's place in the lives of the people who made it.

The purpose of this book is to remedy that lack of information. If the book helps curators and collectors identify baskets from the Mid-Columbia area and understand and appreciate their full significance, and perhaps more importantly, if the book assists these and other educators in presenting the baskets in the context of the lives of the people who created and used them, it will have met its goal. Baskets are works of art, yes, but they also carry stories of human ingenuity and survival in the most generous sense. They can be tangible lessons in history, more easily "read" than a textbook.

I began my research with what first caught my eye, the endlessly varied designs on the flat storage bags known as "cornhusk" bags. The weaving in these bags is similar to needlepoint in appearance. To get a better sense of how the weaver developed her designs, I reproduced some in needlepoint. The results were beautiful, but told me nothing about the design's relationship to the process of weaving. I then asked Julia

Sohappy, the Yakima woman who was like a mother to me, to let me watch her at work. She agreed, and allowed me to photograph her as well.

The traditional learning method among the Mid-Columbia native people is to watch. Small children spent hours with their grandmothers watching and learning the traditional skills. I was accustomed to having things explained to me, and I did not have the child's long lifetime ahead of me in which to learn by observation. "Questions, questions!" my teacher and her daughters would say to me when I asked too many.

Turning to books, I found few sources of information on the twining techniques used by my neighbors. Finally, by studying the bags themselves, recalling my teacher's work, and with much trial and error, I "mastered," in a primitive way, the native twining methods used by the Chinookan-speaking and Sahaptin-speaking people of the Mid-Columbia River.

Understanding the process and something about the traditional materials has helped immeasurably in studying the baskets in museum and private collections. I have examined over five hundred baskets, and have studied photographs of and catalogue information for many more. I have gathered and processed materials, have watched most of the remaining basketmakers at work, and have talked with many others who remember seeing baskets made or who participated in their production in some way.

My awe at the artistry, skill, and sheer industry of the weavers who produced this great body of art is boundless, as is my envy as a basketmaker of the long winter hours available for such creative work. Now that I am a grandmother, I yearn for the time with grandchildren that was enjoyed by a long ago *katła* (mother's mother) or *ala* (father's mother).

In this book, I do not speak for the weavers; they have their own stories to tell. Klikitat basketmakers Nettie Jackson, Marie Slockish, and Elsie Thomas have done this well. I hope others will follow their example. I speak only from my own experience with this art that deserves special attention. My wish is to honor the basketmakers of the Mid-Columbia and their work.

Only a beginning, may this study generate many questions and inspire others to seek the answers.

MARY D. SCHLICK
*Mount Hood, Oregon*

# Acknowledgments

This work could not have been completed without the cooperation and active assistance of many people. I wish to express my particular gratitude to our neighbors and friends from the Colville, Warm Springs, and Yakima reservations who generously shared their lives, forgave my mistakes, and helped me learn.

On the Yakima Reservation: Gracie Ambrose; Lena Barney; Virginia Beavert; Delores Buck; Delores George; Sophie George; Robert and Ernestine Jim; Mr. and Mrs. Johnson Meninick; Joe Jay and Tallulah Pinkham; Elsie Pistolhead; Sarah Quaempts; Edith Sampson; Leona Schuster; Elsie Selam; James Selam; Leona Smartlowit; Julia Sohappy and her daughters Amelia, Lena, Laritta, LaRena, and Viola; Marie Slockish Teo; Loretta Thompson; Violet Tomaskin; Watson and Tilda Totus; Agnes Tulee; William Yallup.

On the river: Sally Slockish Buck; Mary Jack; Maggie Jim; Warner and Linda Jim; Ella Jim; Leonard Kuneki; Maynard Lavadour; Doreen Mahaffey; Sophie and Elsie Thomas; Esther Wilkenson.

At Warm Springs: Ruth Estebrook; Alice Florendo; Daisy Ike; Viola Kalama; Mary Ann Meanus; Madelaine Bruno St. Germaine; George Schneiter; Ernest Sconawah; Lucinda Smith; Gladys Thompson; Blanche Tohet and her daughters Bernice, Prosanna and Verbena; Faye Waheneka; Nelson Wallulatum; the staff of *Spilyay Tymoo*.

On the Colville Reservation: Ann Cleveland George.

Of greater importance than they know are new basketmakers and will-be basketmakers Pat Atkins, Arlene Boileau, Valerie Jim Calac, Bernyce Courtney, Pat Courtney Gold, Lillian Pitt, and Elizabeth Woody.

For general encouragement I would like to thank Violet Rau, Gary Young, Martha Yallup, the staff of the Yakima tribal preschool programs from 1970 to 1980, Violet Carpenter, and the people of Priest Rapids, Rock Creek, Satus, Simnasho, Toppenish Creek, Wapato, and Warm Springs longhouses.

I am also grateful to the following scholars; museum curators and staff; archives and library staff; and private collectors who opened their collections to me, answered my endless questions, and allowed me to examine and photograph their treasures:

Dell Hymes, Don Jackson, Mary Jane Leland, Sally McLendon, Nancy Russell, Helen Schuster, Charles Willson Sellers, and Andrew Hunter Whiteford.

Jonathan King, British Museum; Robin Wright and Pat Blankenship, Burke Museum, Seattle; Judy Thompson, Canadian Museum of Civilization; Rick McClure, Gifford Pinchot National Forest; Susan Harless, High Desert Museum; volunteers at Hood River County Museum; Avis O'Brien, Klickitat County Historical Society Museum; Nancy Blomberg, Los Angeles County Museum of Natural History; Frank Norick, Lawrence Dawson, Lowie Museum, Berkeley; Conrad Graham, McCord Museum, Montreal; Katherine Pettipas, Manitoba Museum of Man and Nature; Linda Mountain, Betty Long, Colleen Shafroth, and Lynette Miller, Maryhill Museum of Art; Bruce Bernstein, Museum of Indian Arts and Culture, Santa Fe; Tim Mulligan, National Archives; Linda Eisenhart, Susan Crawford, Felicia Pickering, Jane Walsh, National Museum of Natural History; Don E. Dumond and Pamela Endzweig, Oregon State Museum of Anthropology; Sally Bond, Peabody Museum, Harvard; Kittu Gates, Portland Art Museum; Dee Ulrich, Southwest Museum; Ann Rowe and Katherine Freshley, Textile Museum, Washington, D.C.

Alice Fleming, Mary L. Goodrich Library, Toppenish, Washington; Kathryn Thomas, June Knudson and the staff of Hood River County Library; the staff of the Huntington Library; James Glenn, Elaine Mills, Stephanie Koziski, Goeffrey Gamble, Paula Richardson, Vyrtis Thomas, National Anthropological Archives; Alden Moberg, Oregon State Library; Janette Saquet, Smithsonian Anthropological Library; Mary Hufner, Ms. Lodico, U.S. Department of the Interior Library.

Ellen Ambuhl, Ruth Berger, Doris Bounds, Frances Connolly, Jeanne Hillis, Geoffrey Hilton, Glenn LaFontaine, Iva Linens, Natalie Linn, June Martin, Janice and Lew Merz, Katharine and Jack Mills, Lee and Lois Miner, Jerrie and Anne Vander Houwen, Lucile Wyers, June Daggett Young.

I appreciate the thoughtful suggestions of filmmakers Bushra Azzouz and Marlene Farnum and the editorial advice of Lori McEldowney of the Oregon Historical Society Press.

Special thanks go to Del McBride, Washington State Capitol Museum, Olympia, for stimulating my interest in learning more; to David French for suggesting resources; to handweaver Martie Holmer and artist Barbara Loken for taking me over the hump from hobby to craft; to Robert Hart, U.S. Department of the Interior Indian Arts and Crafts Board, for encouraging me to write about what I knew; to Dale Archibald, Oregon Historical Society, for proposing a method; to John Gogol for offering a forum; to Kate Duncan for pointing me in the right direction and keeping me on course; to Bruce Taylor Hamilton, director of the Oregon Historical Society Press, for his enthusiasm for the project and encouragement at every step; and to the entire staff of the University of Washington Press for making it all possible.

My deep appreciation goes to Nettie Jackson for her friendship and for showing me what courage means; to Katherine, Russ, and Joseph; and to Bill, Joseph, Alexandra, and Jack for listening and watching with flattering interest. My greatest debt is to my late husband William T. (Bud) Schlick. Without the respect and affection he earned in his work with the Colville, Warm Springs, and Yakima people, this book would not have been possible. For that and for Bud's support always, I praise the junior high English teacher who seated us next to each other in Ames, Iowa, a long time ago.

There are many others to whom I am in debt. I hope those whose names I have omitted will offer me the same generous forgiveness I have received through the years from the native people of the Mid–Columbia.

Native terms used in the book for the most part are taken from the Yakima Language Practical Dictionary and reflect the Sahaptin dialect spoken on the Yakima Reservation of Washington. Unless otherwise noted, photographs are by the author.

Research for this publication was made possible in part by a grant from the American Association of University Women Educational Foundation and by travel grants from the National Endowment for the Humanities and the Smithsonian Institution. I am most grateful for this recognition.

Proceeds from sales of the book will be shared with the Middle Oregon Indian Historical Society of the Warm Springs Tribes and the Yakima Indian Nation Library.

# COLUMBIA RIVER BASKETRY

*Gift of the Ancestors, Gift of the Earth*

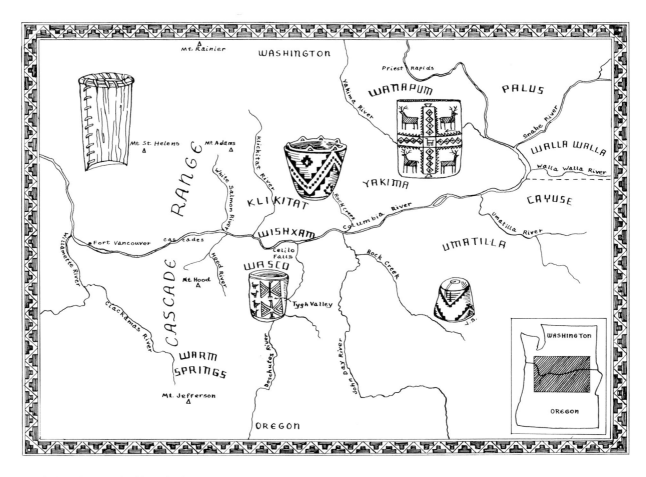

*The basketmaking people of the Columbia River. Drawn
by Joy Stickney.*

# 1. WAP'AT
## *The Art of Basket Weaving*

*"He breathed on her and gave her something that she could not see or hear or smell or touch, and it was preserved in a little basket, and by it all the arts of design and skilled handwork were imparted to her descendants."—Kotai'aqan*

The mighty Columbia River bends and flows across the Northwest from the mountains of British Columbia to the turbulent bar between Washington and Oregon where it enters the Pacific Ocean. Native people made and used baskets along the entire length of the Columbia, but one short stretch of this great river produced basketry that ranks among the best in North America (Schuster 1982, 4).

This stretch extends along the Columbia River and its tributaries—the Yakima, Snake, and Palouse rivers—roughly from the Priest Rapids in Washington State (present site of Priest Rapids Dam) around the big bend where the Yakima River enters the Columbia, downstream along the Washington-Oregon border and through the Columbia River Gorge to the Cascades (present site of Bonneville Dam) where the river cuts through the mountains. This is the region referred to as the Mid-Columbia in this book, which explores the basketry traditions of the talented and resourceful people, past and present, who live there.

Along the Mid-Columbia people lived in small family settlements for thousands of years before the first European ship reached the river's mouth. Archaeologists have found only a few areas where both culture and environment remained stable over such a long period (see Aikens 1984, v). For uncounted centuries, huge gatherings of these families filled the banks of the river during the spring and fall salmon runs. They came together at The Dalles and Celilo Falls, and in smaller numbers at other favored fishing spots such as Priest Rapids and the juncture of the Snake and the Columbia. Native families from all over the Northwest met old friends and prospective relatives, gambled, and, of primary importance, traded for fish, dried roots, berries, and other products of this country bountifully supplied by nature.

And how did they carry these valuable trade burdens back to their settlements? They used containers created by the skilled fingers of the Mid-Columbia basketmakers. Today, when a handmade American Indian basket is sought after as a treasure in itself, it is intriguing to consider the time when the contents were the prize.

## A GIFT OF THE ANCESTORS

Along the Columbia and its tributaries, and on the plateau and the mountain slopes above, families fished, hunted, gathered berries and roots, worshiped and socialized together, enjoying each activity in its own time.

We know from archaeological evidence that the earliest people were resourceful in providing a comfortable life. Their resourcefulness is exemplified in a Wasco legend about a boy who was deserted by his people (Spier and Sapir 1930, 274). Desperately hungry and cold, the boy made string from some bark, used this to trap magpies to eat and to sew the skins together for a blanket for sleeping. A Wasco man remembers that long ago the hunters carried their game tied up with strips from hazel brush. When the men returned home, the women of the family spun the hazel fiber into string and made baskets from it (Nelson Wallulatum, pers. com. 1988).

Most basketmaking, that essential industry, was carried out in wintertime when food-gathering was over for the year and families could settle into their winter homes. Because of the danger of flooding and fierce Gorge winds, the permanent villages were located well back from the river's main channel (Krieger Papers 1934). The bases of the winter lodges

*Fishing camp on the Columbia, October 23, 1884. From original sketch by James Everett Stuart. Oregon Historical Society no. 4461.*

were set warmly into the earth, and the exposed upper sides of the lodges covered with planks or by the versatile mats the women made from the tules that grew along the streams.

Here those especially gifted as basketmakers began the long process of coiling or twining the containers the family needed for domestic tasks, for storage and carrying, and for trading and other important ceremonies in the coming year. It was during these quiet winter days, with the children gathered around to listen, that the grandparents told the stories of long ago. Through these stories the elders taught the youngest generation what they needed to know: the names of plants; how the landmarks came to be; how to become moral members of the group. In this way they fulfilled their responsibility for passing on the culture to the young (Miller 1985, 14).

Although most of the basketmakers were women, and the feminine pronoun will be used in this book, many young boys learned the ancient skills during the long winters when they stayed close by the elders to help with the work. Of the few basketmakers who carry on these traditional arts today, at least two are men, and a few men help with the difficult and time-consuming job of gathering the natural materials for basketry. Most of these men credit their grandmothers with teaching them their skills.

The families living in the Mid-Columbia area were of three linguistic stocks (Zucker, Hummer, and Høgfoss 1983, 49). At the time of the arrival of the newcomers from the east, the Chinookan-speaking people lived on the south shore of the Columbia below the narrow rapids later known as The Dalles. The Wasco Indians today are their descendants. Their relatives, the Wishxam, lived on the north bank at Nixluidix ("spearfish"), opposite Tináyan, the westernmost Sahaptin village. (Although their name has been spelled Wishram in most writings, the Wishxam people themselves pronounce it with a sound roughly equivalent to the Greek *chi,* represented in this book by x.) Other Upper Chinook people whose basketry was similar to the Wasco and Wishxam lived in small family settlements along the river to the

*This five-gallon basket was made in the early twentieth century, possibly by Susan Williams, wife of Indian Shaker Bishop Sam Williams of The Dalles. Its colors are those supplied by nature (see color section following page 96). Private collection.*

*A young Yakima fisherman dipnets for salmon from a scaffold on the Klickitat River, 1986. Photo by W. T. Schlick.*

west as far as the Cascades of the Columbia and others at the mouth of the Willamette River.

At other villages along the river were their neighbors who spoke dialects of the Sahaptin language: the Klikitats; Sk'inpa, Wayam, Rock Creeks, and other western Columbia River Sahaptin groups; Umatilla; Walla Walla; Palus; and Wanapum; and the Cayuse, whose language was distinct. Most of the descendants of the people of the Mid-Columbia are enrolled today on the Yakima, Warm Springs, and Umatilla reservations in Washington and Oregon.

# Mid-Columbia Basketry Style

As in any preindustrial society, baskets were important articles of household equipment for Mid-Columbia families. When one pictures a mother washing a baby in a basket of warm water before lacing it into the security of the cradle board, the basket slips into its practical niche in a family home. For bathing, adults would go to the sweat lodge or wash using a basket of unwarmed water. Food supplies were stored in baskets and in flexible bags. Baskets could be washed and were hung on pegs in the lodges.[1]

Most of these baskets not only were useful in the everyday lives of the people but were beautiful as well, their beauty reflecting the harmony with the environment that was a primary ethical value of Mid-Columbia society. To the people of this region all objects created are an extension of nature around them. From the weaver's view, working designs into the basketry relieves the tedium of a time-consuming and exacting job and allows her to express her artistry in the context of traditional life. Mastery of the art of basketmaking is considered to be a true gift.

This book is about five traditional types of basketry, the native weavers who made them, and the small number who continue to produce baskets. "Ultimately utilitarian and intimately artistic," each form is an example of fine art that expresses with skilled craftsmanship the harmony of values and aesthetics of Mid-Columbia society, as John Gogol writes in his thoughtful essay on values and aesthetics in American Indian art (1984, 10). A fine basket "reaches out with a richness of spirit that was poured into its creation, the soul of the tree still present and alive." To learn from these baskets, we must not look at them as nostalgic remnants of dead and dying cultures, but rather as unique sources of insight into our world.

The five types of baskets will be presented individually in the following chapters; however, each is an essential part of the whole of Mid-Columbia life and none functions independently. Hats, for example, are worn with the round bags

*Wasco Indians pose in their finest ceremonial clothing at The Dalles, Oregon, June 1924. Many women wear the distinctive brimless twined hats and carry the flat "cornhusk" handbags for which the people of the Columbia River are noted. From left, top row: Sam Schooly, Charles Kishwalk, Andrew David, Kennet Wolf, Alex Tohet, Louie Mitchell, John Powyewit, Frank Queahpama, Jr., Charley Stelamita, Jackson Culps, Walter Johnson, Isaac McKinley, Grant Waheneka, Charley McKinley, Henry Thompson, William Ike, Big Ike, Sam Squiemphen, Jake Waheneka. Front: William Jackson, Joe Kuckup, Julia Simtustus, Isabel Keo, Hazel Jewel Queahpama, unknown, Jeffy Wesley, Mrs. Wolf, Meta Tufti, Addie Cushinway, Essie Kate Kuckup, Saddie Brown, Harvey Tohet, Blanch Tohet, Susan Moses, Edna Johnson, Ida McKinley, Mrs. Charley McKinley, Mrs. Jake Waheneka. Photo by De Monbrun, loaned by Mrs. Rova Galloway. Oregon Historical Society no. 27432.*

during the ceremonial digging for the root feast; dried roots gathered in round bags are stored in flat bags; flat handbags are carried during celebrations at which hats are worn; and when the family's coiled baskets are filled, they make cedar bark baskets to hold the surplus.

The making of the baskets was another example of harmonic integration in Mid-Columbia life. From the earliest times tasks were specialized; each person had his or her own talent. Those who were skilled at cutting and drying fish might trade their product for hides to use for blankets and clothing. The fastest berry pickers might trade for baskets. In this way, the people provided for their own needs as they developed their specializations.

## Twined Basket Hats

The first examples of the basketmaker's art to be discussed are the rare twined basketry hats. Usually described as "fez-shaped," these regal hats were common head coverings

for women of the Mid-Columbia when Lewis and Clark came into the region. We associate these hats with wintertime, the season of basketmaking and the time of the winter dances when the people gathered to mark "the day the sun turns around." The women wore their distinctive hats for the ancient religious ceremonies. Today, winter dress has been retained by the people of the Mid-Columbia as their most appropriate ceremonial attire (Shawley 1974, 292). The hats join other prized heirlooms brought out only for feasts and other religious and ceremonial occasions by those families fortunate enough to own such treasures.

The graceful proportions of these hats and the varied execution of the traditional banded zigzag design required great skill on the part of the weaver. She had to spin the finest hemp threads and select the most flexible grass for decoration. In the earliest days, she dyed her materials to achieve the dark and light contrast that gave vitality to her design. And finally, she called upon the extraordinary sense from her heri-

*Wanapum women demonstrate digging food roots for the annual spring root feast at Priest Rapids Longhouse in 1951. The twined hats continue to be worn by the ceremonial diggers from longhouses of the Columbia River people. Photo by Click Relander. Smithsonian Institution photo no. 41,886-V.*

tage that allowed her to visualize a design that met the constraints of tradition and expressed her own aesthetic talent as well. Without chart or pattern, the Mid-Columbia weaver twined a hat perfect in form and design.

## Twined Root-Digging Bags

The soft round bags, often referred to as "sally bags," have retained their traditional use and importance through the centuries. Although few contemporary weavers are making them, the round bags continue to fulfill a vital role in spring and early summer when the roots are ready to harvest. Many of the bags in use today have been passed down through the generations for this important task. The intricacy and beauty of their designs are further examples of the art of a people to whom aesthetics and utility were one.

According to the legends, the people of the Mid-Columbia learned from their earliest prophets about the roots of the earth and how to use them. They were taught to honor and respect these gifts of the Creator, and to be thankful for them (DuBois 1938, 8–11).[2] The rituals of thanksgiving taught so long ago are carried on today among many descendants of the people of the river and these soft bags used for gathering the food roots play an important part in these rituals. The ceremonial diggers wear the bags when digging roots for the root feast. When all have thanked the Creator for the reappearance of this bounty, all the people are free to tie their bags to their waists and move about the hills gathering the families' yearly supply of roots.

The root harvest is greatly diminished today—digging is mainly done by or for the elders or for ceremonial dinners. However, the people of the Mid-Columbia honor and value the bags as they do the roots, as important parts of the satisfying lifestyle that is their legacy.

The complex geometric and human and animal designs on the round bags primarily made by the Wasco and Wishxam weavers of the nineteenth century and earlier have been of special interest to scholars for many years. It has been suggested that there is a relationship between the basketry designs and the distinctive rock art found in the same region. The craftsmanship and mastery of design that the weavers exhibit place these bags among the finest expressions of textile art—the motifs and their arrangement giving the bags a sense of mystery that few other textiles convey.

## *Coiled Cedar Root Baskets*

Baskets decorated in the distinctive surface design technique known as imbrication were made by the people who lived north of the Columbia along both sides of the Cascade Mountains. Although there were makers of coiled baskets among the other groups of the Mid-Columbia, the style of basket woven on the east side of the mountains is known generally as "Klikitat," named for the major weavers of this work. We associate these baskets with the autumn, for the best-known style was the huckleberry basket—round and tall with sides sloping outward toward a looped edge finish at the rim. The Mid-Columbia weavers also coiled many other shapes for storing foods and other valuables as well as watertight baskets for cooking.

Unknown except in the Pacific Northwest, imbrication allows the weaver to create a complex design with the added interest of a textured tilelike surface. The classic Klikitat-style design is a three-part zigzag known as the "mountain" motif and repeats the elegant formality of the zigzag band around the twined hats. The peaks are plain or elaborated with steps and serrations, "legs" and "plumes." At the height of the collectors' demand for American Indian baskets around the turn of the century, Mid-Columbia weavers experimented with color, motifs, and design organization with more or less successful results. At their best, the makers of coiled cedar root baskets have produced objects of great utility and great beauty.

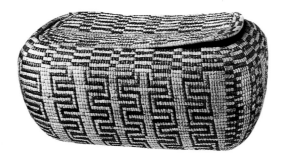

*Coiled and imbricated cedar root storage basket collected on the Wilkes Expedition in 1841. Photo by Victor Kranz. Smithsonian Institution cat. no. 2612.*

## Folded Cedar Bark Baskets

Categorizing this type of basket as artistry may appear to be stretching the definition of art, but the sheer ingenuity required to form the first of these useful baskets brings respect. It was artistry—the conscious use of skill and creative imagination in the production of an aesthetic object—on the part of the first maker who saw in the bark of the cedar tree the material for a container. And it was a sense of the aesthetic, the nature of the beautiful, that led this first maker to fold the bark into the simple and orderly container of pleasing proportions that we know today.

There is no design field in this basket, no variation in color or motifs, only the fibrous bark sculpted by nature in random vertical patterns that add interest to the basket's surface. There is no intricate basket start or braid-finished rim, but there is the artful curve of the base and the careful lacings that, in the basketmaker's effort to avoid splitting the bark, move up the basket's side in a rhythmic repetition. At the top, diagonal stitches hold the neatly trimmed edge piece in place . . . function and order are combined.

We associate these ingenious baskets with the late autumn when families from the Mid–Columbia camped in the
mountains to finish picking and drying their year's supply of
berries. When their coiled baskets were filled, they fashioned
these bark baskets for the purpose of bringing home the surplus berries or products of hunting. Made in the forest itself
to fill this temporary need for a carrying vessel, the basket
repeats, even in form, the tree that provided its material. Of
all the baskets in this book, this simple bark basket is closest
to its source in nature and, because of this, probably best
expresses the people's ethic: harmony with the environment.

*"Wishham Handicraft."* Edward S. Curtis photographed
this collection of important household objects in 1909. Two
chlai (powdered salmon) bowls with mortars flank the collection of fine Wasco/Wishxam twined bags, a sheep horn
bowl, and a folded cedar bark huckleberry basket. Oregon
Historical Society no. 67538.

## Flat Twined Bags

Often described as "cornhusk" bags or wallets, these dust-resistant containers were made originally of Indian hemp and grass to transport and store dried roots and other valuables. Most of the Mid-Columbia makers were the Sahaptin-speakers whose descendants live on the Yakima, Umatilla, and Nez Perce reservations today. The bags are associated with summertime when the families moved about and needed containers for their goods and with the winter when the largest of the bags held the great quantities of foods required for a family. The large size offered the weaver a challenge and an opportunity—two expanses of twining on which to express her artistic visions.

The flat surfaces did not require the integration of structure and design demanded by the round bag or the subconical hat. The weavers were free to work their patterns, the traditional rectangular shape of the bag the only constraint. A look at these bags today shows that the weavers took advantage of this opportunity—covering each side with a unified design limited only by their imagination. As new materials became available, many weavers embraced them, adding

*Cush-nee-yi (known also as Cushinway) family of Warm Springs, c. 1895. From left: Effie Cush-nee-yi, Davey Seymore, Seymore child, Alice C. Seymore, Flora Thompson (La moosh Cush-nee-yi), Martha Lak-away, Thomas Cush-nee-yi, James Cush-nee-yi, and an unidentified woman. Identification by Flora Thompson; courtesy of Dan Macy. Note beaded and twined bags in foreground, especially the bag (center front) with the elk motif worked in false embroidery. Oregon Historical Society no. 44166.*

colors and developing complex combinations of motifs but continuing to use the traditional techniques. The best of these flat twined bags deserve recognition as examples of fine textile art.

Toward the end of the nineteenth century, weavers began to twine smaller versions of these unusual bags for handbags. A few of these are made today. Many families of the Mid-Columbia and across the Columbia Plateau also have fine specimens that have been passed down from former generations which they carry as proud evidence of their people's artistic heritage. (In this book, Plateau refers to the area east of the Cascade Mountains drained by the Columbia River and its tributaries in Idaho, Oregon, and Washington.)

Although other baskets were made by the people of the Mid-Columbia to meet specific needs, these are the main types of baskets that survive today. Fine specimens of these baskets are preserved in most major museums and there is renewed interest among private collectors in the beautiful work. However, nowhere are the baskets, bags, and hats prized as they are among the people of the Columbia River whose grandmothers, aunts, and an occasional uncle created them.

*Woman spinning Indian hemp on her knee* (right), *probably at Celilo, c. 1910. Woman on left is making rope. Oregon Historical Society no. 44184.*

# WHEN DID BASKETMAKING BEGIN?

Baskets are the oldest form of human manufacture. We can guess that they moved through an evolution beginning with simple containers of twigs and leaves which literally freed our ancestors from living "hand to mouth," to more permanent containers for every carrying need. The ability to store provisions was a factor in the successful settled life along the Mid-Columbia. Early in the basket's evolution the makers apparently responded to the urge for beauty by adding designs and embellishments to their work.

We know from archaeological reports and accounts written by nineteenth-century travelers that baskets were made by the early people of the Mid-Columbia. Although these records contain little specific information about the art, we have learned from the few examples of identifiable basketry found by archaeologists that native fibers were used in twining with false embroidery in the vicinity of The Dalles at least nine thousand years ago (Cressman et al. 1960, 73). These techniques are used today by Mid-Columbia basketmakers. *Apocynum cannabinum,* or Indian hemp, the fiber found in many archaeological sites, was used by the twiners well into the twentieth century.

## *Taxos* (Indian Hemp)

"The people kept a supply of hemp weed called *taxos . . .* the hemp grew new from the Earth each season" (Alex Saluskin, Yakima, in Relander 1955, 57). Literature on North American Indian life confirms that many tribes used the strong fibers of Indian hemp, willow, and other fibrous barks for cord or string, but few have utilized them to the extent demonstrated by the people of the Columbia Plateau. Spinning hemp and other fibers was an important skill along the river, where the people used twine for a range of activities from satisfying the humblest household need to creating the most complex object of art. Families used the native twine to tie together the frames for their winter lodges. They used it to sew cattails and tules into sturdy mats to cover these frames and to serve as carpeting, furniture, beds, and utensils in their snug homes. The dip nets, set nets, gill nets, and seines that were necessary for their survival were also made of this important material.

Women twined the soft string into round bags to tie on their waists when digging the staple roots. They created the dust-tight flat bags that held the family's supply of dried roots and other valuable possessions. The native people used the twine to take salmon and other fish from the rivers. Their fishnets were strong enough to hold even the ancient sturgeon, the Wasco and Wishxam people's year-round source of food. Holding such a monster, some reportedly weighing over fifteen hundred pounds, required sturdy line. David Douglas, the botanist-explorer who came into this country in 1824, wrote that cord made from Indian hemp was strong enough to hold a bullock (Douglas 1959).

The fibers are not only strong, but may have another property that made them suitable for use in food containers. The Indian hemp plant contains a glycoside, apocynamarin, that is reportedly lethal to cattle and horses, but not to humans. The name *Apocynum* means "away from dogs," hence the common name, dogbane. The lack of observed insect damage in the hemp-based basketry examined in museum collections for this book may be as much the result of the material's inherent resistance to insects as of careful conservation techniques.

Entomologists have studied Indian hemp as an insect repellent. Although not useful against all insects studied, they found that extracts from the twigs and stems of *Apocynum cannabinum* were effective against the larvae of the codling moth and the black carpet beetle.[3] It is possible, as with the mold-resistant cedar roots and bark for baskets, that the people of the Columbia River, perhaps unknowingly, utilized a natural repellent in the containers they needed to store their important reserves of food roots and other valuables.

Of all the important uses for the Indian hemp along the Columbia River, the *ititamat,* or "counting the days," ball may have the most significance for the people themselves.

From the time of her marriage, a woman would record her life's events on this calendar ball by spinning a length of hemp and tying knots as each day passed. She marked births and deaths and other extraordinary days with beads, shells, or other talismans. As she grew older and the ball grew larger and harder to handle, she started a new ball (Relander 1955, 57).[4]

One Yakima woman remembers her grandmother, who was blind, fingering each knot, each bead, remembering. The soft coil of string grew larger on the floor as the grandmother unwound the ball, recounting the events the *ititamat* brought to mind (Isabelle Yallup, pers. com. 1979). For centuries, this humble fiber known as Indian hemp carried the stories of the lives of the native people along the Mid-Columbia River.

## The Early Record

Meriwether Lewis and William Clark and their Corps of Discovery in 1805 were the first nonnatives to come into contact directly with the people living along this section of the Columbia. The explorers wrote of root-storage bags in use among the Nez Perce (Thwaites 1905, 5: 114), and we know that they returned to the East with at least one round, root-digging bag (Schlick 1979b). This bag, of Wasco/Wishxam type, was collected by Lewis and Clark near The Dalles on the Washington side of the river (see color section, following page 96). The explorers did not mention acquiring this bag in their journals, nor describe its design. This wonderful bag survived that long trip, and escaped a disastrous fire and loss in moves from museum to museum. Now in the collection of the Peabody Museum at Harvard University, the bag stands as an example of the artistry of one woman who lived beside the great Columbia River sometime before 1805.

William Clark told of women near the mouth of the Yakima River cooking fish for him in a basket (DeVoto 1953, 262). Although Clark did not describe the basket, it must have been made by coiling, the local technique used for waterproof baskets. Although the basket could have been made from the nearby willow, more likely it was of cedar gathered during annual trips to the mountains for berries. The explorers also noted seeing distinctive basketry hats in the shape of truncated cones, as did many subsequent Columbia River travelers.

J. K. Townsend (1905) observed women making baskets along the Mid-Columbia in 1834,[5] but commented only that the people downriver traded with those around The Dalles for "silk grass," the silky fibers of Indian hemp. This strong fiber was spun into the string used as the warp and part of the weft in the round and flat bags as well as the hats. Indian hemp was plentiful along the midriver and its tributaries and in great demand among the native people across the continent for everything from basketry to fish nets (Emory Strong, pers. com. 1980).

Early reports include little mention of the folded bark baskets. Simple, perhaps crude to some eyes, these rustic and

*Pi-upt-sun-wei and Anahat Lallashute cook meat and salmon at the family camp during huckleberry season. USDA Forest Service photo by Ray Filloon, 1935.*

practical baskets could have escaped the notice of even the most observant visitor.

What kind of reports would we have if women rather than men had explored this area first? They might have written in greater detail about the place of household articles in the lives of the native families. Perhaps a woman would have been more interested in basketmaking, in the materials her counterparts gathered, and how the weavers achieved the beautiful designs.

## When the Animals Were People

If the written record is incomplete and the archaeological record sparse, at least the ancient myths and legends of the people of the Mid-Columbia tell us that baskets have been important in native life "since time began," as the elders say. These stories tell of tribal beginnings, of how things came to be in the days when animals were people (Beavert 1974, xii). These stories are told from the point of view of the people who were making and using the baskets. They give us something the newcomers' reports cannot, the basket weavers' view (Bernstein 1983).

The legends lift baskets out of the realm of art objects alone. They place them firmly where they belong, in the complex fabric of the life of the people of the Mid-Columbia—not as fringes to decorate the edge of a beautiful shawl, but as threads in the shawl itself.

In the ancient stories, food is paramount—getting, sharing, having the right kind of food. This is not surprising among people who depended on the earth for subsistence and even today give primary importance to gathering, storing, preparing, and honoring the traditional foods. There continues to be a sacramental relationship between the people and the Creator who provides water and food to sustain their life. Because of their importance as containers for these sacred foods, baskets share a role in this relationship. Seasonal ceremonies of thanksgiving as the native foods appear each year continue to be important rituals in the lives of the Columbia River families.[6] Traditional baskets have an im-

*Pi-upt-sun-wei (Mrs. Thomas Yallup) and Ida Billy hold huckleberry branches as they stand amid filled baskets of berries in their camp south of Mount Adams. USDA Forest Service photo by Ray Filloon, 1935.*

portant place in these ceremonies today as they hold the gifts of the earth.

In a Wanapum legend, Naami Piýap (Our Elder Brother) instructed the people to hold the feasts of thanksgiving for the new roots and the first salmon. These ceremonies were to restore the plenty that had existed before the people's downfall when, in their grief at their leader's death, they forgot the sacred practices. These former days of plenty were described as "when there were baskets full of food" (Relander 1956, 26). How better to characterize a life of contentment, free from want, a life in harmony with the Creator?

This relationship between basketry and subsistence may be one explanation for the respect that basketry is given today by the native people. This respect also extends to the few remaining basketmakers who carry on this heritage.

As we look at each type of native Mid-Columbia basketry in this book, we will consider this earliest history of the basket form—the oral history passed down through generations in the legends of the people who made and used the baskets. We will look at the place of the baskets in the lives of the people today as well as those who came before. In addition, I will define the characteristics that help us identify baskets that were made along this stretch of the great river and will describe the techniques and materials used in their manufacture.

## A Gift of the Earth

The native people of the Columbia River did not consider the baskets simply as works of art; the container had little meaning without the contents. A beautiful coiled basket was valuable only when it was full of huckleberries, fresh or dried. A flat twined bag embellished with false embroidery in vivid colors and intricate design had greatest value when it was plump with dried roots. These products of the basketmakers' art when filled with their intended harvest were secure capital for a native family. They represented not only insurance against a long hungry winter, but also barter of high value for obtaining needed food and other items or for ceremonial trading.

We can have greater understanding and appreciation of these magnificent examples of Native American art when we begin to view them in the rich context of the lives of those who made them—as works of art, as fine examples of a basketmaker's mastery of a difficult skill, and as useful articles of

*Charlie Wilpocken, his wife Kil-ess-tum, and daughter holding a child's cornhusk bag. Wilpocken was the blacksmith's assistant on the Colville Reservation. Photo by E. H. Latham. Special Collections Division, University of Washington Libraries no. NA943.*

household equipment. The baskets can represent all of these wonders within the tapestry of tradition, belief, and ceremony of those to whom they mean the most . . . the native people who lived along the Mid-Columbia River and their descendants who continue to live nearby. To these first Americans, and to all of us who admire the work, Columbia River basketry is truly a gift of the ancestors, a gift of the earth.

*Young women of Wapato Longhouse on the Yakima Reservation after the root feast, April 11, 1973. Photo by Joseph Schlick.*

# 2. Patl'aapa
## *The Twined Basket Hat*

*"If the basket hat falls, you will know my child . . . is a girl."*— *The Wyakin*

My first sight of a twined basketry hat was many years ago on the Colville Indian Reservation in north central Washington State. I was dropping off to sleep on our airy back porch at the Colville agency when I heard drums begin . . . far away, but deep and steady like a heartbeat. Startled, I tensed, then relaxed. This is 1951, I thought, and remembered the families gathering that day for the Fourth of July encampment at the Circle grounds just below the hill. I fell asleep, eager for morning and the chance to visit the celebration.

The next day was the first full-dress Indian parade my husband and I had ever seen, and, babe in arms, we lined up and snapped pictures with the rest of the onlookers. The difference was, the participants were our neighbors and co-workers. They were dressed in clothing we had seen only in movies prior to this day. Even the horses were gorgeous. But there was something I had never seen, even on film. An elderly woman sat graceful and erect on her mount wearing a fez-shaped hat as if it were a crown.

The woman was Minnie Yellow Wolf, widow of a famous Nez Perce leader who served with Chief Joseph in that desperate effort to preserve for their people the life they treasured. Minnie had been a child on the long sad "war" through Idaho and Montana that ended in defeat in 1877. The remnants of Joseph's band were forced to settle on the Colville Reservation north of what is now Grand Coulee Dam in Washington after long incarceration in Oklahoma. They lived out their lives far from their homes in the Wallowa Valley of Northeastern Oregon.

The basket hats remind me today of the pride and dignity of the women I knew among those people.

It was years later when I realized these unusual hats retained an important cultural role among the native people of the Mid-Columbia and, to my surprise, were still being made. Some Yakima Indian friends were leaving our house in Toppenish, Washington, saying their goodbyes at the door, when the grandmother reached down and picked up an ear of Indian corn from several that were in a decorative basket by the door.

"What are you going to do with these?" she asked.

"Well—just let them sit there and look pretty, I guess," I told her, puzzled. Then catching the gleam in her eye, I added, "Would you like to have them?"

"Just this part," she said, and twisted off the husk, dropping the varicolored ear of corn back in the basket. "For hats," she explained. We husked the rest of the ears and sent her home with a bundle of the strong dried cornhusks.

A native Iowan, it seemed strange to me that the grandmother would want the husks but not the corn. And then it came to me—she would weave with them! I didn't dream anyone was still twining the basketry her people were noted for, but here was a modern-day weaver in person.

That summer we planted the kernels from the huskless ears. When fall came, we harvested the corn and dried the finest of the husks. Packing them in a huge plastic bag, I slipped the bag under the Christmas tree at the longhouse near Wapato. When the longhouse families gathered for their Christmas, Santa himself delivered the bag to the weaver.

The timing was appropriate, although I did not know it then, for in traditional life near the great river winter was the time for basket making. By the following April, the grandmother had finished hats for two of the ceremonial diggers who gathered, prepared, and served the sacred foods for the longhouse root feast that month. The long winter was over, the weaving complete. It was time to move on to the next season.

## THE BASKET HAT IN ANCIENT TIMES

We know that women along the Columbia have worn these unique basket hats for many generations. The legends tell us so. The earliest stories of the Columbia River people are set in the Myth Age, the time "when the animals were people" before the coming of the human beings, even before Coyote or some other transformer arrived to order the world.[1]

The basket hat serves as an oracle in this short scene from the ancient story of Cold Man and Warm Man.

*The eldest son's wife was with child when her husband was killed. "I have no one left," she told her father and mother-in-law, "I am going away." She took her basket hat from her head and hung it up in one place. She hung a deerskin, white and soft, beside it.*

*"If the basket hat falls, you will know that my child is born and is a girl," she told them. "If the deerskin falls, the child is a boy." (Fletcher 1891)*

Another early tale is the Wishxam story of Little Raccoon and his Grandmother. In this myth, the ancestors used a basket hat to teach children the dire consequences of misbehavior.

*Bad Little Raccoon had a rock and was pounding his blind grandmother's basket hat just for the fun of it. "Bang, bang, bang," he pounded.*

*Soon Grandmother called to him. "Pick some berries for me," she said, "I'm very hungry." Impatient at being interrupted, Little Raccoon grabbed a handful of berries and twigs and tossed them into Grandmother's throat.*

*Choking on the dry berries and twigs, Grandmother cried, "Take my basket hat and get me some water to soothe my throat."*

*Taking the hat, now full of holes from the careless pounding, Little Raccoon filled it at the river. When he brought the hat to Grandmother, it was empty. The water had dripped out through the holes. He ran back to the river five times. Each time he returned with an empty hat.*

*Little Raccoon's grandmother was very angry. She turned herself into a crow and flew away, scolding with a crow's raucous call, leaving Raccoon contrite and alone. To this day she sits where she landed, along the Columbia River near The Dalles.[2]*

Little Raccoon's cruelty was surely a reason for punishment. Children learned another important lesson from this story: Given the importance of the basket hats in the life of the Columbia River people, Little Raccoon's willful destruction of a family treasure was unforgivable.

*"Mnashwai—Wishham." Leona Smartlowit identifies the child in this photograph as her mother, Louise Billy of Pendleton. Photo by Edward S. Curtis, 1910. Oregon Historical Society no. 77181.*

# THE BASKET HAT
## IN COLUMBIA RIVER LIFE

Hats woven of plant materials were worn by native people all along the Pacific Coast of North America. They varied in form, techniques of manufacture, and materials. The original purpose was probably the same as for head coverings everywhere, protection. Along the Mid-Columbia the hat would have been worn for protection from the wind, dust, and occasional rains.

A woman might have worn the basket hat to protect her forehead from the chafing tump line that supported the bag of roots or basket of berries or a child's cradle on her back. In later years a headscarf, which took the place of the basket hat for everyday wear, performed this function.

It is also possible that early in the hat's development it began to be considered important, as did other items of clothing, for personal adornment. In a society where families camped together in larger groups in a seasonal cycle of food gathering and social activities, homes did not have the status value and did not make the personal statement of identity they do in some societies today. Clothing and other portable possessions fulfilled this role.

This life of travel also limited the nonfunctional objects a family could own. Articles of clothing served as mobile means of communication, as symbols of wealth or spiritual power, and as expressions of ethnic identity (Shawley 1974, 243). The hats with their distinctive fezlike form performed the latter function for the Indians of the Columbia Plateau.

The handsome stepped designs that appear on the earliest Mid-Columbia basketry hats that survive today are evidence that much pride was taken in the design and ornamentation as well as in the craftsmanship, at least by the time of contact with nonnatives and probably long before. Such designs decorate a basketry hat now in the British Museum (Cat. VAN197) that was collected in 1792 on the Columbia River by George Hewitt of the Vancouver Expedition. The half-century immediately following Lewis and Clark's arrival

*"A visit at the Indian Camp, Ore." Postcard from the Laura Buzan Collection, no. 1969. 11.15. Courtesy Maryhill Museum of Art.*

in 1805 saw little loss of aboriginal arts and clothing customs, but was marked more by the addition of new materials brought in by the newcomers.[3]

It appears that at the time of first contact with the nonnatives and for many years afterward most native women along the river wore these hats in the wintertime.[4] Although most references state that the hats are worn by women only, there are some interesting anomalies. An unusual carved board figure found at a grave near Beacon Rock appears to be a man in a basket hat with a design similar to the common "mountain peaks" motif (Seaman 1967, 211). Osborne in 1957 described remnants of a basketry hat associated with a man's grave in the McNary Reservoir basin. According to Ray (1942, 167), elderly Klikitat men were known to wear the basket hat; and a young Klikitat artist told me in 1976 of a dream in which he wore such a hat.

From the range of sizes of surviving hats, it appears that they were not made for little girls. A photograph taken at Celilo, Oregon, in the 1930s shows a small child wearing a basket hat which is much too large for her, as if it was placed on her head for the photograph. Geraldine Jim of Warm Springs reports that ties were attached to hold hats on the heads of small girls.

At the time of contact and during most of the nineteenth century, girls were considered of marriageable age when they reached puberty. By the time a girl was twelve or thirteen she had learned from her grandmothers and elder aunts all the skills necessary for her role as wife and mother. Among these skills was making appropriate clothing, including her basket hat, for her new role (Nettie Jackson, pers. com. 1988). This may account for the designation "wedding hat" on one such hat in the Smithsonian Institution that was collected from the Cascade Indians by Dr. James F. Ghiselin, who served in the Columbia River area with the United States Army in the mid–1800s. Although new hats continued to be made, prized family hats also were handed down from aunts or grand-mothers to newly married female relatives.[5]

A compelling use of the basket hat was described by a Warm Springs woman: "They were worn by the old people during the winter when they told stories" (Neda VanPelt Wesley, pers. com. 1987). Her words bring to mind the dark interior of the winter lodge set well back from the river's chilly winds. There on the mat–covered floor below the surface of the ground to preserve the warmth sit grandmother in her stately hat, her work in her hands, and children ready for the story. In the Sahaptin dialects, the word for grandmother and the word for grandchild are the same, illustrating a special relationship.

Beginning in the late 1850s, missionaries and employees of the federal government on the reservations actively encouraged the Indian people to wear "citizen's dress." Most began to dress like the settlers in the area, and the basket hat was brought out only for Sunday Waashat services or other religious or ceremonial occasions.[6] Winter was the major sacred season for the Mid-Columbia people. The winter dances, for example, were held long into the twentieth century, with hats appropriate dress for such occasions (Laritta Yallup, pers. com. 1972).

By 1850 the best land in the western valleys of Oregon and Washington had been taken and midwestern emigrants turned to the valleys of the Mid-Columbia drainage to seek tillable acreage. The presence of the newcomers on their lands limited forever the free movement of the native people. The hats joined other portable objects of importance in providing a link to former times.[7]

When photographers arrived in the area there were some Indian people who feared the power of the camera, but many along the Mid-Columbia posed for portraits. This was another special occasion for which women of the Columbia River brought out their basket hats. Photographer Edward S. Curtis wrote in 1911, "Well-made basket hats were a picturesque feature of dress, and are still worn on gala occasions" (vol. 8).

Photographs taken by Curtis, Major Lee Moorhouse, Indian agent on the Umatilla Reservation, and other photographers in the early years of the century often showed a woman wearing her own prized hat. Some photographers of the day also had "costumes," including hats, available for the subjects to wear, and the same hat appears in several Moorhouse photographs. The basket hat, which by this time had become an article of ceremonial clothing and gave the wearer an aristocratic, dignified appearance, assisted Curtis in capturing the look of precontact days in his dramatic photographic study of the American Indian.

One hat provided a link with the "romance" of the early West for audiences across the world when Susan Papaloit of Warm Springs wore her basket hat for European audiences of Buffalo Bill's Wild West Show (Seymour 1931).

Many families put these treasures away, and only a few twined hats made their way into private collections and museums. Those that did were often described as "very rare" or "very old and scarce." The 1902 catalogue of Frohman Trad-

*Anna Kash-Kash, Umatilla, in twined hat and old style "deer tail" dress. Made from two skins, the dress is beaded in a traditional design that follows the contour of the deer's tail where it is turned with hair outward to form a decorative touch at the neckline. Although this photograph was probably taken by Major Lee Moorhouse, the hat is not the same as that worn by several other Moorhouse photographic subjects. Oregon Historical Society no. 49862.*

ing Company in Portland offered several of the basket hats made in the shape of an inverted bowl by northern California tribes, but advertised no Columbia River hats among other basketry from this region.

The hat was an important possession, full of cultural meaning to the people of the Mid-Columbia. Most hats were passed down in a family, willed to someone at a death, or, occasionally, buried with the owner, as was the hat worn at Nespelem by Mrs. Yellow Wolf. Because of the high esteem in which hats were held from the earliest days, it is not surprising that such a small number have been offered for sale.

## THE BASKET HAT TODAY

Women of the region wear basket hats today, most of them old and prized family possessions. A family on the Warm Springs Reservation prizes a handsome hat that belonged to a great great grandmother who was a judge in the early 1800s. "I call this my hat of wisdom," said a wearer of this heirloom (Bernice Tohet Mitchell, pers. com. 1988).

When seasonal feasts are held to thank the Creator for the return of the sacred foods each year, those women responsible for gathering, preparing, and serving the honored foods wear basket hats if they have them. The Wanapum families living at Priest Rapids treasure four old basket hats that have been in use since the time of Smohalla, the Wanapum prophet who was born in 1815 and died in 1895. They bring them out only for the feasts (Arlene Buck, pers. com. 1988). Members of other longhouses who follow the customs of their ancient religion do the same.

Some traditionalists among the older members of the tribes have objected to women wearing the hat for a pow-wow or any other primarily social rather than religious occasion. For many, however, the celebrations offer a chance to wear with pride something that is uniquely and personally a part of their heritage. These social gatherings are not seen by most participants as exhibitions for an audience but rather a time to renew and reaffirm this heritage. The powwows offer

an opportunity for the people of the Mid–Columbia to represent with pride their own and their ancestors' achievements
through the beauty of traditional dress and the ancient crafts
(French 1955, 111, 48). The traditional eagle fluff or weasel
skin or bells and beads swinging from the stately basket hat
offer another image of kinetic beauty to powwow visitors
and hosts.

The evidence suggests that the hats were made and worn
by all the native tribes of the Mid–Columbia as well as the
neighboring Nez Perce of Idaho and Chief Joseph's band of
Nez Perce that was relocated on the Colville Reservation
in 1885. Where hats are found among other peoples on
the Plateau, they appear to have been traded from the Mid–

*Servers at the Agency Longhouse on the Warm Springs
Reservation circle the longhouse before the root feast in
1984. Photo by Marsha Shewczyk. Courtesy* Spilyay
Tymoo.

Columbia and other southern Sahaptin-speaking groups (Currens 1970, 31, 33; Haeberlin 1928, 139). The people of the Mid-Columbia also made summer hats, quickly woven of grass or reeds, that were worn out by summer's end. The women then crumpled them up and stuck them in between the drying salmon to allow air to circulate (Tallulah Pinkham, pers. com. 1975).

The suggestion has been made that basket hats of the Columbia River Plateau were introduced by the Klamath/ Modoc people who came to the great trade center at The Dalles from southern Oregon, or through horse-trading visits to the Shasta of northern California or the Nevada Paiutes. Weavers in all of these groups made twined brimless hats (Ferrier 1978, 132). However, there are many important differences between the southern hats and those of the Columbia River people. The Mid-Columbia hats generally are taller and have straighter sides than the southern hats, which are more bowl-shaped. The Klamath/Modoc hats are closer in form to the Mid-Columbia hats, but the weavers used a different technique—single element overlay—to form the design, carrying the design strand over from one motif to the next on the inside. These floating weaving elements are not present on Mid-Columbia hats (Gogol 1983, 11).

The Paiutes of Nevada and adjacent areas used diagonal twining in the manufacture of hats, and with the Shasta employed an **S**-twist stitch rather than the **Z**-twist of the Columbia River weavers. The southerners also utilized multiple-strand twining. The weavers of the Mid-Columbia did not use this technique and were the only hat makers to employ full-turn twining.

Until we have more evidence to the contrary, it appears that we can consider the fez-shaped hats, with their distinctive pyramidal or zigzag designs and full-turn twining technique, to be an art form that is indigenous to the people of the Mid-Columbia River and its tributaries as well as the plateaus above.

## Weaving the Hat

The basketry hat worn by the women of the Mid-Columbia is commonly described as "fez-shaped" or having a truncated cone. Twined of *taxos,* or Indian hemp, and *yai,* or bear grass, the hats have, with few exceptions, a three-part zigzag design around the sides in dyed bear grass and other fibers. Hat heights vary from a maximum of ten inches to a minimum of about five; most are six to seven inches high. The diameter of the crown of the hat varies from two to five and a half inches, and is usually about four and a half inches. The diameter at the base ranges from six and a half to seven and a half inches, consistent with the range of hat sizes sold today.

### *Materials*

Indian Hemp. Mid-Columbia weavers used the bark of the Indian hemp as the foundation material for most of their twined basketry. They also utilized other barks, mainly from hazelnut or willow root, but hemp appears to be the preferred fiber for twining hats. The weavers found this perennial shrub in damp ground and along rivers and streams, each weaver cutting the longest and straightest stems from her favorite spot. The time of gathering determined the color—a pale red-brown when the leaves fell and darker if cut later. Cutting time was based more on the custom of the family than on the desire for a specific color. One Yakima family reported they cut it after the rains began, but "before the little people got it" (Amelia Sohappy Sampson, pers. com. 1978). Women had individual methods for caring for the important fiber to retain its greatest strength. One kept the stems under her mattress to cure them, another hung them in a shed, another buried them in the ground or simply left them outside. The stems were from three to five feet long, about the diameter of a finger.

After gathering the winter's supply, the weaver and those who helped her process the hemp split each woody stem lengthwise, opened it flat, and bending it back on itself lengthwise, separated the long strong fibers of the bark from

*Indian hemp* (Apocynum cannabinum) *collected in the fall on the Columbia River near Celilo. Drawing by Kris Allen.*

the woody core, discarding the core. To obtain the smooth inner fibers of the bark, the weaver and her helpers pulled the bark strands across a piece of flint, a rabbit rib, or some other smooth sharp object. Fragments of the outside "skin" would fall away, leaving the long, strong and silky strands they desired. The few who do this work today wear gloves to protect their fingers.

The Columbia River weaver spun the twine on her bare knee or on a piece of tanned hide draped over her leg. A right-handed spinner held the ends of two strands of hemp bast firmly together with the fingers of her left hand while rolling the strands forward across her knee with her right palm. Releasing the left hand and holding the tension with the right hand, the spinner allowed that portion of the strands to spring back into a strong **Z**-ply twine. She repeated this step many times to spin the string that was needed. As each strand of hemp came to an end, another was incorporated into the string to form a continuous strand that could be wound into a huge ball.[8] Considering the time and effort required for this process, it is not surprising that three bundles, each the size of a thumb, or one large bundle of prepared twine were worth as much as a horse to the people of the Columbia (Turner 1979, 171; Ruth Strong, pers. com. 1979).

Preparing the hemp is largely a lost art among the Mid-Columbia tribes today, although there are recent efforts to revive it. Several women on the Warm Springs Reservation have taught the art of gathering and processing hemp to younger tribal members. When the Yakima Indian Nation built their cultural center near Toppenish, Washington, in 1980, a group of women processed and spun enough twine to make the tule mats which covered the museum's winter lodge. These women had learned when they were children to spin hemp by watching their elders and drew on these long-ago memories as well as information from tribal elders to accomplish this task.

Those who appreciate the art treasures of the Mid-Columbia can thank the ancestors for utilizing the strong, long-lasting fibers of Indian hemp for the foundation of the twined hats and bags. With less durable materials, the basketry would not have survived to be enjoyed today. Traders and later newcomers brought other fibers that were soon adopted by some weavers for the round and flat twined bags, but many continued to process and use the native hemp. By the early years of the twentieth century, cultivation had eliminated the important shrub in many of the traditional gathering areas and native women began to turn to more easily available alternatives for most of their twine (McArthur 1911).

Perhaps because of the hat's special place in Mid-Columbia life, it appears that it was not until at least the second quarter of the twentieth century that most weavers replaced the native hemp with cotton string, imported hemp or sisal, and occasionally, plastic cord as warp material.

BEAR GRASS.  Weavers used bear grass (*Xerophyllum tenax*) for the outer surface of the hats from earliest times through the first part of the twentieth century.[9] Although some hats may have been made with bear grass after the early years of the century, it appears that most weavers turned to the softer strands of dried corn husk (*Zea mays*) for their decorative material.

The weavers gathered the bear grass in the summer, taking only the finest leaves with white bases for hats. To make the grass more flexible, the weavers removed the spine on the underside of the blade with a sharp instrument before they tied the grass into bundles to bleach and dry for winter's use. This is a tedious process, for the serrated edges on the grass are swordlike and cut unprotected fingers mercilessly. Families gathered bear grass early in the season for the green color to use in design. Later in the season, after the grasses had dried on the plant, families picked again. The bear grass dried on the plant to a pale yellow or a creamy white and the weavers sorted it for use as background color in the hats (Teit 1930; Verbena Tohet Greene, pers. com. 1986).

*Bear grass* (Xerophyllum tenax). *Drawing by Jeanne Janish.*

OTHER DECORATIVE MATERIALS. To add deeper colors to the early hats, the weavers incorporated the brown "skin" of the willow root in their designs. To obtain black, they immersed the grass in mud at soda springs known for their dye properties. A stronger yellow than that of the natural grass was achieved by steeping the blades in a tealike solution of Oregon grape root (*Berberis* sp.) or the root of the *wak'il-max* or sand dock (*Rumex venosa*) gathered in late summer.[10] There are no reports of mordants being used, with the exception of saliva when the weavers chewed the inner bark of the alder for the brownish-red used in the Klikitat-style baskets.

As soon as newcomers arrived in the area, wool raveled from blankets and clothes became available to the weavers. A woolen cloth usually called stroud was popular in the Indian trade in the eastern part of the continent from the early eighteenth century.[11] When Lewis and Clark arrived at the Cascades of the Columbia in 1805 they saw some scarlet and blue robes among the Indians, evidently traded upriver from the ships that had entered the river's mouth. Meriwether Lewis reported trading a dress uniform coat, navy with red lapels, to the Columbia River people (Thwaites 1905, 3: 185).

Rare at first, the wool was much prized. Of these raveled yarns, the reds appear to have been most popular in the hats. Red wool outlines the stepped design on the early nineteenth-century judge's hat passed down in a Warm Springs family. According to family members, this red came from bundled army uniforms given to the tribes after moths worked their havoc in storage. Soft, silky, vegetal dyed, three-ply wool Saxony yarn from Germany became available sometime around the mid-1800s. The Saxony colors were subtle compared to the dense, saturate hues of the aniline dyes that appeared next. After about 1880, the brighter aniline colors were available in the coarser four-ply, machine-spun yarns shipped to the West from Germantown, Pennsylvania. The Germantown yarns offered a wide range of colors that proved to be unstable when exposed to light (Kent 1961, 9; Kahlenberg and Berlant 1972, 11; Whiteford 1977, 40).

The basketmakers could also color their own materials with the new aniline dyes. The new dyes freed them from gathering and steeping native roots or soaking materials in alkaline mud. They simply dropped the dye package into the kettle of water and boiled their materials until they achieved the color they wanted. A look at the inside face of the basket hat will help determine if aniline dyes were used. If so, the bright ends of the bear grass, cornhusk, or yarn that appear on the inside will contrast with the outside design which has faded to mellow colors resembling those from native dyes.

## The Twining Technique

The sociable times of spring, summer, and autumn give way to the quiet months. The hard work of gathering and spinning is over and the balls of hemp twine for warps and bundles of grass for wefts are stored in dry, sheltered places. The weaver begins to transform these gifts of the earth into objects of beauty and usefulness.

With the materials she needs at hand, and possibly a grandchild or two at her side to watch and learn, the woman of the Mid-Columbia measures her warps, the foundation elements, from the balls of hemp twine. No boards or other measures for warps have been reported in the Mid-Columbia. The weaver may use her arm's length to measure, much as long ago a dry goods clerk rolled out a yard. A short arm's length for each warp will give her enough for an average-sized hat with twine left over for the binding off.

The weaver gathers the warps together in their center and ties them firmly with a strip of hide. The ends of the strip later can hold feathers or shells or beads when the hat is finished, or they will be tied in a loop for hanging the hat, as in the Nez Perce legend, "The Wyakin" (Fletcher 1891, 8). Holding her work in her lap with the hide ties—which will be at the crown of the hat—toward her, she loops a piece of grass over a small bundle of warps and begins to twine around and around from left to right with a **Z**-stitch slant, back weft over front, upper left to lower right.

*Julia Pims Sohappy demonstrates the twining process as she works on a hat to be worn at the Wapato Longhouse root feast in 1973. Photo by Joseph Schlick.*

Twining is probably the oldest preweaving construction technique (Held 1978, 6, 17). When flexible materials are used, the weaver produces a soft "fabric." This ancient technique was ideally adapted to the needs of the Mid–Columbia people who lived a mobile life in a windy and dusty area. Tightly twined items would keep out dust and sand and were easily packed away or carried on horses, dogs, or backs. Early reports describe the twined hats as waterproof, but this could not have been an important consideration in this dry climate. On the other hand, their sandproof qualities would have been welcome.

At the beginning the weaver incorporates several warps between each half twist of the wefts, or serving elements, as they sometimes are called. Apparently both right- and left-handed weavers work in this direction, for an **S**-stitch slant is unusual in Mid–Columbia hats. The weaver lays in a new piece of grass as needed to replenish her wefts. She works with the outside surface of the hat toward her; the new or fag ends of the wefts are visible only on the inside.

As the crown of the hat grows outward, she encloses fewer and fewer warps between each half twist until every warp is held by a twining "stitch." Up to this point the weaver has been working in close, simple twining (Adovasio 1977, 16), using two bear grass wefts of the same color.

As she continues to incorporate only one warp strand between each half twist, the crown of the hat begins to cup away from her and its conical shape begins to develop. At this point the weaver introduces a new color. The earliest weavers worked a row of dark willow-root bark or mud-dyed bear grass to define the edge of the hat's crown. As soon as yarns from raveled woolens and other new materials became available, weavers began using these to define the crown's edge.

At the edge of the crown, continuing to hold the weaving in her lap and working outward, the weaver begins to add warps at regular intervals, two at a time by folding new double-length warps in half and incorporating each half with the adjacent standing warp by the enclosing twining stitches or weft crossings. The weaver may add single warps by incorporating them with a standing warp in the same way. In this case, she usually ties a knot in the end of the new warp to prevent it from pulling out of the weft crossing. When a weft splice is needed, the new weft strand is laid in and is secured by the next row of twining. Occasionally, a weaver will tie the ends of the wefts together at a splice. Much skill is required to maintain an even slope or flare on the hat sides as the weaver builds the dynamic zigzag design.

## Building the Design

To create the design, the weaver changes from plain or half-turn twining, using both wefts of the same color, to a technique known as full-turn twining[12] in which she uses two wefts of different colors (Whiteford 1977, 43). The latter technique allows the weaver to bring forward to the fabric's face one or the other color as needed to build her motifs.

Full-turn twining appears similar to plain twining on the face of the hat: a series of horizontal or slightly oblique stitches. The inside of the hat, however, looks very different. On the inside, the passive weft (the weft that is not brought forward but remains on the inside only) has a horizontal orientation; the active weft that is brought forward to form the design has a vertical orientation (Marr 1988, 55).

Designs in the early hats were worked in full-turn twining. Sometime around 1930 some weavers began to decorate their hats using another traditional Mid-Columbia technique, false embroidery.[13] The reason for the change in technique is unclear. One explanation may be that false embroidery is better suited to the shorter cornhusk leaf which became more easily available in the late 1800s and replaced bear grass in later hats. The Cayuse/Nez Perce artist Maynard White Owl Lavadour suggests another reason: false embroidery uses fewer cornhusks than full-turn twining. The technique can thus save precious material. Not until the middle of the twentieth century, when the art of twining the fine basketry hat was nearly extinct, did a few women of the

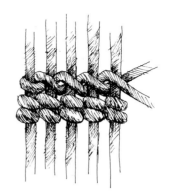

*Close simple twining. Diagram by Peggy Dills Kelter.*

*Full-turn twining, outside face. Diagram by Peggy Dills Kelter.*

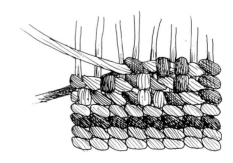

*Full-turn twining, inside face. Diagram by Peggy Dills Kelter.*

*Two design arrangements that are commonly seen on twined hats are three triangles at top and bottom and a three-part zigzag. The weaver used full-turn twining to create the design on the hat at top. The stepped design on the bottom hat is achieved with the less-common technique of false embroidery. Private collection. Photo by W. T. Schlick.*

Columbia River begin to fashion this headgear out of canvas and cover it with beadwork.[14]

Although the function, materials, and techniques used in weaving the hats have changed through the years, the ritually significant shape and designs have remained constant. Art that has protective or ritual value is often resistant to change. The continued use of the rosebush for the bow of the Mid-Columbia cradle board is an example of its enduring protective power.

It is intriguing to think of the designs on these hats as a metaphor for native life at its best along the Mid-Columbia: circular and orderly but changing with demands of space and time. The most noticeable feature of the hat, other than shape, is the three-part zigzag around the body of the hat, identified by most native people as "mountain peaks." This band design covers the entire side area and is bordered by a solid line at top and bottom. The encircling border line at the top of the design field is often repeated in a concentric circle on the crown itself.

Between the bordering circles are an infinite variety of triangle combinations which form the zigzag. The weaver achieves the zigzag effect in one of two ways. She may choose the mountain peak design as her primary motif, with steps or serrated designs as internal and external elaborations. She may further embellish the steps with other geometric forms such as the "foot" or "plume" design.

The weaver may also produce the effect of a zigzag band by weaving three triangles with bases on the border line at the crown and three alternating triangles along the border line at the rim. In the latter design the background or negative space forms the zigzag. Frequently, she embellishes the triangles with stepped or serrated motifs. Rather than treating the surface of her basket as a flat background, the Columbia River basketmaker adapts her stitches to the sloping sides, creating a cohesive design that is integrated with the form of the hat (Cahodas 1981).

It has been suggested that the hat designs are unrelated to the decoration of other basketry articles of the Mid-

Columbia, the weavers having adapted northern California basketry motifs for their designs (Ferrier 1978, 132). However, two other Mid-Columbia basketry forms utilize similar motifs: the coiled huckleberry baskets frequently employ variations on the three-part zigzag enclosed by a single dark border line at top and bottom, and the banded zigzag design is frequently used by weavers of the round twined bags of the area.

## Finishing the Hat

When the design is complete and the hat reaches its proper height, the weaver binds off the warps in the traditional way with a self-edge. To achieve this finish, she carries a warp behind (to the inside of) the adjacent warp to the right, then brings it forward to the workface and to the right in front of the next warp, tucking it down inside between that second warp and the third. She repeats these steps with the warp to the right, and continues around the rim binding off each warp strand in turn. The edge is finished by threading the next-to-last warp into place between the first two warps and threading the last warp forward between the first and second warps and to the inside between the second and third warps.

The weaver using the false embroidery technique employs a different method, known as twining off. She secures the warps inside the hat with the last row of twining, the technique used to finish a flat twined bag.[15] A weaver will occasionally line a hat or bind the edge with a textile.

The weaver's final step is to tie the ends of the hide thong that bound her start together to form a loop for hanging. She may attach feathers, beads, dentalia shells, or other ornaments to the ends.[16] At Warm Springs, one feather hanging from the crown of the hat tells onlookers that the wearer is single; two feathers signal that she is married.

With these finishing touches, the weaver's work is done and one more young girl will join the company of those who wear the symbol of their people and their own womanhood.

*"Mountain peak" design, frequently seen on Klikitat-style coiled cedar root baskets, is similar to the three-part zigzag design of many twined hats. Private collection. Photo by W. T. Schlick.*

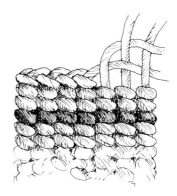

*Self-edge on a twined hat. Diagram by Peggy Dills Kelter.*

*Lena Jim and Puck Hyah Toot (Johnny Buck) pose with a platter of food roots,* skol-kol (Lomatium canbyi)*, at Wanapum Longhouse, c. 1951. Photo by James Rayner.*

# WHO ARE THE MAKERS?

Although at one time weavers from all of the groups living along the Mid-Columbia made twined basketry hats, today only a few weavers are twining hats using the traditional techniques and designs of their ancestors. Helen Jim and Lena Jim have demonstrated their art at the Yakima Nation Museum in Toppenish, and their work is occasionally offered for sale at the tribal museum shop. Their grandniece, Valerie Jim Calac, has mastered the art of twining and has asked them to teach her to make the hats.

Maynard White Owl Lavadour, a young Cayuse/Nez Perce man living in Pendleton, Oregon, learned the difficult art of twining the basket hat from his great-grandmother Susie Williams. He began weaving baskets at the age of five and later studied at the Institute of American Indian Art in Santa Fe, New Mexico. He uses cornhusks and the technique of false embroidery when making hats, round root-digging bags, and flat carrying bags. As a youngster, Lavadour was teased about doing women's work. When he told his great-grandmother he wanted to give up basket making, she reminded him of what a special gift he had—he could do something few other people have mastered (pers. com. 1987).

Lavadour, who is known for other traditional arts as well as basketry, is not the sole male basketmaker in the Pendleton area. Ron Pinkham, Nez Perce, and Morning Owl, Umatilla, also weave basket hats.

This one distinctive object, the basket hat, holds deep meaning for most Columbia River people today. The reasons may lie in its rarity among the families' heirlooms, in its religious and ceremonial significance, or simply in its tie with the long-ago past. As with other art that has ritual or protective value, the technique, form, and design of the basket hat changed little until the last decade.

The traditional twined hat with its three-part design that has no beginning and no end represents a belief system important to survival but that is difficult to live by in today's world . . . a way of relating harmoniously to all life. Like the

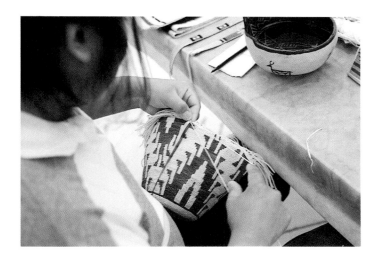

*Maynard White Owl Lavadour, photographed here at the Maryhill Museum of Art in 1987, is one of only a few weavers who make the traditional basketry hats.*

designs that subtly shifted with the flaring sides of the basket hat, life was a series of adaptations for the people of the Mid-Columbia. In the days of living within the cycle of seasons with little outside interference, those adaptations were easier to make.

Although the form remains the same, the introduction of beadwork to the hat's construction allows today's artist greater freedom of design. No longer restricted to geometric motifs, a few hat makers work colorful flowers and intricate personal ornamentation into the newer hats. These innovations reflect the greater number of choices open in other areas of life and the increased opportunity for expression. Many artists find themselves free of the constraints of the old ways while continuing to draw on the old strengths. It appears that the basket hat will adapt and survive with the deepest remnants of those other times.

*Wasco ceremonial bags that caught the author's eye in a
Seattle shop. Private collection. Photo by Wyatt McSpad-
den Photography; courtesy of Bruce Hartman.*

# 3. WAPAAS
## *The Twined Root-Digging Bag*

*"You will make your soft basket . . . facing the sunrise, and then it may address you."*
—*Mary Eyley*

In 1970 I was browsing through a shop in Seattle's University District, drawn in by an old *shaptakay* or rawhide "Indian suitcase" in the window. Known as Artifact, the store was rich in dusty antiques, oriental textiles, and American Indian goods. On a dark shelf at the back of the store I saw a pair of cylindrical twined bags. They leaped at me, asked to go home with me, and, to this day, the memory of them arouses an unusual excitement in me.

The bags were small, about five inches high and three inches across, twined in the intricate full-turn technique of the Chinookan-speaking Wasco or Wishxam people who lived along the Columbia River near The Dalles, Oregon.[1] They were similar, if not identical, and connected by a hide thong strung with light blue and brass beads. More thongs strung with similar beads hung like fringes from the bags' hide-covered rims. Two human skeletal figures in a horizontal position circled each bag. The dealer had purchased the bags from "an old Goldendale (Washington) collection," and said only that he thought they were used as part of a Wasco ceremony.[2]

The pair of bags did not go home with me;[3] they did, however, arouse my interest in a basketry form I knew little about, the round root digging bags made by the ancestors of our friends and neighbors on the Warm Springs and Yakima reservations and used today by these friends and neighbors on their root-digging expeditions. I have accompanied them to root-digging areas among the dry hills that look sterile to those of us who are accustomed to gathering vegetables in lush gardens. Each woman quietly works her way across the barren, rocky hillside, placing the curved blade of her *kapin* (digging stick) beside each plant and gently but firmly pushing it down, deep enough to loosen the bulb. With a careful tug at the plant with one hand and a push on the digging tool with the other, she lifts the root from the ground. She shakes the dry soil from the root and, sometimes twisting off the top, tucks her prize into the soft twined bag tied to her waist.

We encounter this scene again in the Nez Perce legend "Cottontail Boy Steals Thunder's Wife":

*Cottontail Boy knew his grandmother was growing old and needed a woman to do the work. "I am going now," he told her, "to take away from Thunderer that wife who is his most beloved." And, despite Grandmother's warnings of Thunderer's fury, he went.*

*Cottontail Boy say many women digging roots. Among them was Thunderer's most beloved wife. "Put your digging stick aside," he told her, "Put away your bag." Seizing her by the arm, he dragged her away.*

*Learning of the deed, Thunderer followed Cottontail Boy. The clouds thundered, the lightning flashed. Cottontail Boy stared unblinking at the sky, protecting himself and his captive. He vanquished the angry husband.*

*"Only a short time away," Thunderer predicted, "the human race will come . . . and they too will do this thing. Not I, alone, am indignant. Many will be indignant."[4]*

The people of the Mid–Columbia since earliest times have depended for sustenance the year around on the food roots that grow plentifully in the hills above the river. To gather the great quantities needed to last a year, a family had to have containers to hold the roots during the digging and to carry them home. These were the twined, round bags known today as "sally" bags. What may be the earliest reference to this term was made by the western artist and collector George Catlin, who was in The Dalles between 1852 and 1855. He described the bags as utilitarian containers for possessions as Indians "sallye forthe" on their journeys.[5]

Around the turn of the twentieth century the term came to refer to the cylindrical twined bags with human and animal or complex geometric designs made by Wasco women and their relatives, the Wishxam. The popular belief among collectors was that a woman named Sally was the only Wasco weaver who succeeded in making these animated subjects on her bags.[6] The Frohman catalogue claimed in 1902 that "Sally died a few years ago and the few 'Sally bags' on the market enhanced in value. Her work is only in the hands of a few collectors and two museums."

Support for part of this claim comes from an article in the

*The twined bags and digging tools used by the ceremonial diggers are lined up before the 1985 root feast begins at Wapato Longhouse on the Yakima Reservation.*

*Twined hat collected by Velina Nesmith Molson among the Cayuse in 1893. The hat is twined on an Indian hemp foundation with bear grass in the natural creamy color and (dyed) yellow. The red and black are raveled wool or yarn. Molson Collection no. 1657, McCord Museum, McGill University.*

*Coiled basket made to protect feathers or a hand bell. Collected by Louisa Ruch Miller of The Dalles before 1905. H10.5 in., W5 x 3.5 in. Photo by Jerry Taylor. Maryhill Museum of Art cat. no. 1953.03.13.*

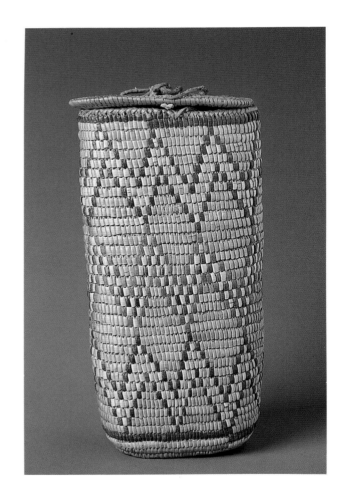

Delores George, of Wapenish Trading Post on the Yakima Reservation, and her daughter, Esther George, wear twined hats as part of their ceremonial dress for a cultural education performance at the Maryhill Museum of Art, 1989.

Colville Indian women parade in their finest during the Fourth of July encampment, 1955. A woman riding in the rear is wearing a basketry hat. Photo by W. T. Schlick.

*Yakima women digging bitterroot, c. 1950. Photo by J. W. Thompson.*

Rodeo scene? Wasco-style bag twined of commercial string and tule or grass reflects other changes in native life. H7 in. W5.5 in. Private collection. Photo by W. T. Schlick.

Cows replace deer and elk on this Wasco bag collected by Brigadier General Nelson A. Miles on the Warm Springs Reservation, c. 1880. Photograph by Joseph Schlick. Southwest Museum, Los Angeles, cat. no. 964-G-90.

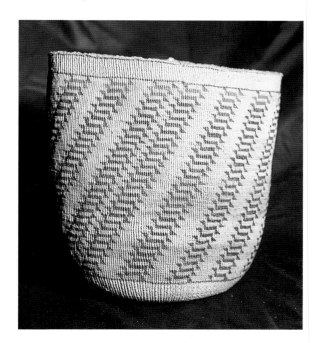

"Steps" design on a twined bag. Southwest Museum, Los Angeles, cat. no. 1499-G.51.

"Very old" is the description of this design on a bag collected by the Reverend William C. Curtis in the vicinity of The Dalles about 1895. Maryhill Museum of Art cat. no. 1951.01.91.

*Cree/Metis-style octopus bag woven of seed beads on the Columbia River in loose-warp technique before 1850. Note similarity of quadruped figures to those on the flat Wasco-style bag. H20 in., W6.5in. Oregon Historical Society cat. no. 1527.*

*An Episcopal missionary, the Reverend R. W. Summers, collected this Wasco-style bag in Oregon in the 1870s. British Museum cat. no. AM 1900C3.98.*

*Flat, twined bag with traditional Wasco/Wishxam images of birds (possibly representing giant condors) and quadripeds. Photo by Jerry Taylor. Maryhill Museum of Art cat. no. 1940.01.97B.*

*Reverse of Wasco-style twined bag. Maryhill Museum of Art 1940.01.97B.*

*The weaver of this bag illustrated the seasonal round of Columbia River life. Four sturgeon lie below the figure of a woman standing beside a motif that has been identified as a box with the tails of two fish protruding from the top. Photograph by Joseph Schlick. Cook Collection, no. 1–903, Oregon State Museum of Anthropology.*

*Another scene on the same bag (upper right): fishermen with dip nets and women holding digging tools for spring root gathering. Photograph by Joseph Schlick.*

*A bird and two figures with hands raised as in a Wasco ceremony decorate this side of the bag. Deer or elk may represent fall hunting. Photograph by Joseph Schlick.*

January 1904 *Sunset* magazine by R. S. Shackelford, a woman from The Dalles whose fine collection of Wasco-style bags now is in the Smithsonian and other museums. "It was christened the Sally bag by a humor-loving Congregational divine, long resident on the Columbia, who still is an ardent basket collector. . . . The name perpetuates the memory of an honest and industrious woman."[7] But here Shackelford disagrees with the Frohman statement that "Sally" was the only successful weaver of these bags. "Good as was Sally's work, several women are still living who can surpass her in her own line of weaving," the collector concludes.

There probably were several, but we know of at least one weaver named Sally who made the Wasco-style bags at the time of these writings. She was Sally Wahkiacus who lived upstream on the Klickitat River, a tributary entering the Columbia at the community of Lyle, Washington. A prolific basketmaker, Sally Wahkiacus was born about 1825 to a Wishxam mother and Klikitat father, and would have been a mature weaver when the great surge of collecting took place at the turn of the century.

Other explanations have been put forth, although not by the people of the Mid-Columbia, who rarely use the term. The Sahaptin speakers among them refer to the bag as *wapaas; aqw'alkt* is used by the Chinookan-speaking Wasco and Wishxam people. One suggestion is that "sally" was a word for a pocket carried by English women and the early traders simply used the same name for this bag which was worn in the same way (James Nason, pers. com. 1980). Another possible explanation is that many of the early bags were twined of hazelnut or willow root bark. The willow was known as "sallow" or "salla" to the British who could have described them as "salla" bags. This explanation is perhaps the most logical.

After the twin twined bags opened my eyes to this unique basketry form, I began to watch for them at the annual spring Speelyi Mi (Coyote's) Arts and Crafts Fair on the Yakima Reservation. There in private family displays of heirloom artifacts were all sizes of root digging and round storage bags.

*Klikitat basketmaker Sally Wahkiacus with two twined bags, 1906. Photographer unknown; courtesy Eva McLavy and Winifred Flippin.*

*Wasco/Wishxam bags in the attic of the National Museum of Natural History, Smithsonian Institution, 1975.*

Many had been woven long ago in the full-turn designs of the Wasco/Wishxam weavers.

These complex geometric designs and human and animal forms that the area is noted for were woven mainly by Upper Chinook basketmakers who lived along the Columbia River. I was too late to meet Louise Van Pelt Sconawah Spino, the last known weaver of these Wasco-style designs, who died in 1971. Those who used these unusual designs in their bags included the Wascos from near The Dalles and their neighbors across the Columbia, the Wishxam; and other smaller bands of relatives whose winter villages were located downstream at the Hood River, the White Salmon River, at the Cascades (present site of Bonneville Dam), and possibly as far as the mouth of the Willamette. Other bags in the family displays bore stripes or bands, usually horizontal, woven in plain twining. A few had designs worked in them in false embroidery. These bags were made by weavers who spoke dialects of the Sahaptian language family. I discovered that some women continue to do this traditional weaving, but all use the plain twining technique of the Sahaptin people.

Among the Yakima weavers was the grandmother who first alerted me to the fact that this ancient work was still being done. She agreed to "teach" me to twine. In the learning traditions of her people, she worked and I watched. In the methods of mine, I asked questions. But when I did, she would go on with her weaving.

Had I begun to learn at the traditional time, as a small child at a grandmother's side during the long winters near the river, I would have had years to absorb the knowledge. As it was, I took in what I could in the time we had left to us. I began to twine. When I needed help, I looked closely at a bag the grandmother had made for my husband. Gradually the awkward process began to make sense. The rhythm I would have learned as a child of the river slipped into place and I learned what my teacher knew: there is peace in twining. It was a generous gift.

## THE TWINED BAG IN COLUMBIA RIVER LIFE

Unlike the twined hats that once were part of everyday clothing but now are brought out only for special or ceremonial occasions, the round bags continue to fulfill their utilitarian purpose for the Mid-Columbia people. However, their use is considerably diminished.

Long ago the food roots that grew in the dry soils of the Columbia uplands provided most of the vegetable portion of the people's diet year around. To look at the land it is hard to believe it is productive, but the roots native to the area have a surprising ability to regenerate each year. The *pyaxi* or bitterroot, one of the most important foods for the people of the Mid-Columbia, is named *Lewisia rediviva* ("lives forever") because of this characteristic. When Meriwether Lewis brought his botanical specimens to Philadelphia in 1807, this plant, of course, was dry and shriveled. But much later, when botanist Frederick Pursh unwrapped the spec-

*Wasco-style bag with stylized faces and geometric designs was collected at the Cascades of the Columbia before 1869 by Dr. James T. Ghiselin of the U.S. Army Medical Department. Smithsonian Institution cat. no. 9041, neg. no. MAH 1773.*

*Wasco-style root bags in a family display at Speelyi-mi Arts and Crafts Fair in Toppenish, Washington, 1975.*

imen to examine the plant, he found the bitterroot was blooming.[8]

In 1841, Lieutenant Robert E. Johnson, USN, a member of the Wilkes Expedition, described the first recorded trip through the Cascade Mountains near Mount Rainier. Johnson observed twenty to thirty women digging camas and wild carrot on the top of a ridge "with baskets suspended from the neck and pointed stick in their hand . . . so intently engaged in the search for them as to pay no attention whatever to a passer-by" (Meany 1916, 27; Wilkes 1970, 428).

From the time of Lewis and Clark on, reports about the people of the Mid-Columbia describe scenes of root-gathering. As late as the mid-1930s, it was not unusual for a family to dig fifty pounds of roots in a day. A supply of twenty-five gunny sacks full of dried roots would last until the next spring when the roots returned. When cooked in boiling water, sometimes mixed with dried salmon, a handful of bitterroots would feed an average-size family (Scott 1941: 209).[9]

Today many of the root-digging areas are outside the reservations or within reservation boundaries but on land that has gone out of Indian ownership. Although the Columbia River people reserved the rights to hunt and gather food on the lands they ceded to the United States in the Treaty of

1855, such access is not easy. In many places fences and gates prevent free movement across traditional gathering areas; in others, heavy grazing has reduced the root crop.[10]

These changes in land use have made a difference in the lifestyle of the people of the Columbia, but, also, the people themselves are more dependent on foods easily obtained from the produce market or grocery store. Not as many root bags are needed today, and very few are made.

In spite of these changes, as in days of old, when the late winter sun begins to warm the hills along the river in February, women especially chosen by the longhouse elders tie their soft root-digging bags around their waists and go out to look for the first green of the year, the wild celery. They are gathering the fresh stems for the first feast of the season, the celery feast.

The people of the Mid-Columbia pick several varieties of wild celery. In late February and March they gather the young sprouts of Gray's desert parsley, known as *latít-latit* to the Sahaptin-speaking people of the Columbia River and as *xásya* in the Northwest Sahaptin dialects. In April the people gather *xamsí,* bare-stemmed desert parsley (*Lomatium nudicaule*).[11] Wild celery is not preserved, but eaten fresh from February through June. The earliest of the celery feasts usually is held at Rock Creek Longhouse on the Columbia and Indians from both sides of the river join in thanking the Creator for the bounty the earth has provided.

Later, usually in early April, the ritual is repeated as the women dig the early roots for the root feast. Feasts are held to honor each seasonal food, the roots, the salmon, and the huckleberries. "The Great Spirit gave the food for us to live on," the people of the Warm Springs Reservation explain. "We didn't have to plant it, cultivate it, or water it. That is why we thank him with our prayers" (Middle Oregon Indian His. Soc. 1987; Relander 1962, 20).

Those who gather and prepare the food for the feast must handle the Creator's gifts with love and kindness in their hearts and begin each day of gathering with songs of prayer. The songs are handed down from mothers to daugh-

*Women from Wapato Longhouse dig roots on the Yakima Reservation for the root feast in 1985. Photo by W. T. Schlick.*

ters to granddaughters as part of their traditional training (Middle Oregon Indian His. Soc. 1987). The day of the feast, the women are up early to prepare the meal as the heartbeat sound of the drums of the Sunday Waashat service fills the longhouses. The digging sticks and root bags are set aside in a place of honor.

When the service ends, the ancient ritual of the meal begins. Each food is served in turn. When all foods have been brought in and the prayer song sung, the leader announces each food, and everyone tastes them in turn: *nusux* (salmon); *yaamash* (deer); *pyaxi, luksh,* and *xawsh* (roots); *xasya* (wild celery); *kw'inch* (black pine moss); and *tmaanit* (berries). The leader then says "*chuush*" and each person drinks the water that is already served in the cups. The people can now eat whatever they wish, joining in a sociable and joyous meal.

In the old days, many families were camped out on the land and each held its own feast of thanksgiving before gathering the year's supply of roots or other foods (Stowell 1980; Nettie Jackson, pers. com. 1987). Several families have described the old custom of burying a bag full of roots, as well as flint and steel for starting a fire, at the camping spot as insurance that the next campers would have food and fire. In recent years, a rancher found such a bag buried at an old camp site near the Deschutes River.[12]

After taking part in the seasonal feast, the people are free to go out and "harvest" the foods for themselves, always careful not to take all the roots at any place where they dig. Many root diggers today replace the turf where the root was removed, as their mothers taught them, leaving the place as they found it.[13]

When a young girl digs her first roots, the family honors this initiation with a dinner. Although a rare ceremony today, the custom among the Wascos and some other Mid-Columbia people was for the youngster to give her digger and bag of roots to an elderly woman guest. The recipient then danced with the gift, singing a song that asked the roots to make themselves available to the child in the future (French 1955, 119).[14]

Today many people continue to dig roots, but only enough for special family occasions, for gifts to tribal elders who prefer the native foods to those from the grocery store, and for dinners at the longhouse. Although air drying was the traditional method of preserving the roots, today they may be dried in an electric food dryer or preserved by freezing. A few of the older women still dig and dry roots for trading.[15]

Round twined bags, made primarily for holding or carrying roots during the digging season, were also used to gather medicines or other foods such as acorns, hazelnuts, mushrooms, and sunflower seeds, as well as to store a variety of household and personal goods. A round twined bag in a Middle Oregon Indian Historical Society display at Kahneeta Lodge on the Warm Springs Reservation was "used for medicine, treasures, potion, and keeper for many things as for medicine singing, Indian Ruge, perfumes, etc." Every family needed many bags. They were the ubiquitous containers—strong enough to last for years (even when buried in the ground), their flexibility allowing flat storage and comfortable carrying.

The smaller quart-sized, root-digging bags were made for children, with adults carrying slightly larger bags. Large bags were used to hold the day's digging, and two loops at the rim and another at the base of the opposite side for a tump line, or carrying strap, to pass through, made them easier to carry on the back (Ray 1932). Even today when the supply of roots is carried out of the hills in a pickup or car and the tump line is not needed, families prefer to carry the day's digging in the old bags if they have them.

Lewis and Clark described great stacks of woven bags, each bag two feet long and one foot in diameter and lined with salmon skin that contained the concentrated powder of dried salmon known as *ch'lay*. This powder is a valued food today and is boiled with dried roots and water or mixed with dried berries for a high-energy food similar to pemmican. The explorers purchased "4 Sacks of fish" on October 29, 1805. The people of the river closed the bags by placing a

*The large bags for carrying food roots or storing dried salmon and other foods were equipped with loops for the carrying strap. The design on this bag is similar to a common motif on coiled cedar root baskets often referred to as "salmon gill." Made from Indian hemp, spun bark of willow root, grass, and cotton string, this bag has a canvas-covered rim. This bag probably was made by a Umatilla weaver using the served twined overlay technique. H12 in., W8 in. Private collection. Photo by W. T. Schlick.*

piece of salmon skin across the opening and holding it with lacings through the loops of string that circled the rim of the twined bag (De Voto, 1953, 262).[16]

These 90- to 100-pound bags of dried salmon pulverized in a mortar of dense wood or of stone were a major item of trade for the people living around the great fisheries of the Cascades, The Dalles, and Celilo Falls and were mentioned as late as 1911 by photographer Edward S. Curtis. Curtis was told that the salmon was "rammed tightly" into the baskets, each of which could hold the powder made from 100 salmon (Curtis 1911b, 173). Families also stored their own winter supplies of the dried fish which, according to one report, were "suspended in trees until cold weather, then boiled and eaten at night . . . causing them to sleep and forget the cold" (Fletcher c. 1891).

The traditional basket sizes evolved as standard measures for trading purposes. The large bag into which the contents of the diggers' own containers were emptied held about a bushel and a quarter of roots and was known by the Nez Perce as *nakts ispalq,* meaning "one bag" (Williams 1896, 103). A twined basket, eight inches in diameter and twelve inches deep, was the standard measure for the pulverized salmon. Dried salmon and salmon heads were offered in a smaller basket, eight inches wide and seven inches deep. One basket of the dried salmon and heads was worth several baskets of dried clams in trade with coastal Indians (Ray 1938, 133).

Over the years the form of the round, twined root-digging bag has changed little. One reason may be that no other shape has been found that satisfies the need quite so well. No commercial containers have taken the soft bags' place, either. More flexible than the old lard bucket or to-day's plastic ice cream pail, the bags are comfortable to wear. Stiffer than a sugar sack or other cloth bag, the bags stay in an open position to receive the roots. With these advantages, the hand-twined bag survives, but just barely.

A few contemporary weavers make the smaller bags, from miniature replicas to those about a foot deep, and sev-

eral young weavers at Celilo Village and on the Yakima and
Warm Springs reservations are learning from their elders.
The larger bags, those made to hold the day's digging, however, were replaced long ago by burlap or other commercial
bags. Requiring quantities of material and time to weave,
these have not been made for many years, possibly since the
early 1900s.

An example of one variation in the common form is the
pair of small bags in the Seattle shop that first drew me to the
Wasco-style weaving. Such bags have been made for a long
time, one pair of "twin" bags was inherited by the late Yakima leader Eagle Seelatsee from his Wishxam grandmother
who was born at Spearfish about 1850 (Lorena Seelatsee,
pers. com. 1979). The Seelatsee bags are connected at intervals by the twining rows on the adjoining sides. One of the
bags features fish, birds, and human figures; the other, dogs,
birds, and men. Another pair of miniature bags, probably
woven in the midtwentieth century is twined with some connecting rows and decorated with simple stripes.[17]

We can only conjecture about the use of such bags. The
Seattle pair (see page 46) reportedly was made for a Wasco
ceremony; others may have been also, or were simply demonstrations of a weaver's virtuosity.[18] One rarely seen variation of the Wasco-style bag is a flat handbag made in the full-
turn twining technique.[19]

# Weaving the Round Twined Bag

## *Materials*

Archaeologists have found remnants of Indian hemp
cordage and textiles in the earliest Columbia River sites. Expert at utilizing the resources at hand, the people also used
the bark of hazelnut and willow root, and possibly of other
shrubs, as well as tule and cattail for the foundation materials
in the soft twined bags.[20]

The ubiquitous burlap bag, or gunny sack, came to the
Columbia River with the settlers. The coarse plain-woven

*"Wishham Basket Worker," 1909. Photo by Edward S. Curtis. This woman has been identified as "Lashcum's ayet (woman)" or as "Old Man's (Martin Spedis) wife." Oregon Historical Society no. 58402.*

fabric of jute, flax, or hemp provided a new material that was free—except for the time it took the weaver to pull out the threads and roll them with the native hemp into twine. Similar to the native hemp in color, these fibers were considered satisfactory substitutes for the traditional material. Older women today remember seeing their grandmothers and other elders raveling gunny sacks for string well into this century.[21]

A Yakima elder told of helping her grandmother by splitting grasses with her teeth to use for the designs in her bags (Julia Sohappy, pers. com. 1975). Most reports from early travelers state that the grass used for decoration on the soft bags was named bear grass. However, several Warm

Springs and Yakima people say that bear grass is too firm for this use. They describe the grass that the weavers used as growing "up mountains," or "back up in the hills," or "like a small tule," or "tall grass growing in mountain lakes."[22]

In 1900, Mrs. R. S. Shackelford of The Dalles sent a Wasco-style bag and a sample of the material used in its manufacture to the Smithsonian "to aid Prof. Mason in his study."[23] She identified the material as *Sparganium eurycarpum,* a pond grass known as bur reed. It is possible that this is the grass described above, which the weavers used for their bags, as well as a variety of other strong grasses such as tough "sage grass" described by a Klikitat family as growing in the lowland (Nettie Jackson, pers. com. 1987).

The husks of the ears of corn were among the earliest of the "new" materials that became available to the Mid-Columbia weavers at the beginning of the nineteenth century.[24] It appears that they were not in general use in the round twined bags until much later. The weavers may have saved the pliable, easily dyed cornhusks for the false embroidery on their flat storage bags. It is difficult to tell from the outside surface if a round Wasco-style bag has been made with one of the native grasses or with cornhusks. The cornhusks are shorter than most grasses and the frequent splices are visible on the inside face of the bags.

Mid-Columbia weavers utilized the yarn from raveled blankets in the twined hats made after the arrival of the newcomers, but only a few of the early round bags had color, usually red, worked into the designs. When worsted yarns became available in many colors, most Wasco/Wishxam weavers continued to work their patterns in natural materials dyed purple with blackberry juice, dark brown from a decoction of willow bark, or black from burying the material in alkaline mud. On the other hand, Sahaptin weavers began to incorporate colored yarns in their round twined bags at about the same time as another substitute, white cotton string, also became available in great quantity and at no cost, around the turn of the twentieth century.

Many native people of the Mid-Columbia tribes began

working in the hop yards after the introduction of the plant in Washington's Yakima Valley in 1871.[25] Many Warm Springs Indians traveled over the Cascade Mountains to the Willamette Valley to work in the hops there also (French 1955, 376; Shane 1950, 15).[26] Entire families moved to the hop ranches at the end of the huckleberry season, the growers providing pasture for their horses.

"For six weeks our house was surrounded by the cheery fires of Indians . . . sometimes as many as 50 teepees," a Yakima hop rancher's daughter recalls. At first the hops were trained up cedar poles, but by 1910 the growers increased their production by stringing cotton twine "about the size of a #9 knitting needle" on high trellises.

*Group of hop pickers in Yakima, 1903. Photo by La-Roche. Smithsonian Institution photo no. 81–13,422.*

At the end of the season, these strings were cut down and the blossoms were picked from the vines. The blossoms were baled in giant burlap bags, and shipped off to breweries across the country. The string remained, thousands of yards of it. The hop grower's daughter remembers seeing the native women winding the hop twine into giant balls to take home for their winter's basketmaking.

This plentiful supply of twining material and the opportunity for harvest work for the Indian people ended in the early 1940s after the introduction of the picking machine about 1939. The machine chops up twine, vine, leaves, and all and returns them to the soil. The string bonanza lasted only thirty years.[27]

Louise Van Pelt Sconawah Spino, who made the Wasco-style bags, continued to base her designs on the traditions of the distant past, using the creatures of the world around her to inspire her work to the end of her life. Like most other mid-twentieth-century weavers, however, Louise Spino used the "new" materials in her weaving. Instead of knee-spun Indian hemp and grass, the more easily obtained commercial string, cornhusks, and imported raffia formed the warp and wefts of her later bags.

## Making the Bag

It is winter. The weaver settles herself on a mat in the warm winter lodge with her materials at hand. Her grandchildren are nearby, boys as well as girls, and they watch her fingers fly along the work, twisting with one hand, holding with the other, stitch by stitch building her designs. Perhaps she tells them the story she is working into the bag, or another story of old that teaches the ways of their people. They listen, but they also watch. The girls, at least, will be expected to do as she does before they can marry, and much sooner, it is hoped.[28]

When she begins, the weaver measures her warps—seeing in her mind's eye the bag she wants to make, knowing just how much extra twine she will need for the binding off. She gathers up sixty or so for a medium-sized bag, holding

*Arlene Brunoe Boileau, Wasco, demonstrates starting a round twined bag. Photo by W. T. Schlick.*

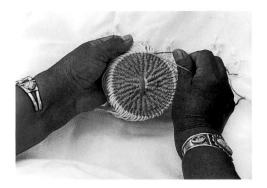

*Sally Buck twines the base of a bag.*

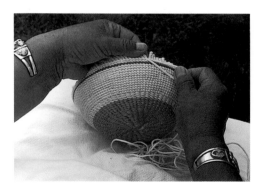

*Twining a solid, dark line around the base to set apart the design field as the bag begins to take form. Photos by W. T. Schlick.*

the bundle by its center. Wrapping the weft string around the center of the bundle, she begins to twine with the two ends of the weft string, enclosing as many as ten warp strands at a time around the center, then fewer, until finally she is twining around each single weft, around and around the bag. If the bag begins to cup up before the base is large enough, she adds more warps, spacing them evenly around the row. After the weaver completes the base and weaves a few rows up the sides, she changes color and twines a solid dark line around the bag. This sets apart the design field.

## Building the Design

In all basketmaking, the weaver's choice of technique determines how simple or complex her designs can be. To make the soft round bags, the Mid-Columbia weavers worked in two major techniques: most Sahaptin-speaking weavers used plain twining; the Chinookan-speaking (primarily Wasco and Wishxam people) employed full-turn twining. Of these, full-turn twining allows the greatest flexibility in design.

Plain twining, also known as simple twining, limits the weaver's choice of designs to vertical or horizontal stripes and simple rectangular accents. Some Sahaptin weavers also used false embroidery, or external weft wrap, to work designs into the bag's fabric. Several Umatilla weavers employed a served twined overlay technique to create their design (Fraser 1989, 94).[29] They call this technique "inside-out stitch." The motifs achieved by false embroidery or overlay rarely were as intricate as those worked in Wasco-style, full-turn twining. (See chapter 2 for diagrams of plain and full-turn twining.)

Between 1971—when Louise Spino died—and 1988, it appears that no Mid-Columbia native woman worked the Wasco-style designs into the bags. Today several young women of Wasco/Wishxam descent are studying this technique. Other than the work done by these weavers, almost all of the bags made today are in plain twining—their designs are stripes or rectangular forms or combinations of both. A few contemporary weavers work their designs in false embroidery.

These ethnic differences are not absolute, of course. A Sahaptian-speaking woman could master the Chinookan technique, and vice versa. Klikitat weavers and some others living upstream as far as the mouth of Rock Creek and at Alderdale were known to use the complex geometric and animal and human figures in the bags also. The groups were close neighbors, spending considerable time together, and intermarriage was common (Minor 1986). The bags with the complex designs are generally referred to as Wasco/Wishxam or Wasco style, to honor those who created the lively vocabulary of human, animal, and geometric forms.

We know that women of the Mid-Columbia were working these Wasco-style designs into their bags before Lewis and Clark arrived in 1805. The story begins on Sunday night, the twentieth of October 1805, when the Corps of Discovery camped on the north shore of the Columbia River near the "Pishquilpah" Indians.[30] Their hand-drawn map shows a camping place across and upriver from the mouth of the Deschutes River (Moulton 1983, Map 76). Clark wrote in his journal the next day: "Those people received us with great kindness . . . we got . . . a fiew pounded roots fish and Acorns" (DeVoto 1953, 259).

Apparently some of these foods were carried away in a twined root bag, for such a bag "prepared of grass by the Pishquilpahs on the Columbia River" made its way back East with the explorers. A "Memorandum of Specimens & Artifacts" from the expedition shows that the bag was in Charles Willson Peale's Philadelphia Museum in 1809 (Jackson 1962, 476). It is a miracle that the bag escaped a serious fire, survived transfers from museum to museum, and arrived unscathed at the Peabody Museum of Archaeology and Ethnology in Cambridge, Massachusetts, in 1899, ninety years later (Cutright 1969; ltr. from Charles C. Sellers, 17 Mar. 1978). The bag remains at the Peabody, perfect in form and proportion, the pattern a sophisticated network of stylized faces bordered by a stepped pattern and divided by groups of small dogs.[31]

The Wasco or Wishxam woman who twined the Lewis

*Wasco-style bag collected on the Columbia River by Lewis and Clark, 1805–6. H11.5 in., W6 in. Photo by Hillel Burger. Peabody Museum, Harvard University, cat. no. 99–12–10/53160.*

*Wilson Charley holds ten-year-old Ralph Nunez on his shoulders to measure the fish caught by Wasco fisherman Joe Estebrook, August 17, 1951. The eighty-two-year-old female white sturgeon weighed nine hundred pounds. Photographer unknown. Oregon Historical Society no. 4063.*

and Clark bag worked figures from her daily life and her people's mythology into her bag. More than a century later, another fine Wasco-style weaver did the same. "There I put elk, water birds, people," said Louise Spino. "That's the way life is, the people are with the animals all together" (Jeanne Hills, pers. com. 1981). "Grandma Louise," as she was known to many in the Mid-Columbia, lived in the village of Wahkiacus on the Klickitat River, a tributary of the Columbia. Born in 1897, she learned to make bags from her Wasco mother and grandmother (Doreen Spino Mahaffey, pers. com. 1985).

Louise Spino's designs were not limited to those she described; she also twined fish and birds into her weaving. Although her birds with wings spread are identical in shape, she varied the designs within their wings. If one compares her fish with those on other makers' bags, the Spino fish are perfectly wrought and uniform in shape.

Many designs on the Wasco-style bags reflected contemporary life along the river. The best-known motifs—the face, the full human figure with exposed ribs, fish, deer or elk, salamanders, frogs and other water creatures, and birds—appear in the weaving from the earliest known examples to the end of the nineteenth century. All of the designs but the "X-ray" human figures, and possibly the face, continued to be used into this century.

The fish, one of the most common of these designs, is notable for the series of stitches in the lighter color of the background that contrast with the dark body. This line of stitches appears to represent scutes, the external bony plates that mark the sides of the giant Columbia River sturgeon. "These people were Wishxam," some Yakima women said, when asked about the design, "They ate sturgeon." They also were making the point that the Sahaptin-speaking people did not eat sturgeon. Anthropologists Leslie Spier and Edward Sapir noted in 1930 that the Wishxam people believed the sturgeon, eagle, water monster, and mountain lizard to be exceptionally brave spirits.

A logical identification of the large figures with outspread wings that usually are labeled eagles or butterflies has been made by Wasco Chief Nelson Wallulatum. "There were condors on the river long ago," he said. "Lewis and Clark saw them. Those birds look like condors." He added that the people on the river kept baby condors in their camps "to keep the thunder and lightning spirit from striking. They called them 'lightning birds.' "[32]

"Some bags had seals on them," Wallulatum also said. "There once were seals up the Columbia as far as the mouth of the Deschutes River. Petroglyphs representing these animals are under the water above The Dalles Dam."

As collectors began to fill their homes with the handiwork of American Indians in the early years of the twentieth century, they were fascinated with the idea of symbolism on this "new" art form.[33] Writers on Columbia River basketry ascribed romantic names from Chinook Jargon to the designs on the Wasco-style bags: the human figure is "tillacum," the jargon word for friend; "mowitch" is deer or elk; "pish," fish; "culla-culla," duck; and "quadudk," frog (Mason 1902; Shackelford 1904).[34] The people of the Mid-Columbia say the inspiration for the designs came from the natural world their mothers and grandmothers knew so well, or from a design the weaver had seen and wanted to adapt (pers. com. Tallulah Pinkham 1975; Esther Wilkenson 1979).

During the time when Wasco/Wishxam weavers were working these distinctive designs into their bags, there were, however, commonly accepted names for traditional elements within the designs. "Hazel rope," for example, was the name for a series of diagonal stripes, as in the twisted fibers of a rope; "human teeth" were represented by a horizontal band with vertical crosspieces at intervals; a stepped pattern was known as "fish gills"; and "hide of a spotted fawn" was an all-over pattern of triangles (Spier and Sapir 1930, 195, 289). Many motifs were passed from generation to generation and from tribe to tribe, their names often changing with each transfer. Each weaver varied the arrangement or execution of the elements to produce a range of complex patterns, only rarely weaving two bags alike.

*Two sides of a twined bag made by Louise Van Pelt Spino about 1969 for her daughter Doreen Mahaffey. This bag shows the "fish, water birds, people . . . all together" that Spino's work depicted.*

*Wishxam names for some common designs, originally drawn by Miss M. W. Bonsall for the University of Pennsylvania Museum (Spier and Sapir 1930, 195): (a) hide of spotted fawn; (b) "very old"; (c) birds or butterflies, deer; (d) steps; (e) loose-fitting dovetailing; (f) salmon stomach; (g) sturgeon roe; (h) steps; (i) steps; (j) hazel withes; (k) eyes.*

Many of the bags told a story, the Wishxam people said (Laura Corpuz, pers. com. 1976). A collector from The Dalles in 1904 reported a weaver's remarks about two bags. One bag recorded the story of a successful hunt, showing two men and a child, a row of ducks that flew up as they went up the trail, and the deer they were stalking. Another bag was titled by the weaver as "The Return of Spring":

*Dancing frogs, girls with flags in their hands, cheerful dogs [portray a time when] nipping cold of winter full of privations is about to end and all nature greets the soft sweep of the Chinook wind as it comes piping up the Columbia river. It is a breeze with a touch like velvet,*

*Woman and girl in typical Wasco dress photographed at The Dalles, c. 1900. Bag at left shows bird and deer figures, center is "very old" design. Flat twined bag held by the girl was described by a Wasco woman as "from Pendleton." Photographer unknown. Courtesy of* American Indian Basketry Magazine.

*and often melts a three-foot snow in a night. It turns the heart of the stockman glad also, and the disconsolate bleating of the herds is soon stilled by the abundance of tender, green bunchgrass it uncovers. (Shackelford 1904, 259)*

The Victorian phrasing and the transition to the stockman's point of view cast some doubt on the weaver as the sole source of this story, but a look at the bag makes the first sentence believable.

The remarkable heritage of myths and legends of the Mid-Columbia people may have offered rich inspiration for these Wasco-style bags (Malin 1965, 5). The stylized faces and the full figures of humans with skeletal details have an

*A rare flat Wasco-style twined bag with stylized images of humans with exposed ribs, birds, and sturgeon. Photo by Jerry Taylor. Maryhill Museum of Art cat. no. 1940.01.97B*

aura of mythology about them. This feeling may come from the fine execution of what in any society would be considered inspired design, or we may be reading the original message of the basketmaker. Without the word of the weavers themselves, we will never know.

In 1926, an amateur anthropologist from Walla Walla was questioning an eighty-five-year-old Umatilla man about the meaning and uses of some artifacts. "Undoubtedly these had a use," the man told the anthropologist, "but many years from now will your grandchildren be able to explain a sickle or a cradle for harvesting wheat?"[35] Although we yearn to know what any work of art from another time is telling us, most interpretations are guesses at best.

The "exposed rib" or "exposed skeleton" motif on the human figures in the old bags has intrigued scholars for years, some suggesting that they represent a "ghost cult" among the Mid-Columbia native people (Strong 1945). Such motifs are actually common in the Northwest, and the people of the river had a natural close association with and understanding of the skeletal foundation of the human body (Bill Holm, pers. com. 1983). They were known to rebury the bones of their dead. Some had family dipnetting sites on the shores of the islands in the Columbia where the remains of their ancestors lay. "He had the blessings of those people [referring to the dead]," a woman said of her grandfather whose fishing sites were on one of the burial islands (Nettie Jackson, pers. com. 1984).

It is possible that the uses of the exposed-rib motif stems from an ancient and widely held belief that the ancestors' spirits reside in the bones. Among some peoples the motif is used as a sign of the spiritual rather than the secular world. The exposed-rib designs could be one way for the early Wasco and Wishxam weavers to depict their ancestors in their art.[36]

From the weaver's view, the full-turn twining technique is more interesting when colors can be changed frequently in the body of the weaving. The ribs, elbows, kneecaps, and spots in between add to the variety of the work. If it takes four days of steady twining to make a bag the size of a five-pound pail (Spier and Sapir 1930, 193), such variations in design would help keep a tedious task interesting.

There are many full human figures on nineteenth-century bags with other than riblike motifs. The figures on a Wasco-style bag in the British Museum, collected by the Reverend R. W. Summers in Oregon in the 1870s (see color section, following page 48), is decorated with parallel zigzag lines across the body (Dalton 1901, 23). Another bag with details so similar that it could have been made by the same weaver is in a private collection on the Oregon coast. One of the human figures on this bag features three diamond designs in a vertical pattern (see color illustration, title page). The other full human figure on the bag has tiny figures of men worked into the rectangle that is the body. The lower figure is upright, the other, upside down. (Could these be the "generations yet unborn" for whom the native people of the Mid-Columbia express such responsibility?)

Whatever their source or explanation, the skeletal details in the large human figures on many of the old bags do serve to identify the work of the Wishxam and Wasco weavers and echo the rib motif that commonly occurs in petroglyphs in the area. Early Wishxams reported that the deeply carved petroglyphs at their traditional dipnetting sites represented water animals who were the particular spirits of their ancestors (Strong 1945, 250). The native people of the Mid-Columbia today simply say, of the old bags with the internally elaborated human figure designs, "Those figures are the old ones," or, "Those bags were made long ago."

It is possible that the Wasco-style designs on the bags were inspired neither by legend nor by the petroglyphs wrought by the ancestors. They may be distinctive artistic expressions within one rich aesthetic tradition that flourished along the river before the newcomers arrived, reflecting the great wealth of ceremony enjoyed by the early people of the Mid-Columbia River.

During the nineteenth century, the Wasco/Wishxam people developed a distinctive style of beadwork that is re-

*"Wasco Sally Bag" pot by Wasco/Yakima ceramic artist Lillian Pitt. Raku-fired; H10 in., W8 in., bead, 1990 Photo by Dennis Maxwell of Lightplay.*

*"She Who Watches," ancient petroglyph that guards the now-inundated Wishxam village of Nixluidix. This face has been suggested as the inspiration for the abstracted face design on Wasco/Wishxam bags. Photo by Joseph Schlick.*

lated to the design tradition (Schlick and Duncan 1991). The earliest known examples were collected about 1850 and feature designs strikingly similar to Wasco-style twined bags from the same period. Often referred to as loomed beadwork, many of the bags were woven without a loom in a manner similar to the twining of the bags. This is evident in the method of binding off at the end of the beadwork on some examples, and in the step (or jog) in the pattern where the new row begins. Patricia Atkins, an accomplished beadworker of Wishxam/Wenatchi descent, discovered this similarity in 1987 when she was studying full-turn twining.

Among the bags made in this way are those beaded by a woman named Taswatha, daughter of Welawa, the head of a Chinookan-speaking family who lived at Ruthton near Hood River, Oregon. The artist lived from 1849 to 1908 and was known as Ellen Lear Underwood in her adult life (Sharon Tiffany, pers. com. 1988). Examples of her beautiful work, made in the late 1800s, are in the Skamania County (Washington) Historical Museum.[37]

As changes came to the people of the river, the bag designs changed, too. Looking through photographs of Wasco-style bags, a woman of Wishxam descent noticed the dark "faces" on two early bags and said, "*Chmukli* (black man), those explorers brought a black man with them." She was referring to the local stories of Lewis's servant, York, who made that long trip with the Corps of Discovery.[38]

It has been suggested that the small solid figures of men with what appear to be hats on their heads are the newcomers (Daisy Ike, pers. com. 1984). Support for this suggestion lies in the language. A Sahaptian word for white man is *shuyapu*, which has been translated by some as "hat on head" or possibly derives from the French word for hat, "*chapeau*." A study of the bags indicates that this motif is not common before the late 1800s. Another motif that appeared in Wasco-style weaving about that time is the horse. Although the animal was introduced to the Plateau region in the early eighteenth century, the Klikitat, Wasco, and Wishxam people had few horses before 1850 (Anastasio 1975, 131).

Cattle were known to the people of the Mid-Columbia after the arrival of the missionaries in the 1830s and perhaps earlier as a result of contact with the native people of the Southwest. Billy Chinook, a Wasco man who served as guide for explorer John C. Frémont, brought a large herd from California to The Dalles in 1851 (Kuhlken 1982). These new animals are documented on a bag made sometime before 1880 and collected by Brigadier General Nelson A. Miles on the Warm Springs Reservation.[39] (See color section, following page 48.)

Other domestic animals made their way into the weaving vocabulary. A bag made by a Umatilla weaver using plain twining with the designs worked in overlay clearly shows a pig and a chicken.[40] Another bag, collected at The Dalles by a pioneer family who purchased land along the

*Beaded bag with Wasco-style figures made by Taswatha (Ellen Underwood), daughter of Wasco Chief Welawa, about 1880. Beads are woven in a loose-warp technique similar to that used in twining a bag. H7.5 in., W3 in. Photo by W. T. Schlick. Skamania County Historical Museum cat. no. 89.32.13.*

*Dancing frogs circle this bag made in 1991 by Wasco/ Tlingit artist Bernyce Courtney for her father.*

*This Wasco-style bag showing frogs and women with one hand raised inspired the design on the bag by Bernyce Courtney. Thomas Burke Memorial Washington State Museum no. 2.4252.*

river in 1856, depicted goats. It is possible that the bag was woven much earlier, for the design could represent mountain sheep or goats that once ranged the Cascades near the Columbia. Such animals are represented in many of the petroglyphs along the river.

Despite the new subject matter, the arrangement of the designs in most of these nineteenth-century bags continued to be orderly and static, with figures placed in vertical columns, horizontal bands, or in a rare all-over pattern.

Some Wasco/Wishxam weavers continued to use the old designs at the turn of the century. Harriet Jackson, born about 1830, was working the network of faces into her bags at The Dalles in the early 1900s. Mary Cloud of the Sconawah/Stahi family and Susan Williams of Hood River were known to use the traditional human figure motif in the same period. Relatives of Sally Buck, a Klikitat weaver making bags today in plain twining and false embroidery, used traditional Wasco-style designs well into the 1900s.[41] In 1991 Pat Courtney Gold, Bernyce Courtney, and Arlene Brunoe Boileau, all of Wasco descent, and Patricia Atkins, Wishxam, began to study the traditional technique.

The turn-of-the-century bags reflected the changes that were taking place in the weavers' lives. As the need to make a living in a cash economy reduced the hours available for weaving, some weavers chose heavier materials for their bags, enlarging the fine stitches. As other traditional lifeways changed, the weavers began to leave behind the conventional motifs of earlier times. Until the recent revival of Wasco-style weaving, the X-ray human form appeared to have died with the nineteenth-century weavers, while the younger turn-of-the-century bag makers began depicting more action on the textile's surface. What the bags lost in artistry, perhaps, they gained in realism, featuring designs that appear to represent rodeo scenes, fish-spearing, a Wasco dance, and other activities.

## Finishing the Bag

*"She would work a while, then do something else, then go back to the bag. Before I knew it, the bag was finished!"*—Eddie Sconawah[42]

When the design is complete, the weaver twines another solid line around the bag. In the newer bags, the twined area above the design field is plain. However, many Wasco/Wishxam weavers in the nineteenth century worked a handsome band of Z-direction diagonal ridges into this border area by enclosing two warps at a time at regular intervals in the twining, creating a twill effect.[43]

The weaver knows from long practice when her bag has reached the correct size. A Wasco-Wishxam weaver finishes the rim of the bag with the same self-edge she uses to bind off a twined hat. (See page 41 in chapter 2 for a diagram of the self-edge technique. Exceptions to this binding-off method are seen on the Lewis and Clark bag and the flat Wasco-style wallet shown in Conn 1979, 252.) To create the self-edge seen in most Wasco-style bags, the weaver works from left to right, the outside surface of the bag toward her, carrying each warp in turn behind the warp to the right, then forward and in front of the next warp, and back between that warp and the next warp to the right, tucking it down and into the basket. On the exceptions, the weaver worked from right to left and involved four warps rather than three in each step of her "braid."

Sahaptian-speaking weavers most often turn the warps back into the bag with the weft strands, in a technique known as twining off (see page 164, chap. 6). This is the edge finish they also use on flat storage bags. In either method, the stub ends of the warps show on the inside.

Depending on what she has at hand, the weaver usually covers the edge of her bag with hide, canvas, dyed flour sacking, or other fabric. Occasionally she also attaches beads or other embellishments to this rim. The blue and brass beads hanging from the Seattle pair of bags are examples. In another bag, the maker attached dentalia shells, blue beads, and

*Twined bag "made before 1898 by Sallie." Collected by Roxa Shackelford of The Dalles. The bag was among the baskets purchased by Ella F. Hubby from Pasadena dealer Grace Nicholson and later given to the Smithsonian Institution. Smithsonian cat. no. 328074.*

*The full-turn twining technique allowed Wasco/Wishxam weavers to create complex designs in bags such as this one, probably made before 1900, which was given to the Maryhill Museum of Art by the granddaughter of Wasco Chief Welawa. H9.5 in., W5.5 in. Photo by W. T. Schlick. Maryhill Museum of Art cat. no. 1940.01.04.*

red yarn; in another, long glass tube beads. In each case, the attachments give the basket a three-dimensional effect, enhanced by the motion of the carrier.

The weaver laces a thong or string around the bag through this binding to form loops. When the bag is full, a woman gathering roots will hold her harvest in place by connecting the loops with a cord. Bags made for digging also have two loops attached to the rim on one side. A root gatherer can run a belt through these loops and tie the bag to her waist, leaving her hands free for the important work.

With these finishing touches, the weaver completes another bag. Perhaps the children who surround her are sad to have the quiet time of learning over, but the new root-digging bag represents the sociable time of spring when they will join their friends and relatives for another round of seasonal activities.

The cylindrical twined bag, worn to gather the sacred roots, is held in high regard by the people of the Mid-Columbia. Its contents are recognized, along with water, fish, deer, and berries, as sacred, essential for life. To the people, the bag means more than a useful container. It is a reminder of the ancient past, a symbol of the earth's great capacity to provide for the people who live on it. As such, the twined root bag is an important and integral part of Columbia River native life.

# 4. Xlaam
## *The Coiled Cedar Root Basket*

*"Shade told First Weaver to weave a basket, so she repaired to the forest
and pondered long over her mission."*

It was September 1969. My family had been away from the West and from fresh huckleberries for five years and I had sent a request up to the berry fields at Potato Hill on the Yakima Reservation for a gallon. Within a day or two a call came from Gracie Ambrose of White Swan. "I have your berries; meet me at Savin' Sandy's."

There in the store's busy parking lot in Toppenish we made our trade—the product of our labor, dollars, for the product of hers, fresh berries—a fair exchange. Except for one thing. Gracie did not deliver the shiny purple berries in the plastic gallon ice cream bucket I expected; she handed them to me in a beautiful coiled Klikitat-style berry basket. A stepped design moved gracefully around its sloping sides, accented by simple "star" motifs. Fresh huckleberry foliage covered the berries and was held in place by strings laced through hide loops around the top of the basket. "I'll get the basket back to you," I said as we left.

"Don't throw away the leaves," she told me, "They need to go back to the mountain." I looked puzzled. "So nothing will ruin next year's crop," she explained.

I had seen many of the coiled huckleberry baskets made by the native people who live near the slopes of the Cascade Mountains north of the Columbia River. But I had seen them in museums. I had never held one in my hands, nor had I seen one full.

The berries brought the work of art to life; the basket became "real" for me. The protecting greenery made it more beautiful. Gracie Ambrose brought to our trade more than we both bargained for—I have never looked at a coiled berry basket since that day without visualizing it full of berries protected by leaves.

I began to look for the basketmakers. The art is dying, everyone told me. Emma Mesplie, an accomplished Yakima basketmaker who had held classes at White Swan, had recently stopped making baskets. We drove down to the Columbia River, then north into the hills above Husum to find Sophie Thomas, a member of a Klikitat Indian family known for many generations for their beautiful baskets. Sophie Thomas was not making baskets at the time, but suggested that we look for her sister Elsie in nearby Bingen, Washington. The two sisters were the last of the Klikitat weavers who

*Filled with huckleberries is the proper role for this much-used coiled cedar root basket. Photographed near Mount Hood by W. T. Schlick.*

used the traditional materials and techniques to make the baskets of their ancestors. We could not find Elsie Thomas. I feared I was too late, my opportunities to learn about the making of these baskets lost forever. Luckily, I was wrong.

Nine years after Gracie Ambrose's basket of huckleberries came into my life, a Yakima tribal councilman, Roger Jim, Sr., told me of Nettie Jackson, a young Klikitat woman. "She's making a book on Klikitat baskets," he said. "Maybe you would like to talk with her."[1]

When I called Nettie, I learned that Elsie Thomas was her husband's mother, and that the basketmaker was teaching her art in a native-culture program Nettie had organized. Sponsored by Clark College in Vancouver, the class was open to Indians of all ages and included bead and feather work as well as basketmaking. She invited me to visit the class held in a Bingen schoolroom.

Elsie Thomas sat surrounded by tidy bundles of cedar roots lying on the table and soaking in tubs of water.[2] Although the women and children in the room were talking quietly among themselves, Elsie was silent. Her pocket knife flew along the surface of a split strand of cedar root she was using as a stitching element. Removing any rough spots in this way, she then cut a pointed end on the strand. She poked her awl into the coil, followed it with the pointed end of the cedar root, and deftly pulled the smoothed strand through the awl's opening. The root made a soft squeak.

This was a bright classroom in a river town rather than a cozy winter lodge set in a sheltered valley back from the Columbia River. However, the scene was reminiscent of long-ago days. It was wintertime, and the teacher was a grandmother going about her accustomed task. The learners were adults; most had wanted to do this for years but had not had the patience to learn from their own grandmothers. The instruction was traditional—silent and by example. I settled back quietly to watch. I was not too late.

"Grandma told me that basket weaving started here," said Nettie Jackson. "Like a vein from the heart will go a long ways and goes deep, it went to the coast, to the mountains, deep into Canada. The looks changed but it started here on the Columbia River, on the Klickitat River."

There is no agreement among anthropologists as to the place of origin of the Klikitat-style basket, a sturdy pail-shaped container coiled of split cedar roots and, frequently, covered with a tilelike decorative layer applied in a folding technique known as imbrication. It has been suggested that this style began on the Interior Plateau (Weber 1982, 26) or among the Salish tribes who lived on the western slopes of the Cascades (Haeberlin, Teit, and Roberts 1928, 136). The Klikitat say that it began in their territory, on the eastern slopes of the Cascade Mountains north of the Columbia.

*Elsie Thomas, one of the few Klikitat basketmakers who has kept her people's tradition alive holds two trinket baskets that she made in the 1930s. Private collection.*

The technique of coiling with cedar roots and incorporating the glossy bear grass as a surface decorative element has been used for many generations by the native people living on both sides of the Cascades and into British Columbia. The art flourished where materials were plentiful and the people lived in one place. Most of the Washington Salish weavers, on the west side of the Cascades near the Klikitats and others to the north, discontinued the industry around 1850 (ibid, 141). Over the years, a few members of other groups have made coiled and imbricated baskets. Nancy, an eighty-year-old Nez Perce woman told anthropologist Alice Fletcher in 1890 that the men wove cooking baskets out of split cedar roots. "We put hot stones in them and boiled water, so cooked our food" (Fletcher 1891, 6). By 1930 the major producers were the Klikitat, and the Chilcotin, Thompson River, and Lilloet groups of British Columbia.

Wherever the art began, the Klikitats developed a distinctive style with a specific history.

*"The first people that had those large great baskets were the* Tatatlya—*today they call them Sasquatch or Big Foot. There were five of them, sisters. Grandma told us about them. . . . They caught little children and put them in the big baskets. They tied the baskets across the top so the children could not get out, and carried them home on their backs to their little ones to eat. The baskets had to be big enough to put children in. We called them* schlkup.

*Grandma told us about the* Tatatlya *so we would not go far back in the woods. She would tell the stories as if they happened to people she knew, and we believed her." (Minnie Marie Slockish in Kuneki, Thomas, and Slockish 1982, 14–15)*

Tatatlya is translated in various stories as ogress, witch, dangerous person, cannibal woman, and "soft basket woman monster." In one version, Owl is her husband and she is striped like her children who eat snakes, frogs, toads, and the like. The Wishxam people had a mask to represent the creature whom they called At'at'ahlia. They used the mask to frighten children to keep them from wandering away from their families.[3]

Another story survives of a jealous Wasco chief who used the family's largest baskets to carry sand from the banks of the Columbia River into his lodge (Ramsey 1977, 65). Spreading this sand around the lodge floor, he looked each morning for footprints of any man who dared to approach one of his one hundred wives.

Such exotic uses of the coiled cedar root baskets appear to have ended with the ancient people of the Mid-Columbia. However, around the turn of the century there was a revival of one of them. It became popular among photographers to place children (and sometimes family pets) in the largest of the baskets to dramatize the basket's great size.

## Coiled Baskets in Columbia River Life

Before buckets and kettles were introduced to the people of the Mid-Columbia in the first part of the nineteenth century (Tyrell 1916, 492),[4] perhaps the most common use for the baskets was in cooking. This was accomplished by dropping special rocks heated in the fire into the basket filled with water and the food. The heat in the rocks would quickly bring the water to a boil.

The tightly coiled baskets held water when the cedar roots were well soaked. Present-day basketmakers say they cannot make baskets that will not leak, but there may be a clue in an interview with the late Cowlitz basketmaker Mary Kiona in the 1950s. Asked if they cooked in these pretty baskets, Mary Kiona replied through her daughter, Minnie Placid, who was serving as interpreter, "These new ones don't hold water." Kiona explained that when berries are picked in a basket the little holes fill up (Gogol 1985c, 13). Perhaps baskets were relegated to cooking only after they had this "sealing" treatment.

Cooking-baskets were wider mouthed and shallower in proportion to width. Anthropologists suggest that the distinctive, tall, narrower baskets are a recent development among the Klikitat (Farrand 1900, 391). Perhaps the shape

*A mythical basketmaker is depicted in a mural by Richard Beyer at Kahneeta Resort on the Warm Springs Reservation. Possibly she represents Tatatlya, the legendary striped witch who, in a large basket, carried wandering children home to her own family for dinner. Courtesy of the Confederated Tribes of the Warm Springs Reservation of Oregon.*

*"Water Baskets—Wishham," 1909. Photo by Edward S.*
*Curtis. Oregon Historical Society neg. no. 67532.*

developed after the introduction of metal cooking pots when the people no longer needed to prepare their picking baskets for cooking duties. James Teit reported that cooking in baskets was rarely seen in 1909 when he visited the Yakima and Klikitat (1928, 356).

Other larger baskets, often more oval, were used to bathe babies or to hold drinking water. A Yakima woman remembers such a basket that sat in the corner of their kitchen with a cup beside it (Julia Sohappy, pers. com. 1974). Edward S. Curtis photographed a woman with a water basket along the river in 1909 (1911b, 120).

Klikitat basketmaker Sally Wahkiacus made a nut-shaped basket with a neck for John Langdon, developer of Klickitat Mineral Springs Company about 1925. Langdon photographed the basketmaker holding his basket under a stream of water and used an artist's rendering of the picture on early labels for his bottled water.

A basket of similar shape except for a slight flare at the mouth is in the collection of the Cheney Cowles Museum, Eastern Washington Historical Society, Spokane, and is identified as "for steeping herbs." This unusual basket is imbricated in vertical stripes in the natural color of bear grass and brown. White and blue beads hang from the rim.

The strong construction of the coiled basket was well adapted to traveling with horses, for carrying feathers and other items that might be broken. Best clothes and other valuables were stored in larger baskets; the smaller sizes, with lids, served as work baskets (Teit 1928, 356). Coiled baskets, as well as the twined bags, held dried foods for the winter.[5]

The Wishxam purchased oblong baskets, similar to the Thompson River trunk, in large quantities from the Klikitat. The larger ones often were undecorated and flattened on the side for carrying on a horse. A basket of this description, said to be more than one hundred years old at the time, was collected by Sir Percy Sargood of New Zealand in 1905 (Harsant 1988, 44).[6] Sargood probably purchased the basket, along with other Columbia River artifacts at the Lewis and Clark Exposition in Portland, from a North Yakima collector.

*Sally Wahkiacus collects water in her basket at the Klickitat mineral springs. She made this basket about 1925 for a bottled soda water label. Photo by John Langdon. Courtesy of Goldendale Historical Museum.*

*The flattened sides of some coiled cedar root baskets made them easily carried on a horse. Drawing by Yakima artist Larry George, c. 1972.*

The smaller, lidded version of this oblong shape was made for carrying feathers and fragile items. Few of these were being made by the turn of the century (Teit 1928, 356). Another lidded basket, tall and slender, also was made for protecting feathers or for carrying the hand bell used in religious services (pers. com. Nettie Jackson, 1984; Bernice Sampson, 1981). Perhaps the earliest example of a Klikitat-style basket is a small, oval basket without a lid that was collected by Captain Edward Belcher of the British exploring ship *Sulphur* when he visited Fort Vancouver in 1839 (Wright 1991, 35). The basket is now in the British Museum.

At the turn of the century, there were three common shapes of coiled cedar root baskets used by the people of the Mid-Columbia: the oblong baskets; the nut-shaped baskets, rounded with the opening just large enough to admit the hand; and the well-known "Klikitat" huckleberry basket, an "inverted truncated cone" (Teit 1928, 356).[7] Often described as pail-shaped, the majority of these berry baskets are graceful in appearance. Their design is logical, the sloping sides of the basket effectively protecting the berries from crushing. Most coiled baskets were either partially or completely covered with imbrication; although small picking baskets, made for children, usually were not.

When iron and copper kettles first came to the people of the river, the new containers were in great demand. Today, however, most Columbia River Indian people do not want to pick berries into metal or plastic. The coiled baskets are considered treasures, and for those families who have them, the baskets are the preferred picking vessels. These cedar root baskets not only receive the berries in silence, they also keep the precious crop fresh. A basket woven by a grandmother evokes memories of childhood as well as pride·in a family heirloom.

The people look forward to the end of summer when they head for the mountains with the family's supply of baskets. "We were taught the Great Spirit created food," Wilson Charley, a Yakima elder, said when recalling berry picking in his childhood. "That is why I love those foods with my whole life. No one can stop me from eating them." He told of going with his grandmother up to Meadow Creek, on the south side of Mount Adams:

*We were there for three weeks. First two weeks picking we dried all the berries. We fell a big dead timber about hundred feet or more long, and we dug the dirt on one side of the log about seventy feet long. She put the tule mats [there] and pour all the berries on these mats. I had to drag dry wood and keep the fire agoing while she stir the berries with a pole made like a boat oar. It took six or eight hours to dry them.*

*Then she would put them back into the cedar baskets and take them back to the camp. She cut some poles and made a table and put these berries on the same mats and let the sun cure them in Mother's ways. I had to stay at camp to keep the squirrels from packing the*

*"Jar" similar to the basket made by Sally Wahkiacus for the Klickitat Mineral Springs Company. Collected by Dr. G. M. Kober at Spokane Falls, Washington. Smithsonian Institution cat. no. 131,246.*

*The preferred container for berries among the native people of the Mid-Columbia is the traditional pail-shaped, Klikitat-style basket. USDA Forest Service photo by Ray M. Filloon, 1935.*

berries away. *The berries had to have that certain dryness so they will keep in good shape all winter. Boy, they made wonderful pies. If I had the chance, I could eat one pie by myself.*

*The following week we would go at daylight until dark and try to fill all the baskets with fresh berries and then we moved home. She canned all the berries she could if we did not eat them too fast (pers. com. 1973).*

In 1925, the *Toppenish* (Washington) *Tribune* (August 19) reported that hundreds of Indians migrated to the mountains for the hot month of August, "not to escape the heat, but in search of the winter's food supply . . . families with children and dogs, wagons and horses and cars." The writer described the berries dried near an open fire as having a "pleasing smoked flavor." Klikitat basketmaker Nettie Jackson remembers that the elders used a certain kind of leaves underneath the mat to give the berries special flavor.

These are not isolated memories among modern-day Indian people of the area. "We were the second people in to Potato Hill," Amelia Sohappy Sampson recalls. Potato Hill, on the north side of Mount Adams, has been a popular Yakima picking site for many years. Today a paved road takes pickers through the area of the reservation that is closed to the public to look for berries in these high meadows, but when she was a child it was a long, tedious trip over rough roads. Her family, too, dried their winter supply of berries in camp, Amelia said, as she made sketches of the log with the fire along it and the paddle they used to turn the berries (pers. com. 1974).

When a cold winter or late spring frost nipped the berries, many families suffered serious hardship. The loss is less serious now because there are other sources of food, but the people of the Mid-Columbia miss this important food in the bad years. In September 1973, the *Yakima Nation Review* (page 7) ran a photo of a Yakima woman in the berry fields surrounded by coiled huckleberry baskets. "This year . . . she didn't get all of her baskets as full as usual," the tribal newspaper said, adding, "Blackberries and salmon berries also are

*Margaret Wanto,* right, *and a helper can berries in their camp near Mount Adams. USDA Forest Service photo by Ray M. Filloon, 1935.*

in short supply in the wilds." The anonymous writer ended with a word of solace, "There are alternatives. We can go without huckleberry pie or we can eat cake," and added, "We'll survive the big '73 huckleberry shortage, but we'll still depend on the earth and what it's willing to produce. Food supply will always depend on the wind and the rain and the soil, and not on the grocery stores."

In the old days, grandmothers saw to it that all the children had their own picking baskets. With only two or three basketmakers coiling the huckleberry baskets today, the people are taking care of those baskets that have been passed down through their families. Susan Brown, a young Yakima woman picking berries near Surprise Lake in the Mount Adams area, told a newspaper reporter in 1986 that she was using the same basket she had picked into as a child.[8] Brown told of being dropped off at a picking spot, when she was a child, with orders from her aunt not to return to camp until her basket was full. "A long time ago, when our grandmas were little, they used to come up on horseback," she said, "Now we come up on trucks."

Children's baskets are smaller, a size that is easy to wear tied to the waist or hung over the shoulders, ranging from two cups for a small child to gallon-size for the older ones. As they fill their baskets, children empty them into larger ones set nearby. The larger baskets, two to five gallons or more, often are fitted with two loops on one side near the top and another near the base on the opposite side. In the old days, pickers would thread a tump line or carrying strap through these loops and slip it over their forehead or shoulders. Today, when they can drive a pickup close to the picking spots, the larger basket and tump line are not as necessary.

Families camped near Brown combined the old—building a traditional sweat lodge next to Cold Springs—with the new—picking two thousand gallons of huckleberries to fill an order from a nearby berry farm. Brown told the reporter that she could pick seven gallons a day, "If I don't get lazy." A local grocery owner estimated that a fast picker can gather a gallon to a gallon and a half an hour.[9]

In the berry basket, the bottom is about half the diameter of the mouth and the depth slightly more than the width at the mouth. Gracie Ambrose's gallon-size basket was eight inches deep, eight inches across the mouth, and four inches across the base. Whether the first measurement is described as height or depth depends on the point of view, like the age-old discussion of half-full or half-empty. A user would talk about depth, for that is what she has to fill. The basketmaker may talk about height, for that is what she has to finish.

How did Gracie Ambrose know that her basket held a gallon, I wondered, accustomed as I was to pails and Pyrex cups with measures marked on their sides. I poured the berries from her basket into standard quart freezer containers. The basket of berries filled four of them generously.

Marie Slockish, who learned to make baskets as a child from her Klikitat mother and grandmother, said, "We could make a bottom without measuring and the basket would come out a gallon." It was a matter of long practice. Children's baskets were more bowl shaped, made faster "so we could get them done," Slockish explained.

*My grandmother had to make sure that each of us children had a small basket to pick in every fall. My two older brothers would have three and five gallon baskets, the older ones carried the bigger baskets.*

*Back when I was 5-years-old, my grandfather was still alive then and he used to take us up to Meadow Creek before the berries were started. He used to have a sweat lodge up there and the whole family had to go sweating before picking or fall fishing. He would have a dinner and a lot of people would come at the first picking. He would have a ceremony and they would serve the berries. We could not eat any berries until that ceremony was conducted. Then after that, we were free to pick, eat and do anything that we wanted. We stayed from then clear on through until almost the last berries were*

*Minnie Marie Slockish, left, picks huckleberries near Mount Adams with her daughter, Washnye, and her sister, Inez Slockish Jackson. The two-cup child's basket worn by Washnye and the larger baskets, far left and far right, were made by the sisters' mother, Mattie Spencer Slockish. The other three baskets were made by an elderly relative, Nah-Wy-Yatt Tahkeal. USDA Forest Service photo by Ray M. Filloon, 1935.*

*gone from the bushes. (Nettie Jackson in Azzouz, Farnum, and Kuneki 1989).*

Before most families begin picking berries each year, the baskets figure prominently in an important ceremony of thanksgiving, the huckleberry feast. On the first or second Sunday in August many people of the Mid–Columbia gather for the annual feast at HeHe Longhouse on the Warm Springs Reservation. Others hold ceremonies in their camps in the mountains to thank the Creator for providing such bounty.[10]

The ceremonial pickers, women selected by longhouse or family elders, take their fine old coiled baskets into the berry fields and gather berries for the feast. With songs of worship, the people follow an ancient ritual of serving and eating the sacred foods. Large decorated conical baskets holding three to five gallons of berries were made especially for these feasts (Smith 1940, 305).

*When a girl learns to pick berries, if she's going to be a good picker, the family could tell. She would fill her basket and they would reserve it and . . . have a dinner. They would give it to an elderly lady that is a distant relative to the girl. She would have to give that basket away of her first picking, berries and all. Traditionally that would promote her to go on when she grew up to be a good berry picker. (Nettie Jackson, pers. com. 1986)*

Each year those women among the Klikitat and their neighbors who were accomplished weavers were kept busy with their basketmaking. They regularly made coiled cedar root baskets with little or no decoration for the family's pick-ing baskets. In addition, they coiled "fancy baskets" for other uses. These highly decorated baskets were given at wedding trades; as payment for helping with funerals and memorials; as gifts for a special event involving women, such as ear piercing, joining (taking part in the religious or ceremonial activities of the group for the first time), or naming; and in trade for needed items (French 1955, 261).

A few families today follow the custom of trading on the occasion of their children's marriage, but the fancy coiled

baskets are so highly prized and so valuable that they rarely are among the goods changing hands. In the days before the newcomers' laws governed the residents of the Mid-Columbia, such trades were the actual ceremony of marriage, the sealing of the contract. When a man wanted a woman for a wife, he sent a messenger with gifts to her father. If the father agreed, the man's family went to the woman's with more gifts and there would be a trade. When they arrived, the woman was dressed by her relatives "with her valuables, with hard baskets." The women of the bride's family distributed gifts to the family of the bridegroom, then brought the woman and all her valuables to the groom (Jacobs 1934, 227).

*Women with baskets full of huckleberries wait to enter HeHe Longhouse on the Warm Springs Reservation at the beginning of the ancient thanksgiving ritual of the huckleberry feast. Photo by Marsha Shewczyk, 1982; courtesy Spilyay Tymoo.*

Trades that included the coiled baskets are within the memory of many descendants of the people of the Mid-Columbia or are part of their family lore. "They Indian-traded on my mom and dad," Nettie Jackson reports. "My grandmother on my mother's side got some baskets from my dad's grandmother. In the olden days, I would be making baskets for my daughter now, for when she marries. They would be prize baskets, the design a fancy design. A five-gallon basket would be traded for a colt. A horse would pay for that basket full of dried huckleberries" (Azzouz, Farnum, and Kuneki 1989). In all of the trades involving baskets, the filled basket is the desirable "gift"; the food has as much importance as the container, if not more.

Goods also are distributed at memorials, usually held a year after a death. Baskets had an important role in these ceremonies in earlier days. The custom is not completely gone: as recently as 1985 a widow who had been brought up in the old ways along the Mid-Columbia presented a beaded bag, an embroidered shawl, and a shell dress all in a large coiled basket to a niece who had helped her. Again, the valuable basket served as container for valuable contents, each enhancing the other.

Other important occasions for the traditional people of the river are name givings. A young woman with promise of becoming a skilled basketmaker might be given the name of a basketmaking ancestor. According to custom, the woman would be expected to produce as many as ten gallon-size baskets to give to relatives and others who knew the owner of the name (Nettie Jackson, pers. com. 1985).

During the great summer gatherings, the fancy coiled Klikitat baskets, with other valuables, were stakes wagered in the horse races and other gambling games at Indian Race Track, near White Swan, and other camping places.[11]

*When a girl went . . . to the mountains, she took her work. They told her, "You must work yonder there at the end of the mountain . . . and then it may address you."*

*That is what the girl did. A woman came to her, she showed her*

*Klikitat basketmaker Nah-Wy-Yatt Tahkeal coils a cedar root basket as Fidelia Meninick watches, c. 1950. See page 87 for examples of her baskets. Photo by James Rayner.*

*a large hard basket, soft basket, and pack rope. "You will make these things, girl. These things will be your products. Everyone will approve of them, they will give things for them, and . . . you will be a satisfied girl."*

*It turned around, it went away, and then of a sudden the girl understood about the woman. "You, yourself, are really Wild Lily." (After Jacobs 1934, 227)[12]*

Baskets were used in the early days as money is today, as a medium of exchange. The Klikitat people were famous for their coiled baskets and Indians came from far away to obtain them. The Nez Perce and Bannock exchanged buffalo robes for Klikitat baskets (Spier and Sapir 1930, 227, 233). Closer to home, basketmakers could trade for fish, roots and berries, soft bags, and other necessities.[13] In 1955, the Wasco people reported that a basket fifteen inches deep and ten inches across at the rim (holding about three gallons) would bring an animal in trade (French 1955, 75). Marie Slockish confirmed that this was true for the Klikitat also, reporting that her mother gave a three-gallon basket for a good mare (pers. com. 1981). Wild Lily's prediction to the young Cowlitz girl was true. A basketmaker would never be poor.

After the newcomers arrived, the change to a cash economy soon created hardship among many of the people of the Mid-Columbia. The skill of basketmaking helped ameliorate the impact of settlement. A basketmaker could exchange her beautiful coiled cedar root basket for cash. An early account of such a purchase tells of one of the founders of Portland, Captain John H. Couch, visiting the Columbia River in 1847 in his ship the *Chanamic*. He purchased a fine round Klikitat-style basket on that trip to carry home to Massachusetts. The basket came around Cape Horn a second time and returned to Oregon to stay. This basket, loaned by Mrs. F. A. Beck, was exhibited at the Portland library in April 1896 (McArthur 1896, 19–20).

We have no record of the price Captain Couch paid for this basket, but we know that a dealer in Portland was offering a large Klikitat "pail" for thirty-five dollars in 1902. A collector from The Dalles asked from seven to eighteen dollars for smaller coiled baskets in 1907.[14] Multiply those prices nearly a hundredfold for similar baskets made today.

At the turn of the century several influences worked together to create a growing interest in Native American basketry. At a time when the Arts and Crafts Movement glorified the products of handwork, prosperous North Americans were building larger homes and decorating them with contemporary handicraft. Travel to the American West was promoted by the railroads; their colorful calendars with paintings of western Indians hung in many homes. All of this encouraged new interest in the arts and crafts of the American Indian. Collections of basketry made during these years have enriched many major museums.

On the Columbia River, the movement's influence was

most evident in the coiled cedar root baskets. The twined bags and hats continued to be made largely for the Indian people themselves, but the coiled baskets had been trade items for many years and the basketmakers were happy to find a growing market for their work. Masters of their technique, the makers produced whatever the collectors requested.

The greatest number of nontraditional baskets appear to have been made around the turn of the century. Museum collections include coiled wall baskets for correspondence,

*Three-gallon basket, right, made by Lucy Cayuse Thomas, would have been worth a horse in trade at the time it was made in the 1930s. H13.5 in., W11.5 in. The one-gallon basket on the left, with similar designs, was made by her daughter Elsie Thomas about 1989. H8 in., W7.5 in. Private collection. Photo by W. T. Schlick.*

*This drum-shaped purse is attributed to Sally Wahkiacus,*
*c. 1900. Private collection.*

footed fruit bowls, vases, and baskets with fragile, double-scalloped edges that would fit into the elaborate decor of a Victorian home. There are fishing creels, cups and saucers, handled pitchers, even hats, all demonstrating the basketmakers' virtuosity. Other baskets are decorated with names and dates or odd assortments of letters. During this period, basketmakers continued to make traditional baskets as well. When there were changes in form and design, the materials and technique remained faithful to the tradition.

One reason for the decline in the making of baskets along the Mid-Columbia is the loss of the original market—other native people. In the early days the basketmakers could trade their products with others who specialized in drying fish or berries or roots or in tanning hides, in this way providing for all of their needs through their art. As the people of the Columbia moved into a cash economy, this barter system no longer could support them completely. They became more dependent on the collectors. Although collectors offered a source for cash, the market was subject to violent swings. Without steady sales of their baskets, basketmakers eventually needed to turn to other work.

The period of affluence that created the demand for Klikitat baskets ended with the Great Depression and the basketmakers lost a market for their fine work, not to be regained until fifty years later. In 1929, when the great surge of collecting was fading with the country's economy, a man in Vancouver bought a large basket from the daughter of the maker for five dollars (Nettie Jackson, pers. com. 1982).

Although prices improved in postwar 1950s, Lucy Cayuse Thomas sold her baskets for a dollar per inch in height. The basket that brought thirty-five dollars in 1902 and five dollars in 1929 probably would sell for seventeen dollars in the fifties and sixties. Lucy's daughter, Elsie, sold gallon-size baskets (approximately eight inches high) for thirty-five dollars in 1974. There was not a big market, mainly because most appreciators of the beautiful coiled cedar root baskets did not know they were still being made. Collectors were paying much higher prices from dealers, but little of the value was reaching the basketmakers (Schlick 1984b, 19).

After Elsie Thomas began teaching in the Bingen culture classes in 1976, word of the basketmakers spread and prices began to increase. Within two years Elsie was receiving ten dollars an inch for an average-size basket (*Hood River News* 1976). By 1984, prices had doubled. But so had costs of the goods for which the basket money was needed.

Time is another factor that has discouraged many young people of the Mid-Columbia from taking up this traditional art. How much time a basket requires, of course, depends on the weaver's skill. A collector reported in 1896, in a period when there were many basketmakers, that one round of a large basket or three of a small one is a hard day's work for an experienced basketmaker (Molson 1896, 13). An expert bas-ketmaker can weave a small basket in a week. This is in addition to the time it takes to gather and process the mate-rials. In 1985 the Washington State Arts Commission asked Nettie Jackson to make a ten-gallon basket that is now in their permanent collection, "Beyond Blue Mountains." This basket, completely covered with imbrication in a complex design, required more than three months of steady weaving each day to complete. Unless they are prolific producers, few young people can afford to become basketmakers. They can make a better living working for wages.

*In my mother's time, when baskets were plentiful, it would take two weeks to make a gallon-size basket and you could only get $5 for that basket. My grandmother used to make a gallon-size basket and trade it for maybe 20 pounds of flour and 25 pounds of sugar and she felt that was quite a bit. Whereas my mother thought that for two weeks' work, that was too much work—too hard of a craft to learn.*

*Why my mother quit making baskets, why my aunts quit mak-ing baskets . . . was just the total influence of the white man coming and buying the old people's baskets for $5. Today, a lot of those baskets are priceless, you can't buy them from anybody. (Nettie Jackson in Azzouz, Farnum and Kuneki 1989)*

*Coiling this ten-gallon basket in 1984 required three months of weaving for Klikitat basketmaker Nettie Jack-son. In addition were the hours spent gathering and prepar-ing the materials. H18 in., W16.5 at top (10 in. base). Private collection. Photo by W. T. Schlick.*

*Only the light color of the new material on the rim reveals that this basket has been repaired. The careful reconstruction was done by Elsie Thomas. This pattern often is referred to as "salmon gill." Private collection. Photo by W. T. Schlick.*

The baskets have always been important to the native people of the Mid-Columbia. Looking at museum collections we find that many of the baskets have been repaired with new coiled bottoms and rim loops; burn holes are calked or covered with old shoe leather or stiff rawhide. On occasion an old parfleche has been cut up for a new bottom. These repairs give us a sense of the respect and care the people of the Columbia gave the baskets. Any piece of handiwork that required so much time and talent to weave deserved to be restored to use.

## MAKING THE COILED BASKETS

*Coyote and his wives came to a creek high with water. Wading across they lost their footing and drifted downstream. Coyote floated on down until he was caught in the roots of the cedar. "Take me out of the water, brother!" he said to cedar. Cedar caught him and pulled him out of the water.*

*"You will be an important one, younger brother. With your roots they will make root strips for baskets and sell them for a great deal of money. . . . You will be valuable, my younger brother!" (After Jacobs 1934, 105)*

### Materials

When Nettie Jackson convinced Elsie Thomas to teach her basketmaking skills to other Mid-Columbia native people, their first task was to obtain enough cedar roots and bear grass for the class. It was November when they decked themselves in rain gear, "not very traditional looking," Nettie observed, and with permission from the U.S. Forest Service went into the Gifford Pinchot National Forest to look for cedar.

Armed with a *kapin*, the traditional root-digging tool, and a hoe, rake, and pruning saw, they sought the roots farthest from the tree. These would be straightest, easiest to use and most pliable, Elsie explained. When they found a new root, she smelled, then tasted it, looking for the fresh damp earth flavor of cedar. Fir and other conifers have a bitter taste.

*Lewis and Clark returned to the East with this finely twined Wasco-style bag acquired along the Columbia from the "Pishquilpah," a group they identified as living across from the mouth of the Deschutes River on the north bank. The explorers were on this part of the river in October 1805 and April 1806. H11.5 in., W6 in. Photo by Hillel Burger. Peabody Museum, Harvard University, cat. no. 99–12–10/53160.*

Large Cowlitz-style baskets such as this one collected by the wife of Senator Levi Ankeny of Walla Walla, Washington, before 1898, frequently were used to hold drinking water. The oval shape, curving sides, and vertical design arrangement are typical of baskets made by the Klikitats' neighbors to the west. Smithsonian Institution cat. no. 200,003.

Lidded basket with strips of red woolen fabric incorporated with bear grass in the imbricated design. Collected by the Reverend W. C. Curtis at The Dalles, c. 1890. H3 in., W4 in. Photo by Jerry Taylor. Maryhill Museum of Art cat. no. 1951.01.76.

The colors in this fine old, five-gallon basket are those supplied by nature. The basket was made in the early twentieth century, possibly by Susan Williams, wife of Indian
Shaker Bishop Sam Williams of the Lone Pine church at
The Dalles. The white bear grass has mellowed to a soft
ivory; the root of Oregon grape or sand dock provided the
yellow; the brown is from a decoction of willow bark, and
the black from alkaline mud. Private collection.

The colors in this "butterfly basket," made by Nettie Jackson in 1985, are achieved by using commercial dyes. The butterfly design also was used by the basketmaker's grandmother to symbolize everlasting happiness or a good event. Private collection.

The designs on this drum-shaped purse, probably made by Sally Wahkiacus about 1900, are imbricated with both dyed and painted bear grass. Private collection.

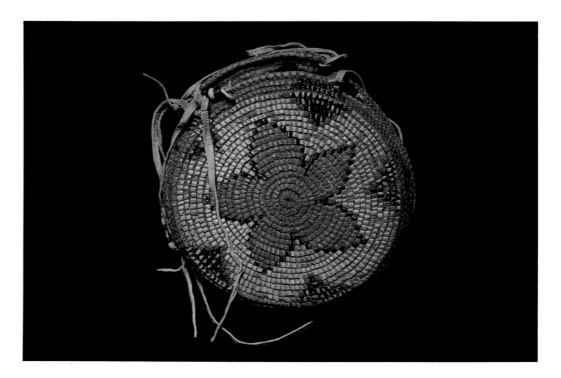

*Coiled cedar root baskets in the John Wyers collection.*
*The largest basket was commissioned in about 1937 from*
*Lucy Cayuse Thomas for Wyers's daughter-in-law. The*
*smallest basket has been attributed to Sally Wahkiacus.*
*Photo by Mark Barnes.*

*Root of the sand dock or Oregon grape root was used tradi-
tionally to achieve this yellow color. Photo by Jerry Taylor. H8 in., W8 in. Maryhill Museum of Art cat. no.
1940.01.14S.*

Small basket or cup with male and female figures. Probably collected in late 1800s by Mrs. John Marden who lived on land formerly occupied by the family of Taswatha (Ellen Underwood) near Hood River, Oregon. Photo by Jerry Taylor. H4 in., W3 in. Maryhill Museum of Art cat. no. 1980.04.17S.

"People of the World" basket by Nettie Jackson, 1983. Fineweave basket with only the figures in imbrication depicts red, white, black, and yellow men. The artist wrote: "First there were red people [here on the Columbia River]; then came the white people. After them came the black people. Then came the yellow people. It was the white people who first visited Grandfather Moon. Basket in art form." H4.5 in., W5.5 in. at top (3 in. base). Private collection.

*Klikitat-style basket from the Mary Underwood Lane
Collection with salmon gill design. Photo by Jerry Taylor.
H16 in., W16 in. Mary Underwood Lane Collection,
Maryhill Museum of Art cat. no. 1940.01.10S.*

"Once you find a good spot for roots," a relative later told Nettie, "mark it. The roots will be ready to dig again in three years."

After they dug the roots they needed, Elsie showed Nettie how to split them with a heavy knife and remove the root's rough outer layer, or "skin," as they call it. The skin usually pulls away as the root divides. They separated the materials into three bundles, the skin to be dyed for decoration, the rougher pieces for the coil foundation, and the long smooth pieces for the stitching material. The tedious job of final splitting, trimming, and smoothing would be done at home. The roots may be gathered at any time of year when the ground is not frozen.

"It took three or four years to learn to get my own material," Nettie says. It wasn't until her former husband, Leonard Kuneki, helped her that she began to understand the process. From his earliest years, Leonard had gone' with his mother, aunts, and grandmother when they dug roots for their famous baskets. This is an important part of the basket-making process and all of the Kuneki children have learned how to dig the basketry materials.

*A long time ago . . . there lived a young girl along White Salmon River. She was Sinmi, brown squirrel. She would sit and dream in the shade of Nank, a huge cedar tree. One day, Nank talked to her. "Nicha, my little sister, you cannot grow up like this, not knowing anything. Go to the mountains and find* yai. . . . (After Beavert 1974, 61)[15]

The other material in Klikitat-style baskets is *yai*, bear grass. In the late summer when the snow is gone and the bear grass has matured, Nettie and her family go up to the mountains to look for the leaves that are snowy white at the base. Because she covers the entire background of her basket with white, the color of the *yai* is important to Nettie. Much of what they find has a purple tinge at the base of the leaf—a color that is difficult to cover with dye.

One good plant will provide enough leaves to cover a gallon-size basket. Picking the leaves does not affect the

*After digging the cedar roots, Nettie Jackson splits the root, removes the bark, then splits the root again into fine strands.*

plant's growth. As her family finds the white bear grass and ties the green ends into a knot to form a bundle, Nettie winds tape on her fingers and thumb and begins to pare off the spine that stiffens the underside of each leaf. The bear grass has a razor edge that will cut unprotected fingers mercilessly. Using a sharp pocket knife to remove the spines, Nettie recalls that her grandmother learned to do this task using an "arrow rock," a knife hand-fashioned of flint or obsidian. As it dries, the bear grass turns white the entire length of the leaf.

Heavy grazing and weed sprays that have destroyed much of the Indian hemp and other plants used by the early people of the Mid-Columbia have not reached high in the mountains where the bear grass grows. However, commercial harvesters have begun to cut thousands of pounds of the grass in the Cascade Mountains to sell for floral arrangements in the United States and in Asia.

The United States Forest Service has asked the Indian people to obtain permits from the ranger districts for gathering bear grass in specific areas so that the agency can keep other permit applicants from encroaching on traditional bear grass gathering places (Barbara Hollenbeck, pers. com. 1988).

## Color

"Traditional colors are yellow, black, brown and white, or a deep red . . ." (Nettie Jackson in Azzouz, Farnum, and Kuneki 1989). The earliest of the baskets bear the subdued natural colors of the materials themselves and of dyes obtained from the land. The cedar root sewing strand, where it can be seen along the braided edge, has aged to a warm tan. The creamy white of bear grass gradually has mellowed to a soft beige. For a major design element, the weaver used the skin of the cedar root turned smooth side out. She colored the root skins black with mud from alkaline springs found in the mountains or brown by steeping them in a decoction of willow bark. The basketmaker's goal was the darkest black or brown she could obtain, for the contrast with the light color of the bear grass gave her design liveliness and distinction.

On the earliest baskets, yellow came from soaking or simmering the bear grass in a dye made from Oregon grape stems and roots (*Berberis* sp.) or from the roots of the sand dock (*Rumex venosus*). The Oregon grape can be found in the forest area; the sand dock grows on the open hills nearer the river.

Although many reports list wild cherry or chokecherry bark as the red element in Klikitat baskets, local weavers say the British Columbia weavers used this material but the people of the Mid-Columbia did not. Nettie Jackson remembers her grandfather making no comment when non-Indians guessed that a basket was decorated with cherry bark. He simply allowed them to think they were correct (Kuneki, Thomas, and Slockish 1982, 32).

An elderly woman from White Swan, Sally George, told a tribal interviewer that long ago she made "ribbons" from the red willow (probably red osier dogwood, *Cornus stolonifera*) for basket decorations.[16] If gathered in the early spring, this bark will retain its deep red color when dried and could be mistaken for cherry. The dogwood may be identified by fine light-colored flecks on the dark red surface that are rounded rather than linear as are the flecks on cherry.

Nettie has tried to dye her basket materials with the native dyes, although her early attempts were not successful and she now uses commercial dyes to produce the traditional colors: black, deep and bright red, and yellow. Just as it was for her great grandmother, black is an important color. "It takes five days to dye the black. I have to keep checking on it or it will go rotten and the skin of the root will pull apart," she says.

A common color on the old baskets was a red-brown from the inner bark of the alder. Saliva evidently provided a strong mordant to help the color penetrate the basket fibers, for most reports describe the weaver chewing the bark to obtain a permanent dye (Mason 1976, 305; Esther Wilkenson, pers. com. 1979). Nettie says, "My grandmother used to put it in her mouth and then, as she was working, she would chew it onto the bear grass, or she would chew it onto the skin of the root. Sometimes they would weave the basket and then dab the red onto the finished basket to dye certain areas of the design" (pers. com. 1988).

The traditional dyeing processes produced complex subtleties of color but it is the process itself, of building the design stitch by stitch, that produces irregularities and unexpected arrangement of motifs that give the basket, whether it was made one hundred years ago or today, a unique surface texture.

*"Then Nank [cedar] showed her how to weave a basket. . . . She worked all day and far into the night." (After Beavert 1974, 63)*

A coiled basket is not woven, it is sewn. The maker "builds" a basket the way the potter can build a clay pot, by winding a long coil of material around and around to form a base and the walls above that base. Unlike clay that will stick together, the basket's coil is made of plant material. The basketmaker must bind these pieces of cedar root together with a sewing material, the smooth longer strands of the split root.

The only equipment a weaver needs for coiling is an awl to pierce the holes through which she threads the pointed end of her sewing strand. Long ago, the sharpened ulna of a bird or a splintered piece of animal bone served to pierce these holes. Today basketmakers use a commercial awl.

The weaver's awl is like a seamstress' thimble, very personal. In 1984, Elsie Thomas found an awl that she had mislaid fifty years ago. The favorite tool had not gone far. That spring, Lucile Wyers of Hood River, Oregon, across the Columbia from Elsie's home, invited Elsie and Nettie Jackson over to look at baskets purchased in the 1930s by her father-in-law, John Wyers. Among the baskets, Elsie identified several she had made before her son Leonard, Nettie's husband, was born. Other baskets had been made by her grandmother, mother, aunt, and two sisters.

At the end of the visit, Lucile brought out a basket start containing a small bundle of prepared cedar roots with a piece of cloth crumpled beside them. "I've never looked in here," she said, opening up the cloth and revealing a pocketknife and a well-used awl. Turning it over in her hand, Lucile looked at the initials carved in the handle. "E.T.—Elsie Thomas?" she asked, holding it out, "Is this yours?"

"Yes," the basketmaker smiled, "that's my 'needle'." Elsie reasoned that her mother Lucy Cayuse Thomas, whose work she identified in the basket start, had "taken sick" and the start was sold by someone in the family, cedar roots, knife, and awl. The awl and the pocketknife went home with Elsie (Schlick 1984b, 19).

*"E.T." on the handle identified this well-worn awl for Elsie Thomas as one she had lost fifty years before.*

*Nettie Jackson uses her awl to pierce the coil to make a hole for the sewing strand she holds in her fingers. She will bend the piece of bear grass forward before pulling this stitch tight to hold the bear grass in place.*

## The Coiling Technique

Like most children of the Mid-Columbia, Nettie Jackson spent much time with her grandmother, Mattie Spencer Slockish, at her home along the Klickitat River, north of the Columbia. "She worked outside all day, year around, tanning buckskins, even when it was cold," Nettie recalls. "At night she would light the coal oil lamp and work on baskets, gallon size. She made a lot of baskets, but she never tried to teach us. We just watched. To keep our attention, she would tell us stories."

With pocketknife and awl ready, the bear grass and skin of the root dyed as desired, the bundles of cedar root soaking nearby, the basketmaker is ready to begin. She trims and smooths the sewing strand to an even width with her knife, then for several inches wraps the strand around and around a small bundle of foundation material. Bending the wrapped bundle into a small spiral, she sews it closed, using the awl to make the holes for her sewing strand.

The basketmaker works from left to right with the outside of the work facing her, sewing the coils close together with noninterlocking stitches until the base is the desired size, approximately half the expected height of the finished basket. She does not measure her base with a ruler. Her practiced eye knows when it is right. Very rarely a basketmaker will weave a design into the base.[17]

The Klikitat weaver begins most of her baskets with a small circular coil start that looks much like the center of a watchspring. Looking at the outside of the base, this coil moves in a clockwise direction. The circular start results in a round basket. Her neighbors on the west side of the Cascade Mountains, members of the Salish tribes of the Cowlitz, Puyallup, and Nisqually, begin with an oval coil, a parallel coil, or a slat bottom—only rarely a round start. This start creates an oval or round-cornered rectangular basket. The sides of the Klikitat basket rise on a nearly straight diagonal line; those baskets made on the west side of the Cascades tend to curve upward from the base (Gogol 1979, 4, 5). During the weaving, the basketmaker adds strands to her foundation bundle to maintain an even coil. When it is necessary to introduce a new sewing element, she pulls a new strand into place, concealing the end of the old strand in the foundation as she continues to weave.

As the weaver starts up the side of the basket, she begins her pattern. Coiling is a widely used basketry technique, but the Klikitat method of decorating the basket as the coils are being sewn is unique to this small part of the world. Otis T. Mason, the curator of ethnology for the Smithsonian Institution in 1904, named the process "imbrication" (derived from the Latin *imbrex,* "tile") because the stitch gives the surface of the basket a tilelike appearance (Mason 1976, 310). Imbrication is known only in a limited area on the Fraser and Thompson rivers, on the Columbia River, and by the Salish tribes of northwestern Washington.

Mason described the technique in this way: The woman catches the end of a strip of grass under a stitch, bends the strip forward . . . [then] back on itself, . . . makes her stitch . . . [forming] a kind of knife plaiting held down by coiled sewing . . . an invention of this region (1976, 427).[18]

## Building the Design

Except for family berry-picking baskets, most Klikitat baskets are completely covered with imbrication and the designs usually cover the entire surface of the basket. In the conical Klikitat basket, the weaver must adapt the design to the expanding surface that forms the sloping sides. As she coils the basket, she folds the design element—the dyed bear grass or skin of the cedar root—on top of each stitch, developing the pattern as she weaves the basket. The two processes, building the basket and creating the design, are inseparable.

The weaver's first imbricated row forms the distinctive black or dark brown line that is the traditional beginning of her pattern. Nettie Jackson explains how she develops the classic mountain peak motif as she makes a basket, "After I

*Nettie folds the piece of bear grass back over the awl point. The sewing strand is ready to be pulled tight to hold the fold in place. Next she will fold the bear grass forward over the sewing strand, forming another bricklike "stitch" in her basket.*

*Imbrication—the folding process used to cover the coils on Mid-Columbia coiled baskets. Diagram by Peggy Dills Kelter, after Mason 1904.*

make the bottom, I find three points and start my design there. As the basket gets larger, the design takes care of itself."

When the weaver makes the three-peaked **V** or "mountain" design, she locates three equidistant points on the base of her basket by eye. Beginning the next row in the natural white of the bear grass, she changes to the darker, dyed material when she reaches each of these three points. In each row her pattern will grow diagonally away from these points, meeting at the top of her basket to form the peaks.

Most Klikitat-style basket designs are variations on this connecting **V** or mountain peak motif. A weaver may work a vertical motif into the basket or, rarely, an all-over pattern. Occasionally only the pattern and not the background will be imbricated. Another technique seen occasionally on Klikitat baskets is beading, where the decorative material is laid along the face of the coil and bound to it by the stitches (Adovasio 1977, 96). This is more common on the Cowlitz-style baskets.

*Cedar Tree said, "Now you must find some designs. . . . Go out in the woods. Look at things of nature. Bring them back in your mind." She walked for many days . . . she saw Patu, the mountain . . . she knelt down by the brook for a drink of water and saw Xaslu, evening star, reflected in the water. (After Beavert 1974, 63)*

Nettie Jackson does not work even the most complicated design out on paper, although occasionally she looks at a photograph of an old basket and works from that, adding her own details. If she is making a basket for a specific person, she thinks about that person when planning the pattern. "I guess my designs come right off the top of my head, like I can be riding along and a design will come to me or I'll see something and I can see it in a design of a basket. Sometimes the design will come to me in a dream, I dream about it."[19]

The Klikitat people told Canadian anthropologist James Teit in 1909 that there had been little or no change in their basketry designs since the earliest times and that few new patterns had been introduced. The only time a weaver used a nontraditional design was when there was a special order for a basket (Teit 1928, 357).

The traditional names for basket patterns suggest the close relationship of the people of the Mid-Columbia with nature. Not only is the basket itself an extension of the earth—of the cedar tree and the bear grass that form the basket's structure—but the designs most often reflect nature.

A vertical or horizontal zigzag is a mountain to many weavers. Marie Slockish said the common "mountain" design represented *Patu,* Mount Adams. This snow-covered mountain has great practical and religious significance to the native people who live near the Columbia. Slockish described Mount Adams as "the corner store"—providing water, roots and berries, animals for food and clothing, trees for homes and baskets, everything her ancestors needed (pers. com. 1981).

Flying geese, flying birds, dogs (tail up or down) and coyote (tail straight out), deer and elk, feet, salmon gills, eyes, snakes, eel trail, shadow, all are captured in the basket designs. What looks like a cross to one weaver may be a star or the crossing of trails or the cardinal points of direction or, simply, a fly to others. Asked why she worked flies into her basket, Nettie Jackson explained, "Indians consider flies their friends. When the flies start to come around the fish, it's time to finish the work."

Marie Slockish and Nettie Jackson explained an ancient symbol in Mid-Columbia basketry—a swastikalike figure— as the four elements of life, the four directions, or as a person running (pers. com. 1981, 1987). An all-over netlike pattern is known as "strap pattern," from the diagonal lines twined into many tump lines or carrying straps. A more common name for this design among the fishing families of the river is simply "net."

Both Klikitat and Wasco/Wishxam basketmakers incorporated human and animal figures in their designs, usually as accent motifs between the connecting Vs.[20] The human figures on the Wasco/Wishxam baskets usually feature two or three fingers on each hand. Some baskets have flowers or

*Three imbricated stitches in bear grass on the bottom of the basket are Nettie Jackson's signature. The basketmaker begins the classic mountain peak design at three points around the base to insure a symmetrical design.*

trees or horses worked into the design field.

Some earlier weavers referred to combinations of traditional motifs as "dream" designs, as Nettie Jackson describes some of her designs. Once used, these new combinations enter the common stock of tribal artistic ideas (Farrand 1900, 399). Basketmakers rarely make two baskets alike, but vary the arrangement, the combinations of motifs, and the color. Often the work of a specific basketmaker can be recognized by the motifs her family was known to use. Through the years basketmakers have left anonymous signatures that were recognized by those who knew their work. This could be a combination of patterns, or a few stitches of a different color or material that might be taken for a mistake by the uninitiated. Lucy Cayuse Thomas of Husum, mother of Elsie Thomas, was known to work flowers and trees into some of her baskets. Susan Williams of Hood River was known to incorporate crosses in her basket designs. As a signature, Nettie Jackson usually imbricates three stitches on the base of her baskets.

When Nettie made a butterfly on a basket for a relative's wedding, her aunt told her it was a good choice. Not only was it a design her grandmother had used, but it represented a good event or everlasting happiness. Her family also incorporated human and animal figures in their basket designs. Another aunt's traditional design was a deer head with a feather lying over it.

*Originally, as told by my aunts, there were five basket weaving families along the river. My grandmothers were both basket weavers and they made the geometric designs, but also animals and people. When I first started to work with baskets, I asked Elsie Thomas and her sister if they could make people baskets. They said not, that wasn't their design. That's when I found out that different families have different designs. When I first started, I didn't know what designs belonged to me, so I thought, "I'm going to make people baskets anyway."*

*I think I made baskets for about four or five years before one of my aunts told me that her grandmother made those kind. It was all*

*Sally Wahkiacus poses with a partially finished coiled cedar root basket about 1900. The basketmaker frequently incorporated human or animal figures into her work. This apparently is a dog because the tail is down. Photographer unknown. Photo courtesy of Jerrie and Anne Vander Houwen.*

*right for me to use that because that was my great grandmother. (Nettie Jackson in Azzouz, Farnum, and Kuneki 1989)*

The complexity of imbrication calls to mind the intricacy of the layered life Nettie Jackson lives in today's world of new and old ways. The basic foundation of her heritage is

*Detail of coiled cedar root basket showing unusual design of a woman in a "Wasco" headdress has been attributed to Lucy SlimJim. Private collection. Photo by Mark Barnes.*

sturdy, a life that is interconnected and circular, rich in traditions and rarely on public view, like the cedar root coils of her basket. Over this foundation the day-to-day happenings fold back and forward, held by the strong binders she creates to keep her sanity and make life livable for herself and her complex extended family. The contemporary basketmaker builds her design stitch by stitch; each stitch, like the events of her life, is an important part of the whole. The pattern is on the surface of her basket only, as are the joys and despairs of everyday life. Like the baskets, the inner and outer surfaces of Nettie's life are intertwined.

## Finishing the Basket

At the top of the peaks, the Klikitat basketmaker again works a row in the dark color, enclosing the design between two dark lines at base and top. Cowlitz and other weavers on the west side of the Cascade Mountains often incorporated designs in the area between the rim and the main design field. Although such rim designs are not traditional for Klikitat weavers, Nettie Jackson has imbricated borders of men and women and, occasionally, animals into her larger baskets.

For the rim, the Klikitat-style weaver usually forms the distinctive Klikitat loops at intervals, finishing the edge with a braiding stitch as she coils the last row. Loops, or, as the basketmakers call them, "ears," around the rim of the Klikitat basket allow the picker to lace strings across to hold down the ferns or berry foliage that cover the freshly picked berries for carrying. To avoid placing strain on the loops, many berry pickers pierce holes below the edge of the basket through which to fasten the braided strings they tied to their bodies. Traditional loops are usually small and sturdily reinforced on the baskets coiled for use. Sometimes two rows of coiling are worked above the loops to strengthen them further. Westside baskets usually were made without "ears." On the large carrying baskets which would be heavy when filled, the users may attach hide loops to accommodate a tump line or carrying strap (Esther Wilkenson and Ella Jim, pers. com. 1978).

To form the loops, the weaver wraps her sewing strand around the bundle only, rather than catching the strand in the previous row. She does this for as many stitches as she needs to form a loop, then catches the next stitch in the previous row in the accustomed method, continuing until she begins the next loop. Nettie Jackson usually continues the imbrication over the loops. Elsie Thomas imbricates only the area between the loops.

The most common edge finish on the Klikitat-style basket gives the effect of a braid, although some are finished in the plain close-coiled stitch used throughout the basket. A simple extra movement forms this "herringbone" edge. After wrapping her sewing strand around the bundle, the basketmaker brings it forward toward her body across the strand, then reverses the strand direction and slips the end from front to back under the stitch she just crossed, pulling it tight. She repeats this process around the basket edge.

Nearing the end of this last row, the basketmaker tapers the foundation bundle so that there is not an abrupt ending. As the end of the last coil makes a complete circle, the weaver cuts off the remaining strands in the bundle and takes her last stitch, securing the end of the sewing strand in the weaving.

*Sinmi took the basket and dipped it in the river. It held water. Nank was very proud of her.*

*"Make five small baskets to give to the oldest women," Nank said.*

*But Sinmi wanted to keep her beautiful baskets. Nank told her, "You will never be a skilled basket weaver if you do not give the first ones away."*

*And so it was. People came from all over to trade with the Klickitat people for their beautiful baskets that Nank taught Sinmi to make. (After Beavert 1974, 64)*

# MID-COLUMBIA BASKETMAKING FAMILIES

Even in the days when the people of the Mid-Columbia used baskets for all of their carrying needs, not everyone was a basketmaker. Many native people of the Mid-Columbia recognize the products of the well-known basketmaking families by their designs and the fineness of their work. They often can identify the specific maker, sometimes naming the various owners of a basket made generations before.

Although all little girls were expected to learn to make baskets, only those who were skilled continued as adults. Perhaps this is one reason for the respect the basketmaker was, and is, given among her own people: the women, and

*Miniature teacup basket and one-cup basket were made by Nettie Jackson in 1990. Private collection. Photo by W. T. Schlick.*

many of the men, learned in their childhood what a difficult task it is.

The talent appeared to run in families. Nettie Jackson came from a recognized basketmaking family. Her great grandmother, Sally Wahkiacus, was born about 1830 along the Klickitat River north of the Columbia and lived there more than one hundred years. She was twelve when the first settlers came into that country. Sally Wahkiacus and her sister Susan Parker were basketmakers. It was Sally's daughter-in-law, Mattie Spencer Slockish, who gave Nettie her first opportunity to watch a basketmaker at work.

For many years, the ability to make baskets lay somewhere in the back of Nettie's mind with the other traditions her Klikitat mother and grandmother had taught her. Born into a generation where the skills of her people seemed outdated and unnecessary, Nettie busied herself with the care of her own growing family for the first years of her marriage.

Nettie's mother became seriously ill and on her deathbed expressed sadness that her children would not carry on the traditions of their family. This was the incentive Nettie needed. Past thirty, she watched Elsie Thomas make baskets and began to learn.

Within ten years, Nettie had learned to gather the traditional materials and to weave the baskets of her Klikitat ancestors to carry on the heritage her grandmother and mother wanted her to learn. Since that time, Nettie has taught her sister, Sharon Dick, and her own children.

The widow of Skookum Wallahee, Sally Wahkiacus's brother, also made baskets. Sally Buck, one of Mattie Slockish's daughters and Nettie's aunt, recalls watching the elderly woman make beautiful big baskets that came "up to her chin" (pers. com. 1987). (It was the custom in those days, and even for some older women of the Mid-Columbia today, to sit on the floor to work.) When Skookum Wallahee and his wife were married, his father, the Klikitat chief, was said to have paid twenty ponies for the bride, for the high value of her talent in those long-ago days (Neils 1967, 13).

An aunt on the Slockish side made high oval baskets that

were flat on one side to carry on a horse (Sally Buck, pers. com. 1987). Another relative, Emma Mesplie of Toppenish, born in 1893, was known for the coiled baskets she made until retiring from basketmaking in the 1970s. Her granddaughter Cynthia has been given Emma's Cowlitz name, *Piliquaya*.[21] One day, perhaps, Cynthia will take up her grandmother's art.

A well-known Cowlitz weaver was also related to the Spencer/Slockish family. She was Mary Kiona of Randle, who died in 1970 at the age of 115. Mary's mother taught her to weave when she was six, and she traded her baskets "for shoes, clothes, moccasins, strawberries." The weaver produced many traditional soft and hard baskets for over 100 years (Gogol 1985c, 9–12). Another long-lived weaver was Lizzie David, a relative of Mary Kiona's, who lived to be over 103 (Beavert 1974, 217).

Nettie Jackson's paternal grandmother, Susan Williams, also produced coiled cedar root baskets. She was married to Bishop Sam Williams who preached at the Shaker Church near The Dalles bridge. Nettie's children also are from a basketmaking family on their father's side. Leonard Kuneki's great grandmother was the basketmaker Mary Hunt Cayuse. The family lived up Rattlesnake Creek behind Husum, Washington, north of the mouth of the White Salmon River on the Columbia. Her daughter Lucy Cayuse Thomas, and Lucy's daughters, Julia, Sophie, and Elsie Thomas, carried on the tradition. Elsie's granddaughter, Sharon Kuneki, shows promise of becoming a fine weaver. Elsie was born in 1910 and learned to weave from her mother as a young girl. She is also skilled at repairing coiled baskets, an art she learned from her mother and grandmother.

Related to the Hunt/Cayuse/Thomas family were other basketmakers, the Stahi family of Rock Creek and Josephine Tanawash (or Tanawasher) of Husum. Among the other remembered weavers are Martha Sconawah Stahi, Mary Sconawah Cloud, Annie Dave, Wahsuse Tahkeal, Lucy SlimJim, and Grace Washington. Perhaps the earliest basketmaker whose name we know was Kommun Bluset, a Yakima woman whose life spanned three centuries, from her birth in 1790 to her death at the age of 116 (Bernice Sampson, pers. com. 1981).[22]

This is only a partial list of basketmakers of the river, gathered from the memories of many Mid-Columbia people. Of these, only Elsie Thomas and Nettie Jackson regularly weave the coiled Klikitat-style baskets today. A few others are beginning to learn. They are slender but strong strands of continuity with the traditional past of the people of the river.

*Samson and wife, "a common figure on the Mid-Columbia in early days . . . settled on the Warm Springs Reservation where he died." Note similarity of woman's headdress to that on the detail of the Lucy SlimJim coiled basket (p. 108). Photo by Bruno Art Studio, Portland, c. 1910; Mary Underwood Lane Collection, Maryhill Museum of Art.*

*Painting of two folded cedar bark baskets by Lt. Johnson
Kelly Duncan, member of George B. McClellan's Pacific
Railroad Survey party on the Columbia River in 1853.
Smithsonian Institution no. MHN1481I.*

# 5. LAP'UY
## *The Folded Cedar Bark Basket*

*"Go look for cedar bark for buckets and dishes for food."*—Cougar to Wild Cat

Treasures do not always reach out and grab us when we see them. Some are sleepers that settle into our minds and lie dormant until something triggers a memory and brings them to consciousness. That is what happened with the rustic, homely at first glance, folded containers known to the people of the Mid-Columbia as cedar bark baskets.

In the spring of 1973 my husband and I were browsing around an antique and junk store at Seaside, Oregon, waiting for the rain to subside enough to let us get back on the beach. There in a case at the back of the store was a small Klikitat coiled berry basket, about two-cup size,· with three rough-looking containers beside it. Taller than wide, the rough "baskets" were tubular in shape with an arched base that had two little "legs" at either side. They were made from a solid piece of cedar bark and in graduated sizes, the largest about twelve inches deep. The dealer had obtained all four baskets from an Indian woman from the Mid-Columbia area.

The bark containers did not look like anything I had seen from the area. The Mid-Columbia woman must have traded for them, I thought. When the weather cleared, we headed for the beach, the memory of the bark baskets embedded in my mind.

As I was looking through photographic archives for pictures of Columbia River baskets, dark forms in the shadows of some of those old photos began to take shape. Gradually I realized that the containers, leaning against a log or stacked in the background, were identical in form to the cedar bark containers in Seaside.[1] Although they were not woven and, strictly speaking, not real baskets, I began to watch for this new type of Mid-Columbia basketry in museum collections. Among the dramatic Klikitat-style coiled berry baskets were usually one or two of these humble relatives. Looking closely at the bark baskets, I began to marvel at the ingenuity of their makers.

Here was a single piece of bark, folded in such a way that it formed an easily carried, commodious, and tight container. Every part of its construction, the body, the reinforcement, and the lacings, came from the western red cedar (*Thuja plicata*). This basket, too, was truly a gift of the earth.

*A folded cedar bark basket,* right, *is easily overlooked in this collection of fine coiled Klikitat-style baskets. Photographer unknown. Oregon Historical Society no. 27040.*

It was not until 1982 that I realized the basket was also a gift of the ancestors. By this time, I had learned that the Seaside baskets were made at Celilo village possibly by Maggie Jim or her brother-in-law Warner Jim. We found a larger example of Warner Jim's work for sale in The Dalles. But a telephone call told me that these makers were not the first of their people to use such ingenuity.

Barbara Hollenbeck, archaeologist/historian with the Gifford Pinchot National Forest headquarters in Vancouver, Washington, was working on an interpretive display for a visitor's center near recently erupted Mount St. Helens. She wanted more information on the cedar bark baskets "made near the huckleberry fields" in the Mount St. Helens and Mount Adams area.

When Hollenbeck described the scars that had been discovered on trees on the Mount Adams District of the forest,
the complete picture of the baskets I knew began to fall into
place. "We found cedar trees with scars from one to five feet
long," she told me. "They looked like open mouths." Most
of the scars were squared off at top and bottom, as if cut.
Examining them, she found the cut marks plainly visible.

At first, Hollenbeck thought the scars had been made by
settlers looking for firewood or cutting cedar shakes. Although she had been told they could be "basket trees" similar
to those found on the coast, she knew the west-side trees had
been peeled up in a wedge shape. The coastal people used the
inner bark of the cedar for their plaited baskets and needed
long strips rather than rectangular pieces for their work.

Scars with the rectangular shape were different, the archaeologist knew. When the district packer told her of seeing Indians making huckleberry baskets from this bark, she
knew she had found an important cultural resource.

The scarred trees remained healthy, the archaeologist
said, because the basketmakers took only one or, at the most,
two strips from each tree, allowing the nutrients to continue
to travel up from the roots. Finding a poor stand that was
destined to blow down, foresters and archaeologists examined cut rounds from the trees to determine the time the
bark was removed. They discovered that some of the trees
were over three hundred years old, the bark removed from
seventy-four to two hundred years ago.

As Hollenbeck talked, my excitement rose. This is the
source, the beginning of these unique folded baskets. Images
of families camped in the Mount Adams berry fields or other
favorite places came to mind, of finding a good cedar tree for
bark, of peeling the bark and forming the basket, and (eventually) of filling this basket with huckleberries. The baskets I
knew suddenly came alive for me, from their true beginning
on the tree to their places today—in a store or museum, or on
my hearth, or filled with berries and bouncing home in the
back of a pickup.

*Marks of a cutting tool show that a basketmaker was here
many years ago. Although scarred by the removal of bark
for a folded basket, this western red cedar still thrives on
the Gifford Pinchot National Forest near Trout Lake,
Washington. Photo by W. T. Schlick.*

## THE BARK BASKET IN ANCIENT TIMES

The trees tell us that people made these ingenious baskets at least as early as two hundred years ago. The tales told from grandparent to grandchild confirm the baskets' presence in Columbia River life for a much longer time. The story of Cougar and Wild Cat tells us that they made baskets of cedar bark as early as the Myth Age when the animals were people (Jacobs 1929, 192–96).

*Cougar had four brothers, Wolf, Fisher, Weasel, and Wild Cat. The eldest, Cougar went about hunting and when he shot and killed game he would take his younger brothers along to that place where they would live until they ate it up.*

*When he shot and killed a big elk, Cougar said to Wild Cat, the youngest, "Now do your work, peel off bark then we shall boil things; we have a kettle and a water pail to make."*

*Wild Cat went on. He got cedar and peeled it and fashioned it so that it would be an object to boil with, and he made another with which to fetch water. "Only if I sing and work at the same time could I do it well," Wild Cat said. And so Wild Cat sang, but in a low voice. Indeed he peeled it off whole.*

Singing as he worked, Wild Cat attracted the attention of a dreaded "dangerous person." With trickery, his brothers fooled the creature; then later in the story, Wild Cat makes another basket:

*When Timber Rabbit proposed that they play a game of scratching each other's backs, Wild Cat told him, "Why no. I do not want to play a game." Timber Rabbit encouraged him. "We cannot merely meet one another and let that be all, at least let us have a game together."*

*Wild Cat reluctantly agreed, showing Timber Rabbit his hands with claws withdrawn. "Look at my hands, they have no claws." Timber Rabbit laughed. "No one about has any claws. Look at these claws of mine." He urged Wild Cat to start the game.*

*"No, my brother, you challenged me. Now you scratch me first," and Timber Rabbit agreed, scratching Wild Cat's back. Wild Cat laughed all the time. When it was his turn, Wild Cat kept his*

*claws withdrawn. Four times he scratched Timber Rabbit, the rabbit
laughing, "hahahaha."*

*The fifth time Wild Cat seized Timber Rabbit and skinned
him whole, saying, "In future you shall be merely food for me."
Thereupon he made a cooking vessel of bark and he heated rocks and
put the hot rocks one after the other into the water to boil the meat of
the rabbit. (Adapted from Jacobs 1929, 192–96)*

These stories tell us that the bark baskets were made for
something more than picking huckleberries. They could be
made to carry water and for cooking.

Another use is described in the Lower Chinook story of
"Wren Kills Elk," a classic tall tale in the Jack and the Bean-
stalk tradition. In this story, Wren, at Grandmother's request, went out and with great cleverness killed Elk for meat.
Grandmother taught Wren to make a basket of cedar bark for
carrying the meat home:

*Wrapping some grease from the huge animal in a skunk cabbage
leaf, Wren carried it home to Grandmother to prove that he had been
successful. Overjoyed, she awakened Wren early the next morning
and they went back to where Elk lay. She taught Wren to skin Elk,
to dry the meat on poles between two sticks over a fire. When the
time came to take the meat home, Wren said. "We can't pack it all
back, grandmother."*

*"Go and find some cedar bark and cedar poles; poles that are
easy to bend." Wren did as she asked. The old woman put the cedar
bark and the flexible poles together, making a basket to carry the
meat. She made a carrying strap. "It will be like that," she said.
"That's how they will pack meat home." (Adapted from Ray 1938,
146–48)*

Although the ingenious folded bark basket has had little
attention from museum curators and basket collectors, these
stories make a telling point about the basket's meaning to the
people of the Mid-Columbia. With cedar bark easily found in
the forests of the Cascade Mountains where they hunted and
picked berries, families could in a short time make something
in which to prepare a meal on the spot or carry food home

that otherwise would be wasted. The trees themselves contributed to the people's self-sufficiency.

Part of the basket's appeal today is its confirmation of
this resourcefulness. These "rough emergency baskets" as
anthropologists called them, fall into the category of "the
other baskets" in Ed Rossbach's thoughtful essay on basketry
(Rossbach 1973, 23). "Temporary baskets," Rossbach writes,
"satisfy a romantic longing of man in an industrial society.
Man can survive free . . . secure in his ability to manipulate
grass, leaves, roots, and twigs to satisfy primary needs without reliance on any tools or machinery."

Many other temporary baskets were made with fresh
materials that dried, leaving a dangerously brittle shell.
Many of the cedar bark baskets retain their sturdy usefulness
today, years after that first hurried manufacture to satisfy a
temporary need.

The telltale marks on the western red cedars of the Cascade Mountains leave an unusual record of cultural use. Not
only do these "culturally altered trees" tell us the shape of the
removed material and therefore the product, but they also let
us know where the people were when they needed the baskets (Hicks 1985).

Foresters and archaeologists have found trees with rectangular basket scars and a few with triangular scars near the
huckleberry fields in the areas of Mount Hood and Mount
St. Helens and Mount Adams.[2] Scars also have been reported
on the Willamette National Forest in Oregon and in Nez
Perce country on Idaho's Clearwater National Forest near
camas beds, huckleberry fields, and good fishing sites (Bergland 1990; Karl Roenke, pers. com. 1987). The earliest documented folded cedar bark baskets are the subjects of a
watercolor miniature in the collection of the Smithsonian
Institution. The painting was done by Lieutenant Johnson
Kelly Duncan on the Columbia River, August 10, 1853 (see
page 114).

According to the people of the Mid-Columbia, nearly
every family knew how to make the bark baskets in former
times—from the Chinookan and Sahaptian people of the Co-

lumbia River and the plateaus above to the Salish-speaking people to the north, wherever there were huckleberries and cedars.

In earlier times the weavers of the Mid-Columbia made most of their baskets in the quiet of winter. In that season, too, the women brought out their twined hats for the winter ceremonials. In spring, the root-digging bags came out with the first green fingers of the bitterroot, the roots to be dried and stored for the following winter in the flat twined bags. In late summer and early autumn, families carried their coiled berry baskets to the mountains. Unlike the other baskets of the Mid-Columbia, this folded cedar bark basket's making cannot be separated from its use; both take place in the autumn and up in the mountains.

Early in September 1983, my husband and I studied the Mount Adams District map at the ranger station in Trout Lake, Washington, trying to find Cold Springs Camp. Friends in Toppenish had told us the day before that Warner Jim and his family were camped up there. We had picked berries closer to Mount Adams that long-ago summer we had worked for the Forest Service on the Packwood District, and had visited friends in the Yakima camps at Potato Hill, just north of the mountain. But this was our first trip to the berry-picking country to the south of Adams, used primarily by the people of the river. Cold Springs Camp is occupied traditionally by families from Rock Creek, most of whom now live near Goldendale, Washington, and by families now living at Celilo.

Following the map, we drove out of the heavy timber into the uplands where the huckleberry brush beckoned from both sides of the road. We found the wooded campsite easily—a large tent and kitchen shelter and a table protected from rain by a sheet of plastic. As we approached we heard singing, and, realizing they were beginning their meal, we waited in the car until the prayer ended. A young boy sent over by his elders invited us to the table. We joined the family at dinner, drinking the traditional *chuush* (water, the source of all life) from our cups in thanks to the Creator for the food.

*The Warner Jim family camp at Cold Springs near Mount Adams, autumn 1983. Families return to traditional camp sites each year when the berries are ripe. Photo by W. T. Schlick.*

With the other foods on the table were bowls of huge huckleberries, to our great pleasure. We all completed the meal with the happy mark of purple on our lips, an appropriate finish at Cold Springs Camp.

## Cedar Bark Baskets in Columbia River Life

At the end of each summer when the berries are ready, the people of the Mid–Columbia come together to honor this gift before going out to pick. Although many families attend the feast at HeHe Butte on the Warm Springs Reservation, others thank the Creator for the sacred foods before the harvest begins at their camps up in the mountains. The bark basket filled with berries joins its cousin, the coiled cedar root basket, as an important part of this ceremony in the Jim camp.[3]

When the meal was over, Warner Jim talked with us about Cold Springs Camp and the cedar bark baskets he makes. The basketmaker remembers his own childhood at that camp. "We picked berries and did the dishes," he says.

Each day when the children arose they had to run to the glacial creek and jump in. "It was like ice," he recalls.

In Warner's childhood, when the family's coiled cedar root baskets were filled and the berries were still coming on, someone would go to a cedar grove, cut the bark, and make the baskets needed to finish the harvest. These baskets were considered as temporary as a paper bag today and often were discarded when they had fulfilled their purpose (Watson Totus, pers. com. 1974; Bella 1983).[4] Although basketmakers have made them in many shapes over the years, the cedar bark baskets observed in museum collections ranged from five to twenty-two inches in height, their width about half the height in most cases. Most of the Jim baskets are made in these proportions, also.

The people of the Mid-Columbia used these bark baskets for storing dried foods as well as for picking berries. Lined with fishskins, the baskets would keep dried and pounded salmon for a long time.[5] Dried roots and meat were stored in the same way. For dried huckleberries, the people lined the basket with large leaves from the swamp or with "deer ferns," putting more leaves on top and tying them down through the loops of string around the basket's edge. A nineteenth-century collector wrote of the bark basket when it was used to transport fresh berries: "All interstices are stuffed with wild bracken to prevent leakage of the juices of the wild berries."[6]

Warner describes the process of drying berries over a fire built in a hole in a slanted hillside, "until they looked like raisins." A Yakima tribal elder told of staying in camp with his grandmother to help stir the berries and to keep the drying fire going along a slowly burning log (Watson Totus, pers. com. 1974).

"In those days," Warner Jim remembers of his childhood, "we had to go up to the camping places by horseback—no saddle, just a blanket and a small rope they made from hemp. Families would leave their belongings at home when they went into the huckleberry fields." In camp they used bark baskets for cooking, in the manner of their ances-

*A grandmother turns the berries that dry on tule mats facing a slowly burning log near Mount Adams in 1935. Forest archaeologists have found evidence of such drying sites near groves of cedars from which bark has been removed for baskets. A burlap-covered coiled basket, bark basket, and large coiled and imbricated basket with salmon gill design, right, are ready for the dried berries. USDA Forest Service photo by Ray M. Filloon.*

tors. The makers covered the side seams of the baskets with reinforcing strips of cedar and sealed them with pitch on the outside where the hot rocks would not burn the pitch.

In the same manner that Wild Cat cooked the elk meat or Timber Rabbit, Warner's family made a fire, heated up a special kind of rock, "half the size of a ball of common twine," and dropped them in the water-filled basket with the food. "They put some kind of leaves in the bottom," the basketmaker recalls, to keep the flavor and to prevent burning from the hot rocks. After adding more rocks, they allowed the food to sit for an hour or so until cooked. Mary Kiona, a Cowlitz basketmaker who lived just over the ridges, near the community of Randle, described propping up the vessel and cooking in the same way (Gogol 1985c, 13).[7]

No one cooks with either the folded cedar bark or the coiled cedar root baskets today. However, there are uses for the bark baskets other than gathering berries or storing food. A small basket may be worn on a necklace; baskets are given as gifts. An anthropologist who received a larger bark basket found inside her gift a miniature replica complete in every detail (Helen Schuster, pers. com. 1981). No one explained to the gift's recipient the significance of the second basket, but a Klikitat basketmaker reports that she may tie a miniature to a larger basket simply to show that she can make baskets in all sizes, an illustration of her versatility (Nettie Jackson, pers. com. 1985). Perhaps the tiny gift basket, too, was the basket-maker's way of showing an ancient skill.

Today, when there are so few basketmakers among the people of the Mid-Columbia, a family may hang a new cedar bark basket on the wall. "I'm making one for the front room," said the wife of a relative of Warner Jim's who showed us her first basket. "I'll save it to pass on to my children" (Iris Billy-Harrison, pers. com. 1983).

## MAKING BARK BASKETS

### *Materials*

"Just anyone can't run into the forest at any time to get bark," Warner cautions. It took him many years to learn to cut the right bark for the baskets. In the 1940s when the basketmaker first was selling his baskets all over Oregon, someone who did not understand the process began to make baskets and offer them for sale. "I didn't know who the person was, but he went in the forest and started making them." Later people began to complain to Warner that his baskets were splitting and falling apart. He discovered when he questioned them that it was the other man who had made the baskets.

Warner's grandmother knew by the feel of the air, the smell of the bark, and from long experience just which cedars to choose and when to peel them. "Indians followed the signs, the place of the stars, the color of the moon," Warner says. "We don't know these signs now." The basketmaker has learned by experience to find the bark he needs.

Basket scars have been found on all sides of the trees near the huckleberry fields. Warner likes to take the bark from the southeast face when possible because the sun will help the tree grow and heal. Leaving a scar on the north side leaves the tree subject to rot and insect damage, the Indians believe.

"Long ago, we had to pray that the tree would be protected and the basket would be a good material for food," he says. Having read the story of Hiawatha talking to the tree about giving bark, Warner acknowledges this as an ancient ritual among the native people of North America. Although cedar is the major material used in bark baskets, the people of the Mid-Columbia, except for the Klikitat, were known to use the bark of the birch, cottonwood, and pine on occasion (Kiefer 1988; Teit 1928, 353).

Forest archaeologists have not yet found basket scars older than about two hundred years. Warner offers an explanation for this: "For thousands of years, the last family camping at Cold Springs at the end of October would gather dry brush, start a fire, and burn a portion of the huckleberry fields before leaving." Huckleberries prosper in sunlight, and this periodic burning prevented trees and brush from encroaching on the valuable crop. It is Warner's belief, as well as that of some archaeologists, that the burning also destroyed the older basket trees, removing evidence of earlier basket-making.[8]

## Teaching the Skills; Learning the Art

One day when Warner Jim was about seven, he did not want to pick berries and stayed in camp with his grandmother. "*Cutla,* Grandson," she said to him, "I want you to take me to the forest. Lead me by my left hand." After walking a long way down the trail, the blind woman told him, "Wait, let me take the lead." She stopped in an open space, "I think it's here someplace."

"I looked around," Warner remembers, "and there was a big cedar. I don't know how she could tell."

She said to the child, "There's *lap'uy* [bark basket] over there." He led her over to the tree. When she felt the bark, she told him to take his axe and cut across the bottom. She took a little tool made of deer horn and worked loose the edge of the cut. "Grab the bottom and pull," she told him. "It won't go up the tree." Warner took a firm hold and pulled up, the bark coming off in a long wedge about seven feet long. Had the child been older, he could have cut the top of the bark piece from the tree neatly with his axe. To cut the bark for an especially large basket, men would stand on horseback.

Then Warner's grandmother turned around, "There should be a smaller cedar tree, a limb." He found a small limb and cut it. She took some hop string from her pocket and tied it to the two ends of the limb, pulling them together enough to form a bow. Laying the strip of bark on the ground with the smooth inner side up she used the arc of the cedar limb as a guide and made a deep bowed mark with her deer horn tool near the center of the piece. She turned the curved "pattern" over and scored the bark again, forming a neatly pointed and gentle oval that would be the base. The oval must not be too curved, she cautioned, or the sides of the basket would split when bending up.

Before sewing up the sides, the old woman showed her grandson how to reinforce the basket with extra pieces of inner bark. The pieces were pushed between the inner and outer surfaces of the bark where the handles would be added

*Folded cedar bark basket. Diagram by Joy Stickney from a drawing by Peggy Dills Kelter.*

and at the ends of the oval where the bark would be bent upward to form the base.

Working on a basket as he tells us this story, Warner uses a commercial straightedge to mark the top and bottom of his basket piece. "This was all done without measuring," he says of those earlier days. As he marks the oval for the base, he recalls, "My grandmother was doing this without looking. It was really amazing how she could do it!"

Whatever its size, the bark basket always has two "legs" at the sides of the concave base. It has been suggested that this bowed shape was designed for carrying on a horse's back.[9] The real explanation is much more practical. It is the method of construction—the scoring and bending the cedar to form a one-piece container—that creates this distinctive arched base. When asked about the horseback idea, Warner simply says, "Well, those legs do help the baskets stand up in the brush."

Bending the cedar and shaping it on his knee, the basket-maker advises, "Take time, you have to use your body to feel the bark. Be easy with the bark. It's delicate."[10] (Warner tells of a basket holding his weight when he was well over two hundred pounds. The Jim family had a basket that had been made by Warner's great grandmother about 1850. Although it has gone out of the family now, he knows that the basket was still in good shape and usable in the late 1940s.)

His grandmother finished that first basket there beside the tree that gave them its bark. She showed her grandson how to use a small cedar limb to reinforce the inner side of the basket's rim, and how to cut a strip from the piece of bark to use, smooth side out, for the outer rim. She taught him not to waste anything—taking the rest of the bark they removed from the tree back to camp to make smaller baskets at a later time.

Today Warner uses an upholstery needle to sew up the sides and around the top of the basket—a larger needle could split the bark and ruin the basket. His grandmother pierced holes for the stitches with a bone awl, then sewed up the basket sides with a needle formed from a crane's lower jaw

*The basketmaker's tools. Strings are tied around new baskets to help them hold their form as they dry. Photo by W. T. Schlick.*

*Warner Jim marks the curve for the fold at the base. Photo by W. T. Schlick.*

or a curved piece of bone from the mouth of a sucker. She taught Warner to place his stitches so that they would not split the bark. "They used to leave a crack or a knot hole to let a little bit of air into the storage baskets," Warner recalls. Cooking baskets, of course, were stitched as tightly as possible.

Many basketmakers used smooth strips of the inner bark of the cedar to sew the basket together, but, until recent years, the Jim family used strong cord spun from the fibers of

Indian hemp. The adaptable people of the Mid-Columbia sewed them with other materials as well: string spun from the inner bark of the sagebrush, cotton hop twine, commercial sisal or hemp, and, today, darning cotton or even plastic cord, anything that holds the basket together securely.

When Warner completes his basket, he ties another cord tightly around it. Keeping it out of the sun, a berry picker can use the new basket right away. The string will hold it firmly during the several months it takes to dry completely and achieve maximum strength. The Mid-Columbia people sometimes put deer fern or grass inside the basket to help it dry more evenly. After the basket is dry the string may be removed.

Warner Jim is perhaps the best known of the contemporary bark basketmakers. Although he learned to make the baskets at the age of seven, he soon forgot the skill and was in his early twenties when his mother, Annie Jim, began to teach him once again. A few others living near them at Rock Creek learned at the same time. Jim feels it was his destiny to make baskets. A hermit named Taksinoo made baskets and gave them to people for huckleberries. "I had to learn because I was given his name," Warner explains.

Hoping to preserve the traditional art, Warner has taught others his methods; the largest group were forty-three youngsters from regional Indian clubs in a workshop at Rock Creek Longhouse in 1982. Another basketmaker, Louise Billy, learned from her father to make the bark baskets in all sizes. The Rock Creek woman lives near Goldendale.[11] Her son Lindsay has also mastered the art.

There may be others today who make these ingenious baskets for their own families' use. Although we do not know their names, we honor them for keeping alive an important heritage.

All Columbia River baskets are richer when shown or used within the originally intended context, as a flat twined bag filled with dried roots or in a wedding trade. All of the types of basketry—the hat, round bag, flat bag, coiled basket—also can stand alone as works of art. At first glance, the

folded bark "basket" is out of place in this prestigious group. However, the happy circumstances of its manufacture—to hold a surplus of food; the quiet time of its making; the ingenious mind of its originator; and the satisfaction its making and use brings to the owners; even its sheer simplicity, when fully understood—all contribute to our appreciation of this container as a representative of plenty and of pleasure and, yes, as a work of art.

The feeling among the people who claim this rough basket as their own is of wonder and gratitude that the Creator provided such useful material so close to the place of need, and gave them the skill to take advantage of it. "Nature provides everything, table or bed of strips of cedar bark, cattails, anything . . . just take the time to feel around."[12]

*Warner Jim demonstrates the use of a folded cedar bark basket; he says, "use your body to feel the bark." Photo by W. T. Schlick.*

*The central design on the beaded bag at left is similar to those found on flat twined bags made after 1850. Similar connected triangles form a banded design on the twined root storage bag, right. Gifts to the author's family on leaving Warm Springs Agency, 1964. Photo by W. T. Schlick.*

# 6. WAWXPA
## *The Flat Twined Bag*

*She gave him a flat carrying bag, saying, "Bring some acorns back for our meal and don't play on your way."*

It was summertime and hot. We jostled up the dusty road above the Warm Springs Indian Agency in the county agent's pickup. Turning onto the street that runs along the hill above the highway, we stopped at a house. Blanche Tohet came out and led the agent into a nearby shed to carry out an old metal suitcase. When he placed it on the tailgate and she lifted the lid, it was as if Marco Polo had opened his trunk of treasures from Cathay.

There lay heirloom textiles that rivaled any in the world. The suitcase was filled with colorful flat twined bags, commonly known as "cornhusk" bags or "wallets," that family members had woven or inherited or received in trade over many generations. Choosing the finest to send with us for exhibit at the Wasco County Fair at Tygh Valley, the woman laid them in a large *shaptakay,* a rawhide Indian suitcase or parfleche, which itself was a work of art.

This was my first exposure to the finely twined flat bags of Indian hemp that are prized by the native people of the Mid-Columbia and their neighbors across the Columbia Plateau. (These flat "cornhusk" bags were used for storing dried foods and other valuables and, later, as handbags, and are not to be confused with the cylindrical bags discussed in chapter 3.) In the early 1960s the bags were little known outside the area except among a few collectors. After examining these bags in several museum collections, I realized that, with few exceptions, those that have remained in the families of the native people represent the finest of the work. The dry climate of the area to the east of the Cascade Mountains and the careful storage and handling provided by the owners have preserved many of the bags in excellent condition. It is not unusual today to see a beautiful twined handbag slipped out of a plastic bag when the owner is ready to carry it.

This is not to say that museums have mistreated these artifacts. Rather, it appears that the flat twined bag holds such importance and requires such talent and industry to create that families have been unwilling to part with the best of them. Rarely made for sale, the flat twined bag changed hands through the most traditional of means—

*Onepennee family members display heirlooms in their tee-pee at a Yakima tribal celebration in the 1950s. Photo by J. W. Thompson.*

trades, ceremonial gifts, and inheritance. Families of the Mid-Columbia needed these practical containers to hold their year's supply of dried roots. Their beauty aside, the large twined bags of hemp and grass or cornhusk were the gunny sacks, the Mason jars, and the freezer bags of long ago.

The handsome bags were slow in coming to the attention of people beyond the native community. Otis Mason's classic 1904 report for the Smithsonian Institution on aboriginal American basketry (that continues to be the most comprehensive book on the subject) includes only a few lines on the flat twined bag (Mason 1976, 437–38). The 1902 catalogue of the Frohman Trading Company in Portland, Oregon, listed no such bags, although the dealer offered many fine coiled

*The small number of flat twined bags available to collectors at the beginning of the twentieth century is illustrated by this photo of Portland dealer D. M. Averill's collection. The baskets in the display are largely from native weavers in Northern California. The design on the bag in the center of the flat twined Columbia River bags in the foreground has been described as "salmon stomach." Oregon Historical Society no. 50027.*

Klikitat-style baskets and a few round Wasco-style bags for sale.

When the time came for us to move away from the reservation, our Warm Springs friends held a picnic among the junipers that rim Lake Simtustus, the reservoir on the Deschutes River behind Pelton Dam. With young children also saying goodbye, the choice was far superior to a farewell party in a fancy hotel or restaurant. And even more thoughtful were their gifts to us—a beaded handbag in a nineteenth-century design and, treasure of treasures, a flat twined storage bag.

The beaded handbag design is similar to those found on twined bags, two horizontal motifs at the top and bottom of the design field with a broad stepped diamond in the center.

The horizontal motifs are similar to those the weaver worked onto one side of the root storage bag, two triangular forms connected at their apexes by a line. The two works of art are out of the same tradition. For some thirty years we have carried these heirlooms with us from our lives at Warm Springs. Today as I look at the fine stitches in the root storage bag and at the handbag's tiny beads in subdued pinks and bronze and cranberry, the talent of the people we lived among, not to mention their generosity, overwhelms me.

Until Christmastime 1970, I assumed that the descendants of the people of the Mid-Columbia considered the twined bags only as honored heirlooms to be displayed at fairs and the annual tribal art exhibitions on the reservations.

By this time we were living on the Yakima Reservation and just before the holiday, a call came for me at the *Toppenish Review* where I was working. "There will be a wedding trade at the community center the day after Christmas," Virginia Beavert told me. By this time I had learned that notice of an event was an invitation to the event, so I gathered up camera and notebook and went out to the huge building south of town that the Yakima tribe used for everything from general council meetings to powwows and sports events.

Christmas is a time of tradition for many people; a time of families getting together, exchanging gifts. This was a traditional family gift exchange, but the fact that it was the day after Christmas was only a coincidence. It was the wedding trade for a young Yakima Indian couple—a ceremony that may be older than most Christmas observances. During this ceremony, relatives of the bride and groom exchanged gifts. These gifts included flat twined bags which were given by the bride's relatives to members of the groom's family. It was my first exposure to these bags as an integral part of a modern ceremony.

## A Yakima Wedding Trade

According to the custom of the people of the Mid-Columbia, the parents of the bride and groom agree on a day when relatives from far and near come together to "trade on"

*A large root storage bag with an overall design is among the treasured gifts acquired by relatives during a 1970 wedding trade on the Yakima Reservation. Photo by the author; courtesy* Toppenish Review.

the marriage. On the day after Christmas in 1970, nearly a hundred members of two Yakima Indian families spent the afternoon performing the prescribed ritual of the wedding trade. In this case, the couple had been married in the White Swan Independent Church the previous June.[1] The young couple missed this wedding trade due to the bride's illness, but their presence was not necessary. Such trades are between members of the two families and not for the purpose of giving gifts to the pair.

The ceremony began when a young woman chosen by a relative from the bride's side to represent the bride knelt on a tule mat on the floor. Other young women did the same. There were as many proxy brides taking part in the ritual as there were relatives who wished to take part in the trade. Each relative had a counterpart to return the trade from the groom's family. If the bride had been present, she, too, would serve as a focus for the exchange of goods between two trading partners.

The bride's relatives placed gifts on and around each kneeling "bride," gifts that were traditional products of a woman's talents: beaded bags, moccasins, buckskin dresses, and, to my astonishment, flat twined bags. This was not the nineteenth century, this was 1970. I had watched the women bring great cloth-tied bundles into the hall before the ceremony began. The museum-quality gifts were taken from these bundles.

In response, a woman or group of women from the groom's family brought gifts of blankets, shawls, and scarves across the hall to each proxy bride. These items represented the traditional contributions of men in earlier days—blankets replacing the elk hides that the hunters provided for their families, shawls and scarves representing the deer hides used in clothing. When the groom's relatives placed a blanket on the floor beside the mat where the proxy bride knelt, they removed the women's gifts. Then the stand-in moved to the blanket. This action symbolized the bride leaving her family and joining the groom's household. As the proxy knelt on the blanket, the groom's relatives dressed her in the gifts they brought and placed combs in the proxy bride's hair. Members of the bride's family removed the combs, symbolizing the ancient custom of braiding the new bride's hair. Following the combs, "bugs" of coins, candy, or gum were dropped on each proxy bride's head while the women and children from her family pulled them off, again, symbolically preparing her for her wedding.

When every family group had traded, "blazing the trails" began. Women from the bride's side carried smaller gifts—roots, dishes, strings of bright beads ("knickknacks," a woman told me)—across to the groom's side of the hall where his relatives waited to give in return lengths of cloth for the traditional wing dresses or shawls. On this occasion,

*During the "blazing the trail" segment of the traditional wedding trade ceremony, Virginia Beavert places a twined handbag on the mat with other gifts for her trading partner from the groom's family. Photo by the author; courtesy* Toppenish Review.

one of the trading women brought a large, twined-root storage bag across the hall. Hardly a knickknack, I thought.

The final ritual of this wedding trade on the day after Christmas in 1970 was the dinner given by the bride's family. The women spread mats in a long line on the floor, covered them with tablecloths and set places for the guests. On this cover they laid out a feast of salmon, berries, bitterroot, camas and other traditional roots, cakes, and pies.

As the bride's family was setting up for the feast, a proxy groom joined the first "bride," and his relatives dressed the couple in blankets and shawls and other finery which included a twined handbag for the bride. When all was ready, the bride and groom and all the members of his family took their places on mats that surrounded the cloth-covered "table" area and the bride's relatives served them. At the end of the meal, those who had eaten gathered up the dishes and any remaining food to take home. This, too, was part of the trade.

At a later time, the parents of the bride and groom would agree on a return trade when the groom's family would be the hosts. The families would spend another day with friends and relatives, exchanging gifts in the time-honored custom. The twined bags again would be brought out and given with other heirlooms to seal an important contract.

## THE FLAT TWINED BAG IN ANCIENT TIMES

Archaeologists report that the people of the Mid-Columbia have used twining and false embroidery, the weaving techniques employed in making the flat bags, for at least nine thousand years (Cressman 1960, 73). The ancient myths confirm that the people have used these root storage bags since the earliest times.

### *Kalaasya and His Grandmother*

*A long time ago there lived little Kalaasya (Raccoon) and his grandmother near a river. One day Grandmother asked Kalaasya to go down to their cache and bring her some* wawachi *(pickled acorns). She pickled the acorns with black coal dirt mixed with mud and buried them deep inside a hole near the river where the dampness preserved them. She gave him a flat carrying bag, saying, "Bring some acorns back for our meal and don't play on your way."*

*Kalaasya skipped off to the river and scooped acorns into the bag until it was full. Covering the hole he headed back to their camp, dawdling and playing along the way. As he played, he stumbled and scattered the acorns in the dirt. Kalaasya knew his grandmother would be angry, so he ate the soiled acorns and returned to the hole for more.*

*On the return trip he was daydreaming again, swinging the bag around his head. Again he fell and spilled the acorns, and again he ate the spoiled acorns. This went on until he had spilled and eaten the food four times. After the fourth fall, and disgusted with himself, little Kalaasya tossed the empty bag into the brush and returned to the hole to eat up all the rest of the winter's supply. As Kalaasya burrowed into the hole to get the last of the acorns only his tail waved at the opening.*

*Grandmother was busy preparing Indian hemp for her weaving, but soon became very hungry. She took her fire stoking stick for a cane and walked to the river to look for Little Raccoon. She saw her grandson's tail waving there at the mouth of their cache as he wriggled to reach the last of the acorns. Grabbing the tail, she pulled little Kalaasya out of the hole. She struck him angrily with the fire poker, and dragging it all the way from his nose to his tail, giving him the black eyes and stripes he wears today. (Adapted from Beavert 1974, 116)*

## TWINED BAGS
## IN COLUMBIA RIVER LIFE

The women living near the river had unique problems to solve—how to protect and transport family belongings during seasonal moves to the great encampments during the salmon runs, to the root digging fields, to the mountains for berries, and home to the winter camps. They needed containers that would keep dried roots and other foods free from

dust, as well as containers for carrying small personal objects, clothing, and jewelry, and to hold the materials for
making more containers. These bags needed to be flexible,
tightly woven, and to take up little space when not in use. To
meet these needs, they devised the *wawxpa,* a bag which
could be woven in one piece. The bag looked much like a
flour sack in form, but was stronger in construction. Like a
flour sack, the bag lay flat when empty, but would expand to
hold a large quantity of food or other valuables.

The ancestors at some long-ago time discovered *taxus,*
the tall plant growing in the damp ground that we know
today as Indian hemp or dogbane (see chapter 1). The inner
bark of this plentiful plant produced soft lustrous fibers that
could be spun into strong string. They used this string, in
turn, to form the sturdy but flexible containers the people
required. Although they made string from other fibers such
as hazel, willow root bark, antelope brush, and sagebrush,
hemp was the favorite.

To decorate the bag, as well as to construct a dust-free
container, the weaver added an outside layer in a technique
known as false embroidery, or by the more descriptive term,
external weft wrap. True embroidery is added after the fabric
is constructed. In false embroidery, the weaver incorporates a
flat weaving strand to create the design during the weaving
process. It is the discovery of fragments of this distinctive
technique in the earliest archaeological sites along the river
that leads us to believe that the early people of the Mid-
Columbia made these bags and even in those earliest of times
decorated them in some way.

The process of creating bags large enough to hold a
family's possessions was a long and tedious one. The materials had to be gathered and cured, and the hemp spun into
twine. By the time a weaver was ready to sit down and begin
weaving the bags, she had spent many hours preparing the
materials. Then came the months of twining the bags, stitch
by stitch. A woman from the river estimates that it took two
to three months to twine a large root-storage bag. It is no
wonder that the Nez Perce women were unwilling to part

*"Wash-us-etan-way" weaving a large storage bag, c. 1907. It may have taken a woman two to three months to complete a bag of this size. Photo by Fanny van Duyn, Tygh Valley, Oregon. Gary Goodwin Collection, Maryhill Museum of Art cat. no. 1991.06.01.*

with any of these valuables on June 7, 1806, when asked for bags "for the purpose of containing roots and bread" by members of Lewis and Clark's Corps of Discovery.[2]

Later explorers reported that the people stored berries, roots, and nuts in bags about one by two feet, and used larger bags up to three feet long for clothing and other personal effects. Early visitors to the Mid–Columbia also described piles of filled bags in the corners or hung along the wall in native homes (Miller 1986, 61). A Yakima elder remembered seeing great stacks of the bags beside the race track near White Swan on the Yakima Reservation when he was a boy. They were piled with other valuable goods being wagered

(Watson Totus, pers. com. 1974). Sizes of the flat storage bags in collections today average about fifteen inches wide by twenty inches high. Smaller square bags, about eight inches by nine inches, held trinkets and small household articles (Ray 1932, 33; Delores Buck, pers. com. 1974). The bags' flat shapes and flexibility because of the soft, strong materials made them ideal for carrying on horseback.

As a medium of trade or barter, the bags in the early days were considered only the wrapping or container for the dried roots they held. The quality of the roots inside determined the value of the item in trade (Nettie Jackson, pers. com. 1985). When filled for such trading, the bag would be bulging and the contents held in place by string laced across the opening between the cord loops that the maker had added just beneath the top edge. Trade values varied somewhat by the location of the trading and the condition of the goods, but the quality of the container itself was not the deciding factor. The largest of the bags described above would hold just under a half bushel or nearly four dry gallons of roots. Such a sack filled with camas and another of bitterroot could be traded for a *shaptakay* (Indian trunk or parfleche) filled with a blanket, dress material, shawl, and a scarf. If the material in the trunk was especially valuable, the owner would expect an extra bag of roots in exchange.[3]

Through trade, the flat twined bags have traveled far from their weavers' homeland. A Canadian Blackfoot medicine bundle on display in the Provincial Museum of Alberta in Edmonton has been made from a very old flat twined bag with the designs worked in colored wool in the false embroidery technique. The Indian hemp background of the bag is in plain twining. The Crow and Blackfeet people of Montana also were known to use flat twined bags from the Plateau in similar medicine bundles, which held important personal and sacred objects (Miller 1986, 72).

Other bags that have reached Canadian collections include a large root-storage bag and three handbags from the Columbia River that are on display at the North West Mounted Police Museum of Canada in Fort McLeod, Al-

*Anna Kash Kash (Wannassee) holds a small twined handbag with central design. Photo by Edward S. Curtis, 1899. Smithsonian Institution photo no. 76–15868.*

berta. Several other fine bags were collected in Gleichen, Alberta, for the Canadian Museum of Civilization in Ottawa, evidence of the "centuries old cultural ties between north-central Plains and the Columbia River area."[4]

Today, the *wapanii sapk'ukt,* or "twined handbag," is the most popular form for the flat twined bag. For many years after the settlers brought burlap bags and other containers that could be used to store foods, the native people continued to cling to the tight dust-free twined bags. The weavers also began to make many smaller bags with handles for handbags. These bags ranged in size from seven inches wide by eight inches high to twelve inches by fifteen inches. Many of the bags from the Columbia River area can be seen in formal portraits taken by turn-of-the-century photographers. These include photographs of native women living far to the east who would have obtained them in trade. Although rarely carried by men except on ceremonial occasions, the bags often are displayed in such portraits of Plateau men.

The twined *sapk'ukt* was, and still is, carried with great pride by native people throughout the Columbia Plateau. Considered to be a necessary article of clothing for ceremonial or dress-up occasions, the twined handbag emphasizes the particular and distinct heritage of the people of the Mid-Columbia (Cheney Cowles 1974, 3). On the few bags still being made, some weavers add fringes of hide across the bottom, giving the wearer another accent of kinetic beauty when dancing. Weavers also make small handbags for children and miniatures to be worn pinned to clothing or on a necklace.

The Mid-Columbia weavers use similar techniques and materials to make the popular foldover belt wallets or side purses that are worn by both men and women. In earlier days, other products also were created by virtuoso weavers—vests with intricate designs, arm bands, belts, even a martingale for a rider's mount.[5] About 1940, a woman from the White Salmon area decorated a complete dance outfit in false embroidery (Nettie Jackson, pers. com. 1988).

Although the twined bags rarely wear out, they occa-

*Two bark baskets collected by H. W. Krieger at the Wish-*
*xam village of Spedis, Washington, in 1934. Apparently*
*made for the anthropologist as an example of the form, one*
*basket, right, is unusual in that the rough outer bark of the*
*cedar is on the inside. Smithsonian Institution cat. nos.*
*374,063 (left) and 374,062.*

*Pauline Wahsise and young Beatrice Sampson display a twined bag full of food roots, a valued possession representing the generosity of the earth. Photo by J. W. Thompson, c. 1950.*

*The flat twined storage bags and the rawhide* shaptakay *(Indian suitcase or parfleche) were suited for travel by horseback. Photo by J. W. Thompson, c. 1950. The horse has been identified as belonging to Lena Sohappy of Toppenish.*

A popular variation of the flat twined bag was the "foldover" or side purse, a wallet that is worn on the belt by both men and women. This fine example could also be carried by the handle. H8 in., W7.5 in. Photo by Jerry Taylor. Maryhill Museum of Art cat. no. 0.544.

The Maryhill Museum foldover purse with the flap lifted to reveal another design.

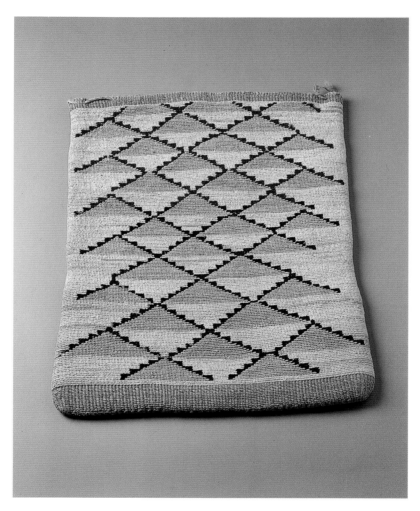

*Twined storage bag from the Mary Underwood Lane Collection, Maryhill Museum of Art. This green color is found on many late nineteenth-century bags and may have come from green lichen. H18.5 in., W14 in. Photo by Jerry Taylor. Maryhill Museum of Art cat. no. 1940.01.91.*

*Reverse side of twined storage bag showing a complex banded design. Photo by Jerry Taylor. Maryhill Museum of Art Cat. no. 1940.01.91.*

*Twined handbag held by Cecelia Totus in the photograph on page 159 features elk figures similar to those found on round Wasco-style bags. H12.5 in., W11 in. Lee and Lois Miner Collection.*

*Reverse side of elk bag. The central star motif in the five-part design is found on other bags attributed to Cecelia Yumpty Totus's family.*

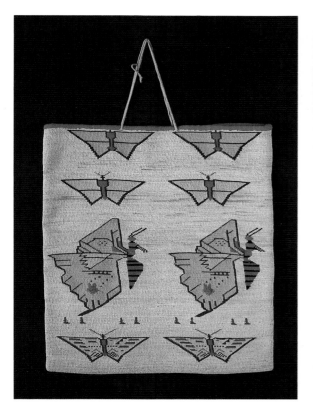

*Butterflies decorate this spectacular twined handbag made about 1880.*
*L16 in., W14.5 in. (See page 161 for a photograph of the bag taken*
*in 1902.) Lee and Lois Miner Collection.*

*Stylized birds march across the reverse side of the butterfly twined bag.*

*This overall design is an example of the symmetry and rhythmic repetition of motifs that are characteristic of many of the flat twined bags of the Columbia Plateau. Gift to Yakima Indian Nation Museum in memory of William Condit Schlick. Photo by Robert Pace.*

*Reverse side of flat twined bag. Triangles, diamonds, and lines create this lively banded pattern. Photo by Robert Pace.*

*Detail of a twined root storage bag made in the 1920s by Susie Walsey Billy of Rock Creek. This bag has had good care over the years, for the colors on the outside are as bright as the original colors revealed on the inside (shown below). Photo by W. T. Schlick.*

*Detail of the inside of the Susie Walsey Billy bag shows knee-spun Indian hemp wefts in the top border and cotton string wefts that are concealed by the cornhusk false embroidery in the body of the bag. Photo by W. T. Schlick.*

The distinctive elk, sturgeon, condor, and human motifs on this flat twined handbag identify it as the work of a Wasco or Wishxam weaver. H13 in., W10 in. Photo by Joseph Schlick. Doris Sweazey Bounds Collection, High Desert Museum, Bend, Oregon, cat. no. 5.1.112.

*Embellished triangles form a banded design on the reverse
side of the facing bag. Photo by Joseph Schlick.*

*Cecelia Totus on horseback, c. 1960. The horse regalia
and the large bag decorated in Wasco-style figures are examples of twining with false embroidery. The bag is illustrated on page 167. Photo courtesy Lee and Lois Miner.*

*Klikitat-style coiled basket presented to the Smithsonian Institution in 1902 by the wife of Senator Levi Ankeny of Washington State. Smithsonian Institution cat. no. 214,455.*

*Woman's work basket collected at Fort Simcoe on the Yakima Reservation before 1876 by Indian Agent James H. Wilbur. Smithsonian Institution cat. no. 23,872.*

*Wasco-style twined bag collected before 1899 on the Warm Springs Reservation by Miss E. T. Houtz, a matron at the boarding school. Smithsonian Institution cat. no. 204,223.*

*Turn-of-the century Klikitat basket showing the unusual negative images of birds, possibly giant condors. H20 in., W13 in. at top (7 in. base). Private collection.*

Roxie (also Roxa) Shackelford of The Dalles sold this
fine coiled cedar root basket with attached twined carrying
strap to the Smithsonian Institution in 1900 for twenty
dollars. The collector wrote on a note with the basket,
"Said to be of Lewis and Clark time." Smithsonian Institution cat. nos. 207,758 (strap) and 207,759 (basket).

Distinctive, partially imbricated Klikitat basket in W. C.
Curtis's collection. (See illustration, page 182, right fore-
ground.) H15 in., W12.5 in. Photo by Jerry Taylor.
Maryhill Museum of Art cat. no. 1951.01.81/80.

*Twined bag woven by Wasco basketmaker Patricia
Courtney Gold, 1993.*

*Chief Wolf Necklace (Harlish-Washshomake), Palus, visiting Washington, D.C., from his home on the Snake River in 1894. He poses for this formal portrait holding a twined handbag. Photo by C. M. Bell. National Archives neg. no. 106-IN-2901A.*

sionally are chewed by mice, stained by mildew, or damaged by fire or water. Ingenious owners salvage the untouched portions of the bags to make smaller handbags, belts, or other useful items. No handwork as valuable as this can be wasted.

One use of bags today could not have been predicted by the early weavers of the Mid-Columbia. The Appaloosa Horse Club, Inc., with headquarters in Moscow, Idaho, has established standards of personal dress for their members when participating in horse shows and parades—dress that recalls the ceremonial clothing of the native people who first rode the distinctive horses of the Palouse country (Connette 1970, 6). Standard dress includes a flat twined handbag. For the proud Appaloosa owners, the bags represent their tribute to the beauty of the region, the ties with the past, and the artistic talents of the first residents along this great river—the ancestors of the people of the Mid-Columbia.

# WEAVING THE FLAT TWINED BAG

## *Materials*

For generations, the weavers of the Mid-Columbia used Indian hemp for the basic fiber of all of their twined weaving. The strength and beauty of this material made it ideal as the foundation for hats and bags of all kinds.

Cotton twine probably came to the Mid-Columbia with the fur traders in the early 1800s, for it had been a standard trade item in North America since the middle of the seventeenth century (Whiteford 1977, 58). Probably some weavers adopted this new pre-spun cordage for their weaving as soon as it was available. Women also used raveled burlap bags for the foundation twine in some bags, although this appears to have been more common in the round twined bags than in the flat storage bags. It was not until growers began using cotton twine to train hop vines about the turn of the century that such made materials became available in large quantities and for little or no expense.

For many years, weavers continued to prefer the more traditional appearance of a bag made with Indian hemp warps and wefts, at least in the exposed rows of plain twining at the bottom and top of the bag. The plentiful cotton twine from the hop yards, however, replaced hemp in the body of many bags made in the twentieth century—in the portion of the weaving concealed by the false embroidery. Gradually the twine replaced the hand-spun hemp completely in most of the bags.

Although hop growers replaced the cotton twine with a rough jute cord in the early 1940s, weavers continue to use commercial cotton twine in their weaving, ordering it by the cone from local suppliers (Sally Buck, pers. com. 1988). Several weavers today also use warps of jute twine, the natural color reminiscent of Indian hemp.

The oldest of the flat twined bags are made entirely of Indian hemp with the false embroidery in a species of grass. On the earliest bags, the weaver worked only her decorative elements—usually overall arrangements of rectangles, triangles, and lines—in false embroidery. The background was in the warm tones of the plain twined hemp foundation (Julia Sohappy, pers. com. 1974). For variety in color, she gathered the grass at different times of the summer. By drying it in the shade, she was able to retain some of the green of midsummer grass. The grass gathered later in the season provided a light beige. The contrast in these natural colors is still visible on very old bags.

Although most early reports list bear grass as the material used for the false embroidery, it rarely has been identified in a bag (Miller 1986, 119).[6] Bear grass was used on the twined hats of the Mid-Columbia, its stiffness giving the hat

*Elsie Pistolhead, Yakima, is weaving a flat twined bag using cotton string for the warps. Photo by J. W. Thompson, c. 1950.*

form and body. However, it appears that in precontact times a softer material was used for the flat twined bags. The people of the Mid-Columbia say, as they do of the material in the round twined bags, "They used a grass that grows up in the mountains." With their hands, they describe a bunch grass. It also is possible that the bur reed (*Sparganium eurycarpum*) sent to the Smithsonian by Mrs. Shackelford of The Dalles was used in these bags as well as in the round bags. Whatever the grass species, it has not been used in the flat bags for many years.

The first change in material for the flat bags came from the newcomers' gardens, the husks from ears of corn (*Zea mays*). Corn originating in the Mexican highlands gradually made its way north to what is now the American Southwest, but those varieties originally were not hardy enough for the climate of the Columbia Plateau.[7] Through a circuitous journey, the plant was carried across the Atlantic to Europe where it was adapted to northern growing conditions. From there the Europeans brought it back to North America.

Although it is possible that the people of the Mid-Columbia had obtained corn with the horse, directly from the Southwest, or from the Mandans, Missouris, or other natives to the east (Eugene Hunn, pers. com. 1988), we know the plant was introduced into the Northwest at least by 1820 by the fur traders. At that time, the Hudson's Bay Company encouraged their posts, one of which was at The Dalles, to cultivate gardens to eliminate the costly import of staples and to relieve the monotony of the diet (Gibson 1985). By 1833, 150 bushels of corn were harvested at Fort Walla Walla. By the next year, Nathaniel Wyeth reported that Indian corn grown on the east side of the Columbia River at Wallula produced 80 bushels to the acre (McKelvey 1955, 512, 608). Missionaries began arriving soon after this and planted corn as well. Many Indian people, especially among the Umatilla and the more-settled Wasco and Wishxam, planted corn (Kuhlken 1982, 15).[8]

For women accustomed to using several varieties of plant fiber in their basketry, it is not surprising that they soon

*Yumtobe Kamiakin (1855–1910) holds a fine flat-twined handbag for this photograph taken at Fort Simcoe in 1902 by Gill. Smithsonian Institution photo no. 2871.B.*

began to weave with the strong new material that dried to a pale cream color and took the native dyes easily. The strands of cornhusk were shorter than the grasses, but this was no handicap in false embroidery. Rather, the shorter pieces made it easy for the weaver to change color frequently. Cornhusks probably became more readily available to the native weavers after 1860. It was about then that the choice land in the Willamette Valley was taken and emigrants began to settle in the valleys of the Columbia and its tributaries, bringing their gardens with them. A plentiful supply of cultivated corn allowed the weavers to cover the entire bag with the false embroidery rather than only the design areas as had been the custom when only grass was available. This third layer created an even tighter, more dust-resisting container.

For the few weavers today who make the flat twined bags, cornhusk is the material of choice for the background. An elderly Yakima weaver told of helping her grandmother make bags when she was a child, using cornhusks for false embroidery. "They need to be tough, white, and soft, in long pieces," she said. The weaver especially prized the corn with variegated kernels, known as Indian corn, for the strength of its soft interior husks (Julia Sohappy, pers. com. 1973). As recently as 1973, a Yakima woman complained about the farmer who left a gate open into a field of harvested corn and allowed cattle to trample her yearly supply of twining material (Barney Dunn, pers. com. 1973). Although some weavers today reportedly use the cornhusks sold commercially for wrapping tamales (Miller 1986, 137), these generally are more fibrous and less desirable for false embroidery than the finer husks closer to the kernels selected by the weavers. Klikitat weaver Sally Wahkiacus was known to use some imported raffia which she purchased around the turn of the century in Goldendale, Washington, where she shopped (Sally Buck, pers. com. 1987).

Weavers raveled yarns from blankets, trade cloth, and woolen clothing for the decorative elements in twined hats during the first half of the nineteenth century. A few of the early bags include small areas of red, dark blue, or green, but most weavers of the flat bags continued until midcentury to work their designs in the subdued hues of the natural grasses contrasted with the brown hemp background. Under the terms of the treaties with the Columbia River people, ratified in 1859, the government issued blankets and clothing to them. The most common colors were red, dark blue, and green. The greater availability of woolens may be one reason for an increase in the use of wool after that time. In addition to raveling woolens for yarn, weavers boiled cornhusks with them to dye the husks.

Bright aniline-dyed yarns from Germantown, Pennsylvania, were readily available by the 1870s and became popular. In many cases, the soft colors we see today on the twined bags are simply the subdued result of age and light on these once-vivid colors. Even after the first commercial yarns became available, weavers continued to use dyed cornhusk as well as the woolens in their patterns, frequently čombining the two materials in one bag. This practice continues today.

A study of Plateau twined bags demonstrates the variety of materials available to the weaver from the mid–1800s on (Schlick 1977). Whether from need caused by scarcity of materials or by ingenuity, the basketmaker used all possible combinations of native and commercial materials. On one bag studied, an area of the design was worked in dyed cornhusk, worsted yarn, and strips of cloth, all in the same color of pink, the differences among the materials only visible on close examination. A Nez Perce bag in the Smithsonian Institution collection, once owned by Buffalo Bill Cody, has a bold woven design with wide horizontal lines applied in red paint.[9] A weaver's relative describes a bag in her family that has a twisted candy wrapper worked in for color (Nettie Jackson, pers. com. 1981).

TWINING THE BAG. In a few Mid-Columbia families today, children can watch their mother or father, aunt or grandmother twine these flat soft bags, just as children always had watched to learn the skills needed for successful living along the river. Most of these children, however, will never see

*Twined handbag, unusual in the use of dyed cornhusk for the background. Doris Sweazey Bounds Collection, High Desert Museum, Bend, Oregon, cat. no. 5.1.70.*

*Reverse side of the twined handbag in the Bounds Collection.*

Indian hemp spun for the warps of the bags. With few exceptions, weavers today have replaced the knee-spun hemp twine with commercial string.[10]

The materials may have changed, but the method of weaving has not. The weaver begins by measuring the string for her warps with a practiced eye. The number of warp strands depends on the desired width of her bag and the dimension of her material. Depending on the fineness of the material, a large handbag, eleven inches wide and twelve inches high, requires up to a hundred warps—over eighty yards of string—and much more than that for the wefts. The warp length must be twice the height of the bag plus at least six inches for the binding off. With her warps laid out before her, the weaver measures off a weft strand that is six or more times the desired width of her bag, to insure that she can complete the base of the bag without having to splice the wefts (Shawley 1975, 29). To keep the ends from tangling during the twining, the weaver might shorten the length of the wefts by making a series of loops held by slip knots, starting from each end (Mary Jim Chapman, pers. com. 1976).

The basketmaker begins weaving by doubling her long weft strand and looping it over the center of the first warp. This gives her the paired wefts needed for twining. A right-handed weaver will work from the left to the right, twisting the paired wefts by bringing the back weft forward over the front, the front weft moving to the back.[11] This creates a **Z**-twist stitch, from upper left to lower right, on the workface (outside) of the bag. She continues twining in this direction, picking up warp strands in each stitch, one by one, until all are incorporated in the weaving. At the end of the row, she turns her work around and twines again on the last warp, moving back across the warps to the end. To create a wider base, some weavers add one or two extra warps at the end of the row, usually after the first round. These added warps are treated in the same way as the final warp on the first row— twining twice on the warp strand to prevent twisting.

Illustrations in early books showing native weavers making twined baskets in Virginia and Alaska led several

*Diagram showing start and turn for a flat twined bag. Drawn by Peggy Dills Kelter.*

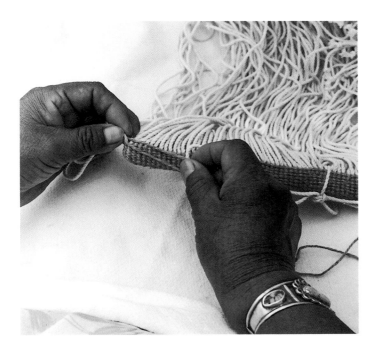

*Sally Buck brings the paired wefts around each warp strand in turn, then twists them. She has tied a stick inside the base of the bag to keep the corners from twisting. Photo by W. T. Schlick.*

writers to assume that all twiners suspend their work from a support, weaving in a downward direction. The Mid-Columbia weaver works in a more comfortable position. Rather than reaching out or up to weave, she holds her work on her lap, twining outward from the closed bottom of the bag, her arms resting at her sides. The work in progress is flexible and may be picked up and carried from place to place. With no loom or frame to move, the weaver makes her bag wherever she is. As the weaving progresses, the bottom of the bag begins to cup upward. After several rows, some weavers will place a stick or slat cut to the width of the bag inside at the base to keep it from twisting.[12] As each weft is exhausted a new weft strand is laid in; the tightness of the next row of weaving holds it in place.

## False Embroidery—External Weft Wrap

When making a root-storage bag, the weaver works several rows in simple, or plain, twining before she is ready to begin adding the third weaving element to create the false

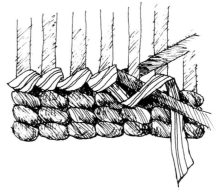

*Diagram of false embroidery technique. Drawn by Peggy Dills Kelter.*

embroidered surface. When making a handbag or other false embroidered article, she might begin the false embroidery immediately, with no initial rows of plain twining.

In false embroidery, the weaver introduces a strand of flat material between two warps and wraps this around each outside weft as it comes forward. The technical name for this technique, "external weft wrap," describes this action. This third element covers the twining stitch completely on the outside and is not visible on the inside except where it is introduced or changed.

The false embroidery stitch slants in the opposite direction from the plain twining of the first rows of the bag—upward to the right in an **S**-twist. The unusual technique creates a tight fabric and offers design opportunities limited only by the stitch–by–stitch construction.

There are a few weavers today who work their designs in the flat bags using full-turn twining instead of false embroidery, and several weavers in recent years have used false embroidery only for the design itself, working the background in close plain twining, as did their predecessors.[13] In rare cases, both full-turn twining and false embroidery are found in the same bag.[14] One possible explanation for this variation in technique could be that the bag was started by one weaver and finished by another.

Mid-Columbia weavers occasionally constructed another type of bag that is airier and more open, with bands of compact plain twining with false embroidery and twined openwork. In this latter technique the weaver encloses two warps in each twining stitch, moving over one warp at the beginning of each row to create a twill effect (Mason 1976, 234).[15]

## Designs

*"Fine art [exists] when exceptional creativity is accompanied by exceptional technical skill" (Dockstader 1961, 21).*

The oldest known examples of flat storage bags from the Mid-Columbia area are decorated in some way. In early times, the long process of preparing materials would be brightened by the prospect of winter days spent weaving new patterns into the hemp bags. Today, although the weaver purchases most of the materials and twines the bags throughout the year, the creation of a beautiful bag continues to offer an opportunity and to pose a challenge.

The challenge is to weave a fine, even textile. In all art, mastery of the technique is vital to the successful execution of design ideas. In twining a bag, the weaver must have perfected the rhythm of her fingers' movement and the control of the tension of the wefts in order to provide a smooth, even fabric.

This technical skill allows the weaver to express her artistry in the weaving of designs. Actually, the opportunity is dual—each side of a flat bag presents a surface for design. Although James Teit reported that designs usually were alike on Yakima bags of long ago, few of the people of the Mid-Columbia have seen such bags (Teit 1928, 360), and other reports confirm that similar designs on the two sides are rare (Dockstader 1978, 126; Mason 1976, 283). Generally each side of a twined bag can stand alone as a work of art. In many cases the design on one side is complex and on the other is a simpler repeat geometric design. This variety is not surprising when one considers that the bags are not made to hang on a wall but are mobile art—to be carried, moved from place to place, turned this way or that, danced with or ridden with. Both sides are never seen at the same time (except in free-standing museum cases or when reflected in a mirror).

It may be, as described by a Yakima man, that the simpler repeat pattern could be the weaver's signature (Don Umtuch, pers. com. 1974). A young Yakima woman reported that her aunt always wove "pine trees" into one side of her bags (Ernestine Jim Connor, pers. com. 1973). This recognized use of specific patterns by known weavers appears to be one of the few ways observers can tell where a bag was made. Some well-known designs were considered the personal property of the weaver and her family (Dockstader 1978, 126).

In Mid-Columbia life, the bags are one way for a weaver to express her own artistic talent and to achieve recognition and status. If the bags have stories to tell, they are of the skill and pride of their makers who lived (and live) among a people to whom such works of art are a much-appreciated part of everyday life.

DESIGN ORGANIZATION. Most weavers of the Mid-Columbia and the Plateau coordinate geometric motifs into a unified design. In an attempt to define a Plateau aesthetic tradition, studies have identified some factors commonly seen in the organization—the overall spacing and placement—of these designs. Shawley describes the Plateau philosophy of aesthetics as formal, with accented repetition and symmetry (1974, 246). Miller has developed five descriptive categories of design organization: overall, banded, central, five-part, and naturalistic (1986, 156).

Generally, the earlier bags can be identified by a balanced repetition of a single motif on each side. This repetition often gives a rhythmic feeling to the overall design. Some overall designs are arranged in vertical columns, an arrangement popular among Yakima weavers into the 1930s. The overall pattern is the most common design type.

In the banded design, which is another frequently observed arrangement, repeated individual motifs form horizontal, vertical, or diagonal bands. The common horizontal motifs—for example, triangles connected by a central diamond or other figure—also are seen on beaded bags and ceremonial clothing among the Plateau people.[16] Whether the beadwork was inspired by early false embroidery designs, or the two design organizations developed concurrently when smaller beads made more complex motifs possible, is an area for further study. The diagonal bands on these flat bags generally are in an **S** or lower left to upper right direction. Because of the **S** twist of the stitch, this gives a smoother edge to the diagonal line than would occur in a diagonal line in the **Z** direction.

In an arrangement with a central focus, weavers coordi-

*Mrs. Baker, left, carries a twined handbag in a vertical banded design, and her sister, Lily Harding (Tsitwats), holds another twined handbag with a central design in this 1902 photograph by F. A. Young. Addie Cushingway (Cush-nee-yi) is on the right holding a fine beaded bag in the floral style of the Plateau. Mr. and Mrs. Bert Morse Collection, Maryhill Museum of Art cat. no. 1951.06.03.*

*This twined storage bag collected at Warm Springs, c. 1940, by Edythe Burt Jermark, illustrates the overall design, the most common organization on flat twined bags. Photo by Jerry Taylor. H23 in., W18 in. Maryhill Museum of Art cat. no. 1963.03.69.*

*The weaver created a banded arrangement of bird figures and geometric designs on this twined handbag made about 1880. H16 in., W14.5 in. Lee and Lois Miner Collection.*

*This handbag (right), attributed to the family of Cecelia Yumpty Totus, illustrates the central design arrangement. H12.5 in., W10 in. Lee and Lois Miner Collection.*

nate from one to seven different motifs into a unified design. An example of a central design is a large star or elaborated diamond that is framed by triangles.

For a five-part design, weavers repeat the same motif five times to form a coherent pattern, placing the largest in the center and smaller versions in the corners. An example is a central, eight-pointed star with smaller stars in the corners. This design type differs from the central design in that the four-corner motifs repeat rather than frame the large central motif.

A small number of bag designs are naturalistic and their subject matter encompasses all recognizable natural forms, including the "tree of life" design, animals, butterflies, dog-wood blossoms, conifers, even scenes from everyday life. Prior to nonnative contact such motifs were confined to Wasco/Wishxam and some Klikitat and Tenino weaving. These designs have become more common in the twentieth century and many of the more literal representations of flowers may have been inspired by popular needlework patterns.

Using pattern books as the source of these designs is another example of the native weaver's command of her technique. Superb technical skill enables the weaver to experiment with new forms, materials, and design ideas as they become available to her. Given the apparently inherent ability of the artist to visualize the design before actually building it (Boas 1955, 158), the Mid-Columbia weaver could use the newly available patterns simply for inspiration.

Because of the long tradition of basketmaking along the Columbia, the preservative quality of the dry climate, and the comparatively settled lives of the people for many generations, weavers have had many bags to turn to for design inspiration, giving them a wide command over a multitude of forms. Through the years they have not copied each other's work, and, although they use the same elements in their weaving, weavers pride themselves on never weaving the same design in the same way. This tradition of artistic independence has created the subtle diversity of design that is the trademark of the flat twined bags of the Plateau.

Writing of the basketry of native weavers across the continent, Otis Mason said, "It is considered a reproach to violate the rules of bilateral symmetry" (1976, 283). The weavers of the Mid-Columbia are no exception. Symmetry is an important design tradition in the flat bags. Most bags exhibit horizontal symmetry—mirror reflection of size, shape, and relative position of parts on opposite sides of a vertical axis (Boas 1955, 33). Among these bags, the majority also exhibit vertical symmetry, although there are often slight variations in color or design elements on either side of the horizontal axis.

The weaver's skill in judging the size of her pattern in

*Cecelia Yumpty Totus (1902–78) photographed on the Yakima Reservation about 1920 holding a finely twined handbag. Photo courtesy Lee and Lois Miner.*

*A root storage bag collected on the Nez Perce Reservation shows naturalistic feathers arranged in a traditional banded design. Gift to Yakima Indian Nation Museum in memory of William Condit Schlick. Photo by Robert Pace.*

*On the reverse side of the root storage bag, the weaver has combined traditional motifs into a more complex design. Photo by Robert Pace.*

relation to the desired shape of her bag varies and affects the symmetry of the bag's design. Many designs, on expertly made as well as beginner-made bags, are not completed at the top of the bag. It appears that the traditional proportions of the bag and consistency in motif size were more important to the weaver than a completed design. If the weaver began with warps that were too short, it would be a tedious task to splice them. From a practical standpoint, when the weaver is near the end of her warps, she must end her design.

Two other characteristics appear to be important in the design tradition and elicit a strong optical response in the viewer. These devices are the outlining of forms and the contrasting of dark and light. The weaver adds life and dimension to her designs by incorporating simple outlines or steps or serrations in contrasting values of dark and light. These may be added inside or outside the motifs, or both.

MOTIFS. Although the basic motifs used in the flat bags are the same, the organization of these motifs into a coherent design has changed over the years since the middle of the last

*Naturalistic yellow and red butterflies decorate the bag in this photograph taken in 1902 by Dr. E. H. Latham. Before the development of panchromatic film, photographers used film in which blue appeared as a light color and yellow and red as dark, hence the dark butterflies at lower center. (See color illustration, following page 144.) Photo courtesy Lee and Lois Miner.*

century. More sources for design color and material, and possibly freedom from traditional expectations, have allowed the basketmaking artist to create a great variety of patterns on the flat "canvas" of each bag side. Tradition determines the shape of the bag, but allows the weaver to use her own creativity to develop designs appropriate to that shape. The challenge is to create a work of art within the traditional outline of the bag, using available materials.

As with the designs on other Mid-Columbia basketry, only the maker knows their meaning. The earliest bag designs make use of elements that have been in the design vocabulary of the people for many generations. Although many of the designs on the Wasco/Wishxam round twined bags had commonly accepted names, this does not appear to be true of those on twined flat storage and carrying bags (Teit 1928, 359).[17]

The introduction of new materials allowed the weaver to combine these traditional motifs in more complex ways, and naturalistic designs began to appear on the bags toward the end of the nineteenth century.[18] The great variety of designs are seen on bags made after the people of the Columbia began to feel the impact of the newcomers. These distinctive bags helped proclaim a separate and special identity for the native people (Cheney Cowles 1976, 3).

Some scholars have attributed the designs on the flat bags of the Mid-Columbia and the Plateau to influences from the Pacific Coast, the Plains, or from northern California Indians (Coe 1977, 166). However, the age of the art form and the relative stability over time of a formal design style that features symmetry and rhythmic repetition of motifs suggest that the weaving has a distinct character in its own right. The Plateau people traveled great distances, but influence from these contacts with other Indians did not eradicate their own culture. Much remains of their old ways, and the twined bags are among the treasured remnants of the very earliest days.

All twined designs are created stitch by stitch and row by row around the surface sequentially. This does not limit weavers to simple geometric forms. The tradition among all but a few Plateau groups, however, appears to favor geometric designs. Most bag designs, even those woven in this century, are arrangements of traditional geometric elements into larger motifs.[19]

Weavers used the triangle most frequently as a design element in the flat twined bags. This is followed by the diamond, rectangle, parallelogram, and line. Common accent motifs are zigzag, chevron, rhomboid, cross, and "foot" or "leg," also known in California basketry as "quail plume." The artist combined all of these forms in endless variety to create the primary designs on each bag side. Steps, serrations, and other motifs embellish larger forms both internally and externally (Schlick 1977, 27).

## *Colors*

At the time of contact with newcomers, weavers decorated their bags only with grasses in their natural colors of green, yellow, and white. These colors, in bags surviving from the first half of the nineteenth century, have mellowed to subtle tones of light and less light. After the introduction of cornhusk and woolens, weavers began to use all colors in a variety of combinations.

Studying a number of bags, we find the weavers using from two to seven colors in one design. Red in all its values and intensities was by far the most popular color, followed by blue and green. Red and blue were the most popular combination, and blue or green was rarely seen without some form of red; these three colors were the first available on the Plateau in trade cloth and blankets and their popularity continued. Other common colors observed in the bags were bluegreen, yellow, orange, purple, and pink. Brown and gray were used infrequently (Schlick 1977, 22).

The weavers of the flat bags evidently did not use dyes on their early work. After the adoption of cornhusk, the new fiber's dye-absorbing properties allowed the weavers to achieve a rainbow of hues, ranging from the purple of huckleberries and mountain blackberries to a pale red from the juice of chokecherries or a bright red from the earth in central and eastern Oregon. Other natural substances completed the palette: larkspur, lichen, or duck excrement for blue; juniper, sage, snowberry leaves, or slime for green; Oregon grape bark or roots, or wolf lichen, or the root of the sand dock for yellow; and the inner bark of the alder for red-orange. "Pound it and put a little water with it," a Yakima elder said of the alder bark (Grace Washington, pers. com. 1978).

Most of these natural dyes were fugitive, as demonstrated by the pale, soft colors on the early cornhusk bags, and the weavers must have embraced the new yarns and their brighter colors with enthusiasm. An examination of the inside surface of bags reveals the weaver's original color choice. Color retention appeared to depend on the bag's use. Many handbags in normal use were exposed to the sun and air, and

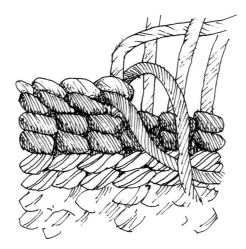

*Diagram of the edge finish on a twined bag. Drawn by Peggy Dills Kelter.*

their colors faded. Further study on dyes and yarns used in these bags will add much to our ability to date their manufacture. For many years the people of the Mid–Columbia have considered the bags as heirlooms and have treated them with care. Like the bags of the Warm Springs woman who was sending her family treasures to the Wasco County Fair, many of the large storage bags remain brightly colored. Treated as valuable possessions, they have been carefully stored, rarely seeing the light of day.

## Finishing the Bag

Most weavers work several rows of plain twining at the top of the root storage bags before binding off the edge. This plain twined area in natural hemp at the top and bottom of most of the larger bags gives the appearance of a border. Handbags rarely have this upper band of plain twining, nor do later storage bags made entirely of cotton twine. A few bags have dark border lines at the top and bottom of the design. These lines are customary on round twined bags and coiled cedar root baskets of the Mid–Columbia but usually are not woven into the flat bags.

To bind off at the top of the bag, the weaver continues to

*A hide string threaded around the top of a root storage bag, as on this bag, makes it possible to lace across the opening to hold the contents in place. Dried food roots displayed here are, from left, bitterroot; a lomatium known as punko; sup'lil, a biscuit formed by pressing fresh-ground roots in the fist; and ground skolkol, another lomatium.*

work from left to right on the workface or outside of the bag. She makes a twining stitch around a warp, then brings that warp strand forward and around the warp to the right and tucks it down on the inside of the bag. She locks this warp in place with another twining stitch, then repeats the step— bringing the next standing warp forward and around the warp to its right, tucking it down on the inside of the bag and locking it in place with a twining stitch. (See facing diagram.) If a weaver is left-handed, or for some other reason twines in the opposite direction, she will finish her work from right to left. This twining-off technique differs from the self-edge used to finish a round Wasco-style bag. When all warps are twined down and she has worked around to the beginning again, the weaver will draw the outside weft to the inside through the loop made by the first warp. She then pulls it tightly downward to complete the procedure. The weaver cuts the ends of the warps off close to the edge on the inside, the tightness of her work holding them in place.

In the larger storage bags, the weaver threads a hide or hemp string through the weaving at intervals around the top just below the edge. Users would then lace string back and forth across between these loops to close the bag when full.

To finish a handbag, the weaver usually binds the edge in hide or woolen, canvas, velvet, or other fabric. She adds handles for carrying, sometimes sewing them on each side, and occasionally provides ties or a button and loop for closure on the rim. A closing frequently seen on Nez Perce bags is described by Spinden as "double handles made by passing a single thong twice through each side of the top" (1908, 192). The weaver may hang beads, shells, brass beads, or other ornaments from the rim or handle. Occasionally a storage bag has a bound edge.

## THE MAKERS OF FLAT TWINED BAGS

All the people of the Plateau of the Columbia and Snake rivers harvested the food roots that grew plentifully in the earth throughout the area. The flat twined bags that the peo-

*Realistic buffalo figures by Cecelia Totus are forerunners of the lifelike scenes in beadwork for which she became noted. H13 in. x W12 in. Lee and Lois Miner Collection.*

ple developed for storing these valuable foods are unique products of the area. The work of the Plateau weavers can be differentiated from work of other Indian groups by the use of soft materials, the technique of twining with false embroidery, and by the organization of design.

The only other native people to decorate their twined basketry with false embroidery are the Aleut, Haida, Tsimshian, and Tlingit of the Northwest Coast. The baskets manufactured by these northern weavers are of stiffer construction, without the durable flexibility of those made on the Plateau. At the time of contact with the first Europeans, weavers among Eastern Woodland groups also decorated twined bags and carrying straps in false embroidery. Using Indian hemp for the foundation and the inner bark of the basswood tree for the decorative element, these weavers produced a flexible fabric similar to that woven on the Mid-Columbia. However, the use of this technique died out in the eastern region before the early nineteenth century (Brasser 1975, 37–40; Phillips 1987, 84).

## Regional Preferences

It appears that Mid-Columbia weavers made the flat twined bags long before Lewis and Clark arrived. The Klikitat and the Wasco and Wishxam people may have made fewer of them, trading their own coiled and round twined basketry with their neighbors for the flat bags (Teit 1928, 354). The Nez Perce were well known for making the bags, and the bags often are attributed to them when provenience is unknown (Cheney Cowles 1974, 2).

In the early 1700s when the people of the Plateau acquired horses and contact among distant neighbors became easier, the technique of twining the flat bags probably diffused from the Mid-Columbia and the Southern Plateau to the north, to the ancestors of those now living on the Colville, Spokane, and Coeur d'Alene reservations (Miller 1986, 105).

Except for the rare flat bags identified as Wasco/Wishxam because of their motifs and use of the full-turn twining technique, it is impossible to identify the tribal affiliation of the weaver without knowing a bag's history. Because few bags were obtained by collectors from the weavers themselves, collectors' records and those of museum are usually limited, sometimes with only inferential information. These bags were traded eagerly among the native people and we cannot assume that a bag was made where it was collected. Weavers married into other groups taking their skills with them. Other weavers found design inspiration in the work of those they saw regularly at seasonal gatherings. Unless we know the maker of the bag, we can only guess about its source within the Plateau region.

Among the people of the Plateau, individual makers usually were identifiable because of the fineness of their work and commonly used designs (pers. com., Mr. and Mrs. Steve Iukes, 1976, and Don Umtuch, 1975), but in recent years the makers' names have been lost as the bags passed from one family to another. Most of the people of the Mid-Columbia

*The Wasco-style human figures on the bag at left are unusual on a flat bag decorated in false embroidery. H17 in., W13 in. Lee and Lois Miner Collection.*

*Reverse side of the facing flat bag. Similar figures of "deer" with triangular bodies are frequently found on nineteenth-century Wasco root-digging bags.*

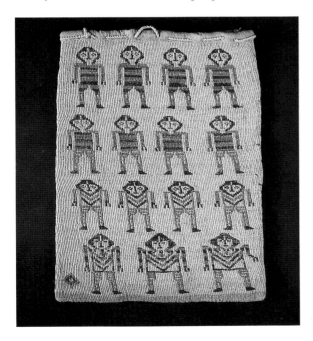

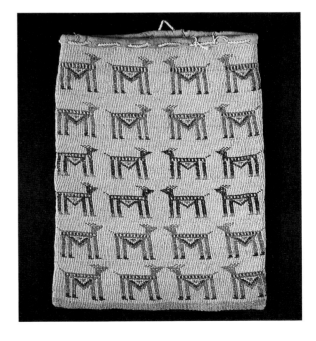

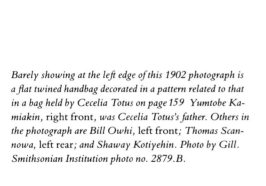

*Barely showing at the left edge of this 1902 photograph is a flat twined handbag decorated in a pattern related to that in a bag held by Cecelia Totus on page 159 Yumtobe Kamiakin, right front, was Cecelia Totus's father. Others in the photograph are Bill Owhi, left front; Thomas Scannowa, left rear; and Shaway Kotiyehin. Photo by Gill. Smithsonian Institution photo no. 2879.B.*

today say they cannot identify the source of the bags with any certainty, but suggest general differences: According to Tallulah Pinkham, "Nez Perce bags have an up and down feeling; Warm Springs and Rock Creek are strange and bold; Klikitats are really nice." Johnson Meninick, a Yakima, says, "We use sharp things, mountains, arrows, birds." A Nez Perce woman identified a bag with columns of repeated designs as the work of her people. Spinden stated that designs appeared to be more uniformly geometric among the Nez Perce (1908, 235). There appears to be some agreement among tribal people that Nez Perce designs are bolder, often with black outlines;[20] that Cayuse are well designed, bright, and innovative; and Yakima designs are simpler, dignified, primarily geometric. The butterfly is reported to be a favorite motif among the Joseph band of the Nez Perce who live on the Colville Reservation (Daisy Ahrens, pers. com. 1976).

## *Dating*

It is also difficult to date most bags. Appearance is no criterion. Although no two twined bags are alike, the technique and general design style of bags produced within recent years are surprisingly similar to those of the bags from the late nineteenth century. The relative dryness of the area to the east of the Cascade Mountains and the care the owning families have given these heirlooms have helped preserve many of these bags in fine condition for generations. On the other hand, newer bags that have had hard use may appear to be very old.

There are some clues to the time of manufacture in the shape of the bags, in the materials, and in the complexity of design.[21] We can speculate that the coming of the horse to the Plateau in the early 1700s caused a change from small bags, which would be lighter burdens when carried on foot, to larger bags for carrying on a horse or horse-pulled travois. Then, as access to root-digging areas dwindled and other foods replaced the traditional roots in the diets of Mid-Columbia native families at the end of the nineteenth century, the making of the large root storage bags began to decline and the handbag became more common. It appears that few of the large bags were made after the 1930s.

Settlement on traditional gathering grounds limited the native people's access to natural materials. At the same time, the coming of the settlers and traders expanded the use of new materials. The first post-settlement change in materials that we know about came with the use of cornhusk and raveled wool. Later commercial yarn and dyes and cotton string were introduced. The new materials and possibly an increased desire to express their tribal identity among the native people led to greater innovation in design.

The number of weavers of the twined bags has decreased steadily since before the beginning of this century. In a 1901 article in *The Indian's Friend,* Mrs. F. N. Doubleday commented on the flat saddlebag "occasionally" made by Nez Perce weavers, adding that "in Oregon, only two Indian

*Riding a horse pulling a travois loaded as if for traveling, Annie Johnson, Yakima, carries a flat twined bag in the Pendleton Roundup parade, c. 1950. Photo by J. W. Thompson.*

women practice such basketry" (1901, 8). A 1934 survey of Indian arts and crafts for the Bureau of Indian Affairs listed sixty-one "cornhusk bag" makers on the Nez Perce Reservation, three on the Umatilla, and only Mrs. Hampton Lumley of White Swan on the Yakima.[22] Kathrine French (1955, 78) found no bags produced at Warm Springs in 1955, although recent reports indicate that there are a few weavers there today (Bernice Mitchell, pers. com. 1980; *Spilyay Tymoo,* 22 April 1988). In all, only a small number of the descendants of the Mid-Columbia people carry on this tradition of weaving the flat twined bag.

Interest in learning the art is growing among young women and a few young men, and the Warm Springs, Yakima, and Nez Perce tribes have held basketmaking classes. A common comment is, "When my grandmother wanted me to watch her, I was too busy; now I wish I knew how." A Yakima woman who learned to twine in a workshop on the

Ollie Spencer and her sister Mattie Spencer pose for a formal portrait in 1899 with twined handbags in a banded design (left) and a central design. Both young women were basketmakers on the Yakima Reservation where their descendants live. Ollie's great granddaughter, Valerie Jim Calac, carries on the tradition of twining and is learning to coil the cedar root baskets. Mattie's granddaughters Nettie Jackson and Sharon Dick and Nettie's daughter Sharon Kuneki make coiled baskets. Smithsonian Institution photo no. 91–19930.

reservation said, "Now I can teach this to my kids!"

"The weaving of vegetable materials [is] a culturally far more complex matter than any grass basket . . . in a glass showcase might suggest all by itself" (Barre Toelken 1983, 35). The most notable characteristic of Plateau bags is the infinite variety of lively and dynamic designs. Perhaps it is enough to recognize and enjoy the beauty of these unique works created by anonymous artists. Although few are made today, the bags are much treasured by the families and neighbors of the makers and deserve larger attention and apprecia-

*The eagle and shield motif, frequently seen in twentieth-century beadwork, is unusual on this flat twined bag made by Cecelia Totus. (See page 165 for reverse of this bag.) Lee and Lois Miner Collection.*

tion as expressions of an ancient North American art.

Only the makers know the stories of the designs on the flat twined bags. However, the bags themselves do carry messages to those who take the time to see them—messages of a life where everyday objects were invested with beauty and meaning, of ancient skills passed down to "generations yet unborn," of the earth's generosity, of changes wrought by time, and of responses to these changes. Looking at these bags in the context of the culture that the basketmaker shares with relatives and neighbors can give a new dimension to these works of art. We may never know who the weavers were, but we can know much about their lives and times.

# 7. EPILOGUE
# NAKNUWISHA
## *Caring for Something Precious*

*"Whatever is done to preserve this material from utter loss cannot be much longer delayed."*

When the superintendent of Indian education for the United States ordered an elegant ballgown from Paris to wear to the Presidential Inauguration of 1900, she did not dream that the dress would dazzle visitors in a museum nearly three thousand miles away and three-quarters of a century later. Nor could she know the extent to which the native basketry and handcrafts that she gathered in her visits to the reservation schools would help later generations of children of Toppenish, Washington, learn about themselves and their classmates on the Yakima Indian Reservation.

Superintendent of public schools in Wyoming before the turn of the century, Estelle Reel was the first woman elected to public office in the United States. When President William McKinley appointed her to the United States Indian Service position, she became the first woman whose appointment was confirmed by the United States Senate.

During her years in Indian education (she was reappointed by Presidents Theodore Roosevelt and William Howard Taft), Reel brought an attitude to Indian Service schools that would surprise the critics of Indian education. Finding no written curriculum to aid those she supervised in the far-flung system, Reel wrote *A Course of Study for Indian Schools of the United States*.[1] In her book, the educator urged agents and superintendents on reservations to encourage the native art of the people. She suggested they find basketmakers to teach the children, thus keeping the art alive. As her own personal effort to encourage the arts, Reel gathered a representative collection of baskets, beadwork, and other native handcraft as she visited schools across the country.

On a trip to the West in 1910, Reel scheduled a stop at the school at Washington's Fort Simcoe on the Yakima Reservation. Cort F. Meyer, a local cattleman and important community figure, was invited to the station to meet this distinguished visitor's train. According to a local historian, the two must have sized up one another and liked what they found for they soon were married and Estelle Reel Meyer moved to the Yakima Reservation (Dick Delaney, pers. com. 1971). She brought with her a small but fine collection of American Indian art collected during her travels to reservation schools.

Before her death in 1959, Estelle Meyer gave the collection, now enriched by the basketry and beadwork of Yakima tribal artists, to the Mary L. Goodrich public library in Toppenish where it lay for many years in display cases in an upstairs room. Knowing that the baskets and other articles of native life could help Yakima children learn more about their own past as well as help other children know and appreciate the Indian people they lived among, librarian Alice Fleming asked for assistance. Fleming wanted to know where the baskets were made and for what purpose. The information would help her answer the questions asked by children who came regularly to the library museum on field trips. An educator, Meyer could have answered these questions, but she had left no records.

The librarian's request began a process that has been repeated in countless museums across the world—giving a voice to silent artifacts. In this case the interpreter was Delbert J. McBride, curator of the Washington State Capital Museum in Olympia, who volunteered to look at the collection. Of Cowlitz-Quinault ancestry, McBride brought the eye of a scholar and the heart of a participant to this study. As those of us who were involved in this project watched, he did what any gifted curator can and must do. McBride brought alive that dusty cache of treasures whose very presentation in the locked cabinets spoke of sterility and decay.[2]

As he talked about each one, we could see the Pima Indian potter putting the finish on the large coiled olla as the visitor watched; or the Ute weaver pulling the tray out of a trunk and telling of its use; or the Sioux mother beading the tiny moccasins. The objects were no longer "curios," a curious assortment of handiwork that appealed to an intriguing but long-departed collector. With McBride's comments, each object became a representation of life, far away perhaps, but no less immediate and real. What the collector had preserved now became the interpreter's job to bring alive.

Estelle Meyer's collection is only one of thousands in public and private ownership. The Meyer artifacts illustrate a major problem in working with collections. Basketmakers did not sign their work. They were known by their own people for the fineness of their stitches or sometimes for specific designs, but few collectors either knew or recorded the names of the makers. Frequently, information about the tribal location was lost when baskets changed hands.

Were it not for the collectors, the art of the past would be

*"Underwood Fair," c. 1911. An unusual photograph of an exhibit of native Columbia River art that was held annually for many years at Underwood, Washington, by a Wasco family. Martha Ellen Dark, a great granddaughter of Ellen Underwood (Taswatha, Chief Welawa's daughter) poses in a hide dress with an antler-handled digging stick in her hand. Many of the bags and baskets pictured were made by members of the Underwood family and are now in the collection of Maryhill Museum of Art. Photographer unknown. Maryhill Museum of Art cat. no. 1940.01.168.*

preserved only in the minds of the elders and in the tales they pass along to the young. Despite the collectors' best intentions, however, much information about the artists or the meaning of their work in the lives of their people has disappeared. This story of the Meyer collection is a reminder to those who acquire native basketry: take the time to record the name and place of the maker, the use for which it was made, the materials and the technique of manufacture and any other information that can be discovered. This is not a new message. The curator of ethnology at the Smithsonian Institution gave the same advice at the turn of the century (Mason 1902, 5; 1976, 539).

We know that we can learn about a people from their art, but only if their art is accessible to us, and if we understand its significance to the people who created it. When packed away in storerooms and closets, the baskets are useless. The Meyer story is also a plea to museums and other collectors to bring out their baskets, making them available to scholars, to school children, and to the descendants of those who made them; and to continue collecting the work of contemporary native basketmakers to document the survival, however limited, of this native art.

The third message of the Meyer collection is of the need to interpret the work. A basket may be displayed as an example of fine art, its intrinsic beauty speaking for itself. The viewer can appreciate the art without understanding the artist. However, when we are displaying art that represents the rich culture that has flourished along the Mid-Columbia for thousands of years, we have an opportunity to help the viewer understand the artists and their river-centered society as well. Some people believe that Indians have been assimilated into the larger society; others, who know they exist today, may believe that tribal groups are alike across the continent. Museums can dispel these stereotypes by conveying the level of satisfaction achieved by a group's lifestyle, inspiring respect for the technological challenges that basketry and other works of art represent (Lester 1972, 25).

## WHO WERE THE COLLECTORS?

The glorious array of heirlooms displayed on the county agent's tailgate described at the beginning of chapter 6 is an example of the first important collections of Mid-Columbia native basketry—those preserved by the families themselves. Whether made or traded for or purchased, the basketwork of their own people was admired and treasured. At the time of an important event, such as a naming, joining, wedding, or death, the pieces of any one collection changed hands as gifts given or received. For the most part, this basketry did not go far but stayed within the great social network of the Plateau. Consequently, many examples survive today.

The earliest nonnative collectors on the Mid-Columbia were Lewis and Clark and the Corps of Discovery, who descended the Snake River and entered the Columbia in October 1805 (Thwaites 1905, vol. 3). Collecting was not a stated goal of the expedition, although observation of native life was. Sent by President Thomas Jefferson to find a transcontinental route for trade between the Atlantic and the Pacific oceans, the explorers were asked to make themselves acquainted with the "ordinary occupations in agriculture, fishing, hunting, war, arts, & the implements for these; their food, clothing, & domestic accom[m]odations" of the native people they encountered (DeVoto 1953, 483). Lewis and Clark not only recorded such information, they also sent a large consignment of natural material objects to President Jefferson in 1805, before crossing the Rockies. Despite the extreme hardships of the return journey, they arrived in St. Louis in 1806 with a surprising amount of additional material.

William Clark displayed many of the items he had collected in his Indian museum in St. Louis. Jefferson sent a large number of the objects he received from the explorers to the Philadelphia artist Charles Willson Peale whose "Repository for Natural Curiosities" became the nation's first popular museum of natural science and art (Sellers 1980, 187). The Lewis objects also came to Peale's museum and probably included three basketry items from the Mid-Columbia that appear on Peale's "Memorandum of Specimens & Artifacts" of December 1809. These are listed as: "Cap, worn by the women of the Plains of Columbia"; "A Bag prepared of grass by the Pishquilpahs on the Columbia River"; and "A Water-cup of the natives who reside in the Plains of Columbia, made of the same grass" (Jackson 1962, 476, 478). We do not know where the cup and cap are today, but the bag is in the collection of the Peabody Museum at Harvard University and is the earliest dated example of Mid-Columbia River basketry in a North American museum (Schlick 1979, 10).[3]

Other collecting continued as an incidental result of the exploration and fur trade that brought nonnatives into the country.[4] The artifacts gathered on the first government-sponsored scientific expedition, the Wilkes Exploring Expedition of 1838 to 1842, formed the nucleus of the famous contents of "America's attic," the Smithsonian Institution. The Wilkes explorers apparently did not probe inland as far as the Wasco, Wishxam, and Klikitat villages when they came up the Columbia in August of 1841.[5] A ship's surgeon, Dr. J. L. Fox, did collect several fine examples of related work—coiled baskets of the Cowlitz people—that are in the Smithsonian Institution's National Museum of Natural History.

Missionaries, early settlers, soldiers, and other representatives of the government also obtained examples of the handiwork in the course of their lives among the people of the Mid-Columbia. One of the earliest reported Klikitat baskets was collected in 1845 by the mother of Mrs. Levi Ankeny of Walla Walla, wife of a United States senator from Washington State. This basket was exhibited at the Portland Library in 1896 (Portland Library 1896, 26). Mrs. Ankeny presented a Klikitat-style coiled basket to the Smithsonian Institution in 1902.[6] It is not known if this is the same basket. Many museums received important examples of Mid-Columbia basketry gathered before the turn of the century, in most cases collected because of the baskets' appeal to those who had day-to-day contact with the native people.

Two women who were instrumental in presenting an

exhibition of basketry at the Portland (Oregon) Library in 1896 were the daughters of another U.S. senator (and later U.S. representative), Colonel James W. Nesmith, who came to Oregon in 1843. Harriet and Velina Nesmith became interested in native basketry as children in the mid-nineteenth century, and the interest continued after their marriages: Harriet to Oregon circuit court judge Lewis Linn McArthur; Velina to a Canadian, William Markland Molson (son of a prominent Montreal family), who was raising hops in the Willamette Valley (Lewis L. McArthur, pers. com. 1987). The resulting collections include many fine examples of Columbia River work. Housed today at opposite ends of the continent, the McArthur collection is in the State Museum of Anthropology at the University of Oregon at Eugene, and the Molson collection is in the McCord Museum at McGill University in Montreal, where the Molsons moved in 1898.

A Maryland physician, James F. Ghiselin, stationed with the United States Army in Oregon before 1869, purchased a twined hat and round, Wasco-style root bag somewhere near the Cascades of the Columbia. These early examples of the complex work of the Chinookan-speaking people are now in the Smithsonian by way of the Army Medical Museum.[7] Another basket, a Klikitat "work basket" (see color section, following page 144), in the National Museum collection came from the Reverend James H. Wilbur, school superintendent and, later, agent on the Yakima Reservation from 1860 to 1888.[8] E. T. Houtz, a former matron at the boarding school on the Warm Springs Reservation, sold a small collection of Wasco-style bags to the Smithsonian in 1899. Houtz was one of the few collectors who recorded any information on the bags' former owners, noting that she acquired the bags from a Miss Tyismun, Etta Haliday, and "a Wasco woman but not the maker."[9]

An English clergyman, R. W. Summers, served Episcopalian churches in Washington and Oregon from 1871 to 1880 and donated a number of baskets to the British Museum through the Reverend Selwyn C. Freer. Included among these is an unusually fine Wasco-style bag decorated with large and small human figures, as well as with fanciful creatures of the earth.[10]

Maryhill Museum of Art, the startling "castle on the Columbia" of American "good roads" advocate Sam Hill, houses an unusually large and representative collection of Indian baskets.[11] Among these is a group of Mid-Columbia baskets assembled between 1888 and 1898 by the Reverend William C. Curtis and his son Winterton C. Curtis. Twenty years before the more famous (and unrelated) Edward S. Curtis began to photograph the Indians of the Gorge in 1909, Rev. Curtis moved across the continent from Maine to be pastor of the First Congregational Church at The Dalles. His son Winterton was thirteen when they arrived, and it was not long before he "caught the fever for relic collecting" (W. C. Curtis 1956, 10). Winterton Curtis returned to the East in

*Basket collector the Reverend W. C. Curtis beside the Columbia River, c. 1895. Photo courtesy Maryhill Museum of Art, cat. no. 1951.01.208.*

1895 to attend Williams College and, later, Johns Hopkins University. After a distinguished career in zoology, he retired in 1946 as dean emeritus of the college of arts and sciences at the University of Missouri and presented the family collection to Maryhill Museum.

In biographical notes he made of those days, Winterton Curtis told of writing a poem, "after a day of negotiations for baskets on the streets of The Dalles and at Celilo" (1956, 7). A verse from that poem is poignant:

> *Togged in the cast-off garments*
> *begged from the frontier town*
> *Klickitats, makers of baskets*
> *workers of fame and renown.*

Curtis believed, as did many others of the day, that the end of the nineteenth century was the end of the American Indian. His poem ends with the common phrase used to describe native people at the time, "the last of a dying race."

It was this belief, that the people and the art were disappearing, that led to the great institutional collecting movement that began in the mid-nineteenth century. Many of the major museums of the nation, including the Smithsonian Institution, were formed to house the incidental collections of explorers and others on reconnaissance missions for the government. A group of scholars soon realized that the ways of life of the native peoples were changing radically and would be lost forever. It was during this period that the discipline of anthropology was born, and researchers began to travel systematically among the tribes recording languages and customs and collecting artifacts from the lives of the people.

Others whose work brought them in contact with the native people continued to collect artifacts, but on a larger scale. Among the Mid-Columbia material in the Smithsonian are several early Klikitat baskets that Lieutenant George T. Emmons of the United States Navy purchased in Victoria, British Columbia, in 1902. Emmons was in British Columbia with an expedition to locate Canadian/Alaskan boundary monuments. In 1903, he sent a group of twenty-two baskets,

including two additional Klikitats, to the Smithsonian Division of Ethnology for display at the Louisiana Purchase Exposition.[12]

By the turn of the century, several movements converged to increase interest in American Indian basketry. Scholars not only were studying the arts of the American Indian, but they also felt a responsibility to write about their findings. The great fairs and expositions of the period—the United States Centennial Exposition in Philadelphia in 1876, the World's Columbian Exposition in Chicago in 1893, and the St. Louis Universal Exposition of 1904—brought ordinary citizens in contact with Indian artifacts as well as with the basketmakers themselves. Concurrently with the scientific study and collection of articles from American Indian life, this late-Victorian period was an age of peace and prosperity. Many Americans were building larger homes and decorating them with the arts and crafts of the time. The railroads, in an effort to capture a share of the new prosperity, promoted travel to the American West and encouraged the growing interest in American Indian arts and crafts. All of this stimulated the collecting of American Indian art.

Otis Tufton Mason, who later became curator of ethnology for the Smithsonian Institution, wrote prolifically on basketry for popular magazines and scientific journals, beginning in 1884. His final work, *Aboriginal American Indian Basketry: Studies in Textile Art without Machinery,* was published in 1904 as a report to the United States National Museum and was also published privately the same year. Mason's book has been reprinted several times since then and is considered the most complete work on basketry available today.

Mason's writings and those of his contemporaries inspired a special interest in American Indian basketry. Collecting, which previously had been incidental to fieldwork or travel among the basketmakers, became a passion for many. Turn-of-the-century collectors filled their homes with baskets from across the country. Photographs taken at the time show baskets nailed to walls, baskets hanging across mantel-

*The Curtis collection of baskets is arrayed for photography in the minister's study in the First Congregational Church at The Dalles, c. 1890. Many of the baskets and bags in the photograph are in the Maryhill Museum. Photographer unknown. Maryhill Museum of Art cat. no. 1951.01.186.*

pieces, baskets on stair steps and stacked in corners. Frequently, baskets seen in these astonishing photographs can be found in major museum collections. [13]

Dealers had been selling American Indian artifacts for many years before 1900; however, the growing popularity of basket collecting enticed others into the picture and this larger market encouraged many weavers to increase production. The Frohman Trading Company of Portland published a twenty-seven-page catalogue in 1902, picturing hundreds of baskets made by weavers from California to Alaska. Although no flat twined bags, twined hats, or folded bark

*Louisa Ruch Miller of The Dalles collected Columbia River basketry through her close association with the native people who sought her out as a friend and photographer. Several of the baskets in this photograph, which was taken in her home about 1905, are now in the Maryhill Museum of Art. Courtesy of Old Wasco County Pioneers Photo Collection.*

baskets were offered for sale, there were a few figured, round "sally" bags listed for ten to twenty dollars. The coiled Klikitat-style baskets were prominently displayed, with nearly fifty illustrated in one photograph alone. Prices for these beautiful baskets ranged from seven to thirty-five dollars. Business must have been good, for the company opened a branch in the nation's capital. A copy of the photograph on the back cover of the catalogue is in the National Anthropological Archives with the caption: "Alaska and Northern Indian Baskets and Curios on exhibition and for sale at Mrs. Frohman's Basket Rooms—121 13th Street, Washington."[14]

During this time, Otis Mason corresponded with dealers and private collectors as well as with the nation's major museums to obtain information and photographs for his comprehensive report on basketry. A photograph of an unusual Klikitat basket with men, horses, and a vertical, diamond-backed snake design, pictured on page 18 of the Frohman catalogue, is in the Smithsonian Anthropological Archives with the notation "Klikitat" written in Mason's distinctive handwriting. The photograph does not appear in Mason's

*Coiled cedar root baskets from the collection of Anne M. Lang, The Dalles, Oregon. Published in Mason 1976, Pl. 160; courtesy Maryhill Museum of Art.*

*Aboriginal American Indian Basketry;* however, baskets from two residents of The Dalles, Anne M. Lang and R. S. Shackelford, are illustrated in the book (1976, Pls. 11, 159, 160, 161).

## The Collectors' Network

Studying several major collections of Columbia River basketry, we find the names of the collectors listed in Mason's book appearing like intersections on a spider web: Ankeny, Curtis, Frohman, Hubby, Lang, Lowe, McArthur, Molson, Shackelford (1976, 541–44). One name stands out as the center of the web, linking many others—Grace Nicholson of Pasadena.[15]

In 1901, at the age of twenty-four, Nicholson came from Philadelphia to Los Angeles for her health. With some experience as a stenographer, she opened an office on West Fourth Street. Recognizing the growing interest in American Indian art, she began to learn about Indians and to buy baskets. Before a year had passed, Nicholson had opened a shop in Pasadena offering Navajo and Moqui blankets, choice antiques, and Indian baskets (Apostol 1976, 23). It was not long before the list of her clients, correspondents, and other contacts read like a *Who's Who in America*—from anthropologist C. Hart Merriam, western painter Joseph Henry Sharp, and naturalist John Muir, to Franklin Delano Roosevelt, photographer Edward S. Curtis, and curators of major North American museums (Grace Nicholson Collection).

A few examples will illustrate the weblike network of early twentieth-century basket appreciators. On buying-trips to the Northwest in 1905 and 1911, Nicholson visited The Dalles and purchased baskets from Mrs. Roxie (also identified as Roxa) Shackelford and Anne Lang, both of whom had contributed photographs to Otis Mason's book. Nicholson sold some of these baskets to Ella F. Hubby of Pasadena, whose collection subsequently went to the Smithsonian.[16] Roxie Shackelford herself had sent a basket to Otis Mason at the Smithsonian as a gift, for study, and the Smith-

*"Mrs. Shackelford seated on a rock with baskets," is the notation on this photograph in the Smithsonian Institution. Another copy of the photograph in the same collection is titled "Klikitat squaw and baskets." The woman apparently is not Roxie Shackelford, who was not Indian, but the coiled basket beside the woman's left hand is similar to one sold to the Smithsonian by Shackelford in 1900. The large coiled basket, lower right, appears to be the same basket as Smithsonian Institution cat. no. 207,756, described by Shackelford as "Klikitat basket from Cascade Massacre Mar. 26, 1856." Photo by Benjamin A. Gifford, The Dalles, Oregon, 1900. Smithsonian Institution photo no. 56,789.*

sonian purchased Columbia River baskets from her in 1900 and 1901.[17]

Anne Lang was mentioned in a 4 May 1914 letter to Grace Nicholson from Reverend Curtis, after he left The Dalles and was living in Columbia, Missouri (Grace Nicholson Collection). Her name appears again in the records of the Lowie Museum at the University of California. A Wasco-style bag first collected by Lang was given to the Lowie by Mrs. P. A. Hearst, who acquired it from the collection of E. L. McLeod of Bakersfield, another of Nicholson's correspondents.[18]

Among more than five thousand American Indian objects that came to the Smithsonian in the 1930s from a bequest from the family of Washington, D.C., Indian claims attorney Victor J. Evans were many fine examples of Mid-Columbia and Plateau basketry purchased from Grace Nicholson. At least one Wasco-style bag in the Evans bequest, purchased in 1911, was among those Nicholson obtained from Lang on visits to The Dalles in 1905 and 1911.[19] Other Evans gifts to the Smithsonian from the Columbia region were originally collected by artist Joseph Henry Sharp for use in his western paintings and for his personal pleasure. Sharp sold much of his famous collection to Nicholson in 1919.[20]

Another collector visited by the Pasadena dealer on the 1911 trip up the West Coast was Sarah J. Henderson of Portland. Although Grace Nicholson did not purchase baskets from Sarah Henderson, she did comment that many of the baskets in the fine collection came from Harriet Nesmith McArthur.[21] Several Klikitat baskets from the Henderson collection are now owned by the Oregon Historical Society in Portland and are pictured in *The Heritage of Klickitat Basketry.*[22]

An early twined hat given to Maryhill Museum by the family of W. M. Fitzhugh of San Francisco was purchased in 1924 as part of the "Lowe Indian Collection" from Professor and Mrs. T. S. Lowe of Pasadena. A photograph of this collection is pictured in one of the Nicholson albums.[23] Another example of Mid-Columbia basketry that has at least an indirect, and possibly close, connection with Grace Nicholson is in the Paul Seashore Collection at Texas Memorial Museum, University of Texas at Austin. Sometime between 1930 and 1950, Seashore obtained a finely woven Wasco-style bag as "part of the Comstock Collection" (Evans and Campbell 1970, 55).[24]

In 1904, Mrs. A. J. Comstock of Ventura, California, wrote Grace Nicholson about a large collection of baskets she was eager to sell. She described a "fine specimen," a sally bag, in a photograph she was sending with the letter (Grace Nicholson Collection). Although no photograph accompanies the letter in the Nicholson Collection at the Huntington Library, a photograph annotated in a flourishing hand similar to Mrs. Comstock's is in a Grace Nicholson album at the Lowie Museum. On this photo "to the right and near the top," as described by Mrs. Comstock, is a fine Wasco-style bag. If not the Seashore specimen, it is a close relative. Spinning more strands on the web of connection between Grace Nicholson and the best-known collectors, the Comstock letter also refers to collectors McLeod and Hubby.

George Wharton James, another Nicholson correspondent who wrote extensively of baskets and their makers, coined an apt description for these turn-of-the-century collectors when he announced his "Basket Fraternity" in 1903 (Gogol 1985a, 12). In references to Columbia River baskets in his 1909 book, *Indian Basketry,* James mentions some familiar names: the Reverend W. C. Curtis, Mrs. J. Frohman, Mrs. Velina Molson, and H. K. McArthur.

## Basketmaking in the Twentieth Century

The bibliography of James's *Indian Basketry* illustrates the growing interest in Indian art at the turn of the century. It lists no titles of books or of articles in journals, magazines, or newspapers on Indian basketry before 1890. For the last decade of the nineteenth century, James lists twelve references of which five were published in 1899. Twenty titles then appeared during the years 1900 to 1902 (1972, 232–33). This growth apparently continued another year, for John Gogol wrote in 1985 that "in 1903 more important work on Native American basketry was published than any other year up to the present time" (1985a, 17).

During the first two decades of this century, the greater popularity of American Indian basketry led to increased production by many basketmakers. We know that dealer Grace Nicholson not only preserved Indian basketry, she actively encouraged two Central Pomoan-speaking (Northern California) basketmakers, Mary Benson and her husband William, and perhaps others, in their basketmaking (McLendon and Holland 1979, 112). In the Mid-Columbia region, the greatest effect of the new demand for baskets appeared to be on those coiling the Klikitat-style cedar root baskets. Although diminished during the previous half-century, the production of other types of basketry—the twined hats and bags and folded bark baskets—continued, but primarily for native use rather than for sale to outsiders. The Mid-Columbia baskets that dominate the Frohman catalogue and the photographs of local collections at the turn of the century are the handsome, imbricated berry baskets of the Klikitats.

The great interest in American Indian art had dwindled by the early 1920s, after World War I turned North America's attention toward Europe. Although the preoccupying trauma of the Great Depression in the 1930s left little energy for collecting anything other than life's necessities, a few individuals continued to purchase baskets. One of these was John Wyers of White Salmon, Washington, who encouraged at least one Mid-Columbia basketmaking family to keep their traditional art alive (Schlick 1984, 19).

Wyers managed the Columbia Fruit Union, a hardware and general merchandise cooperative serving growers of the Mid-Columbia region. Buying the business in the early 1930s, he changed the name to Wyers Trading Company. He was known to be a fair dealer, buying baskets outright or making loans on them, whatever the weaver needed, and over the years acquired a fine personal collection of Mid-

*An unusual coiled cedar root basket with Wasco/Wishxam designs was given to Maryhill Museum by the family of M. Z. Donnell, an early pioneer who was a druggist in The Dalles. Maryhill Museum of Art cat. no. 1980.04.03.*

Columbia basketry that remains with his heirs. Wyers and other "traders" in communities serving the Mid-Columbia reservations provided a much needed source of cash for many weavers at a time when the basket market was practically nonexistent.

Hollywood actor and consultant on American Indian films, Nipo Strongheart was another admirer of Indian art who continued to collect when many had lost interest. Although not of Indian descent, Strongheart was reared on the Yakima Reservation by a tribal member and willed his extensive collection of books and artifacts to the Yakima tribe. This gift served as the nucleus for the tribal museum and library in the Yakima Indian Nation Cultural Center which opened in 1980 near Toppenish, Washington (Schlick 1979a).

Through the first half of the century, the production of baskets continued to decline among the Mid-Columbia people for many reasons, most of them tied to the great social and economic changes brought by settlement. By the 1950s, only a few basketmakers were working, the demand for their baskets largely limited to the diminished requirements of their traditional society. The young were not learning the cultural skills of their people as they had in former generations. It took another great social movement to arouse interest in the art among collectors again—and to establish new markets for American Indian basketry.

Klikitat basketmaker Nettie Jackson credits "the hippies" with the revival of interest among collectors. At the end of the chaotic 1960s, the great back-to-nature movement of thousands of North American young people inspired them to look at the American Indian with new and appreciative eyes. The Indian people's skill at surviving, and in many cases thriving, by understanding and utilizing nature's gifts was a model for many disillusioned products of affluence. The movement also brought renewed interest in handmade goods and processes: quilting and embroidery; canning and drying; building and repairing; and basketry. With time, these interests mellowed into the general culture. Magazine photographs featured baskets as part of interior design, often

*John Wyers of White Salmon purchased this fine example of Wasco/Wishxam twining with duck and condor motifs about 1935. Photographed on the banks of the Columbia River by W. T. Schlick.*

displayed, as Otis Mason had recommended, as single works of art. The market for baskets opened up once again for the small number of Mid-Columbia basketmakers who carried on their traditional art. This influence of the "counterculture" on Native American art offers possibilities for further study.

## BASKETRY—ART WITH CULTURAL MEANING

A concurrent movement was affecting the art world. After decades of relegating American Indian artifacts to anthropology museums, art professionals began to see and to present the indigenous heritage of this continent in a new light—as works of art that fuse artistry in design and construction with deep cultural significance.

A torchbearer for this movement was the 1931 exhibition, "Introduction to American Indian Art," curated by John Sloan and Oliver LaFarge. No Mid-Columbia baskets are shown in the catalogue, but Nez Perce work was represented in the show. Recognizing the economic importance of arts production to the Indian communities, the federal government in 1935 established the Indian Arts and Crafts Board in the United States Department of the Interior to encourage Indian and Eskimo arts and crafts. In 1939, the board organized an exhibition of historic and contemporary American Indian and Eskimo arts for the Golden Gate Exposition in San Francisco. This exhibition was presented again in 1941, with some revisions, at the Museum of Modern Art in New York (Libhart 1989, 41). In the introduction to the book based on the New York exhibition, *Indian Art in the United States,* authors Frederick Douglas and René d'Harnoncourt recognize that "increased familiarity with the background of an object not only satisfies intellectual curiosity but actually heightens appreciation of its esthetic values." Although the book includes basketry of the Southwest, there is no Columbia River material (1941, 11).

More than thirty years later, in 1972, the Walker Art

Center, Indian Art Association, and the Minneapolis Institute of Arts assembled the first of over eight hundred examples of native art, including basketry, from museums and private collections for "American Indian Art: Form and Tradition." Richard Conn's catalogue essay on the arts of the intermontane region included a discussion of Plateau basketry and photographs of a flat twined storage bag and a coiled and imbricated basket (Conn 1972, 72–73).

The native artistry exemplified by the flat twined bags of the Columbia and Plateau received popular exposure in 1975 in Stephen Shawley's comprehensive article in the magazine *Indian America.* In its third issue (Summer 1976), *American Indian Art* acknowledged basketry as an American Indian art form with an article on the work of the Mission Indian weavers,"The Rattlesnake Basket," by Hubert Guy.

Ralph T. Coe, curator of the Nelson Gallery–Atkins Museum in Kansas City, Missouri, mounted·"Sacred Circles" in London in 1976 and in Kansas City in 1977, a survey exhibition of 850 pieces. The Art Institute of Chicago presented another 550 objects in its survey exhibition, "The Native American Heritage," curated in 1977 by Evan Maurer. The events were significant enough to warrant coverage by *Newsweek* magazine.[25]

But the art of the Columbia River was not yet recognized on its own merit. In the "Sacred Circles" catalogue, a twined Wasco-style bag is included in the Northwest Coast section. A twined hat and two false embroidered, flat twined bags are presented with Plains material. Coe credits the Crow and Blackfeet with great influence on Plateau art, describing the hat as "California style," and states that beadwork on a Yakima trade blanket "show[s] patterns derived from neighbouring west coast Salishan basketry" (1977, 157, 185, 166). This assumption that Plateau culture is largely derivative persists and needs critical study. Although no Mid-Columbia basketry is included in the Chicago catalogue, a fine, early example of a Wasco beaded bag with designs inspired by the basketry tradition does appear (Maurer 1977, 281).

In *Native American Art in the Denver Art Museum,* published in 1979, Conn included photographs and discussion of ten excellent examples of Mid-Columbia basketry in the "intermontane" region, a term that allows the work an identity separate from the coast or the plains (1979, 248–52).

It was also in 1979 that John Gogol, a former professor of Russian language and literature and a longtime student of American Indian art and culture, launched his *American Indian Basketry* magazine in Portland, Oregon. The magazine combined scholarly research with reports on contemporary basketmakers and events in the native art world. The theme of the magazine was "the preservation of information on the rapidly disappearing traditional skills" of a complex culture that often is represented as primitive.[26] Gogol's magazine was well-received by Indians and non-Indians alike, but it was the classic story of a critical but not financial success. The magazine ended publication after twenty issues on 30 December 1985. Gogol did much to focus attention on the art of the people of the Plateau as separate from that of their neighbors.

By the end of the 1970s, the "country" look had taken over American homes and the "natural" look described American clothing. American Indian art had entered contemporary consciousness once again, and basketry emerged as a widely recognized art form (Collings 1982).

In the decade that followed, many museums included Mid-Columbia basketry in their exhibitions of American Indian art. The 1980s brought the recognition that traditional Indian arts are alive and, although produced on a smaller scale than in the nineteenth century, are continuing with surprising vitality. Ralph Coe spent a decade collecting contemporary examples of traditional work in North America for a traveling exhibition, "Lost and Found Traditions," in 1986. Coe's quest allowed him an unusual opportunity to tie the works of art and the artists together, and the catalogue documents the process as well as the results (Coe 1986). Two fine examples of flat twined bags represent the work of the Columbia River basketmakers in the section on the arts of the

Plateau. A photograph of Lena Barney captures the Yakima weaver in the process of making one of the bags that appears in the exhibition (1986, 30, 167, 182–83).

In seeking art for "Lost and Found Traditions," Coe commissioned works by many native artists, another revival of a turn-of-the-century practice. A few museums and private collectors are moving in this direction, adding contemporary work to their collections.

This form of encouragement is taking place among the basketmakers of the Mid-Columbia on a small scale. In 1982, photographer Eduardo Calderon included several Columbia River native artists in his "Indian Artists of the Pacific Northwest," a traveling exhibition of photographs of artists at work and their comments about their work. Among these were traditionalists Nettie Jackson, Klikitat, coiled cedar root baskets; Sarah Quaempts, Yakima, twined hemp bags; and Louise Billy, Rock Creek, cedar bark baskets.

In 1985, the Washington State Arts Commission, forming a collection of art made by Indian artists to be used in the Art in Public Places program in the state, commissioned a large imbricated basket from Klikitat basketmaker Nettie Jackson (Wash. State Arts Comm. 1988, 23, 24). Other Jackson baskets were commissioned for the permanent collection of the Yakima Indian Nation Cultural Center near Toppenish and for the Skamania County Historical Museum in Stevenson, Washington. The basketmaker also was asked to create a series of baskets in process for an interpretive display at the Hood River County (Oregon) Museum. The Whitman County Historical Museum in Walla Walla, Washington, commissioned a twined hat by Cayuse/Nez Perce artist Maynard White Owl Lavadour (pers. com. 1987).

Among the contemporary art commissioned by the Thomas Burke Memorial Washington State Museum for the state's 1989 centennial exhibition, "A Time of Gathering," were baskets made by four Yakima tribal members: a twined bag of Indian hemp by Sarah Quaempts, a twined hat by Helen Jim, a coiled cedar root basket by Nettie Jackson, and a folded bark basket by Warner Jim.

*Cameraman John Campbell focuses on Nettie Jackson's hands during filming for the documentary on her life and work, ". . . and Woman Wove It in a Basket."*

The Burke exhibition, which was designed with the advice of Washington State tribal groups, included as a major feature a traditional tule mat house made by James Selam and his relatives and friends from the Yakima Reservation. The basketry technique of twining with knee-spun Indian hemp was used to make the mats that formed the covering for the structure.

The question arises: Has this new interest in the native arts of North America come too late for the artists of the Mid-Columbia? It is probably too late for basketmaking to flourish as it once did as an artistic expression for many weavers of the region. But it is never too late for the aesthetic heritage of a people to receive recognition and support. The time for such acknowledgement is, as the people of the Columbia say, "from time immemorial to the time of generations yet unborn." Those few who practice these time-honored arts along the Columbia work against difficult odds, but their creative drive and the deep roots of their craft help sustain them. They are the connections of the past with the future.

American Indian baskets are more than objects. When presented creatively, they help us sense the soul of the people, and lead us to marvel at the aesthetic and cultural contribution to North American life by the native people of this continent. Museums and other educators have the responsibility of helping the general public "feel the soul" in an honest, factual, and inspired way.[27] It is difficult to accomplish this without complete collection information, but there is a contemporary resource that is often overlooked—the native people themselves.[28]

The move toward tribal museums, exemplified by the Yakima Nation Museum in Toppenish, Washington, and the Museum at Warm Springs, gives the tribal people a voice in interpreting their own artistry. The tribal museums of the Mid-Columbia people, as well as many other such museums and displays across the country, can offer the artist's view and that of the original user and appreciator in presenting the indigenous art.

*Students from the grade school at Warm Springs visit the display of baskets and other traditional artifacts and heirlooms at the Agency Longhouse in January 1983. About 1974 the Middle Oregon Indian Historical Society began acquiring these artifacts from tribal members for the tribal museum which opened at Warm Springs in 1993. Photo by Donna Behrend; courtesy* Spilyay Tymoo.

Among the descendants of the Mid-Columbia people are many with extensive knowledge of tribal tradition. Where they are called upon as resources for interpreting the art, the impact is tangible. In addition to seeking information from the elders, the Yakima Indian Nation Cultural Center each year schedules demonstrations by basketmakers and others skilled in native arts at the museum. Basketmakers also have received enthusiastic responses to their demonstrations in off-reservation galleries and museums.

An artifact purchase program by the Warm Springs tribes makes it possible for many family heirlooms to remain on the reservation, where they will be available for study, artistic inspiration, and as a source of pride for future generations. Before this program, when families needed to sell baskets or other works of art for income, their only market was to dealers and collectors away from the reservation.

Many of the collectors of the basketry of the native people of the Mid-Columbia were, and are, the descendants of the original makers and users. Others were, and are, those who wanted to learn from and enjoy the products of a society that expressed its wholeness and harmony in its art. All of these collectors deserve our thanks. They are *naknuwisha;* they are caring for something precious.

*Surrounded by her basketmaking materials, Nettie Jackson poses for photographer Eduardo Calderon in her home in 1982.*

# Afterword

## A Klikitat Basketmaker's View of Her Art

### Nettie Jackson

I am pleased to be able to share my feelings about basketry. It is a reward in itself to be able to do this. There are many cultural values that are gone because of the ignorance of not sharing. I regret that there are a lot of things lost because somewhere along the generation line my people thought it was no longer important. Today, I have so many questions about how my people first learned this basketry art—questions in my mind about how this beautiful art started.

My gratitude goes to my late mother for her concern that she was leaving me and my brothers and sisters without enough knowledge of our culture and traditions. Now, I can share what she felt because I am a mother. I do this work to please my family and myself and because I know that if my mother were here she would be pleased. I know that my grandmother would be very pleased at the traditional work my sister, my daughter, and I do. We not only make baskets, we also dry salmon and eels, and make *ch'lay* out of salmon. We salt and can salmon in the spring; we dig bitterroots and wild carrots. We are not as strong as our mother was, but we do what we can. This is what I tell my children.

Making baskets is important, but it is just one part of our way of life that follows the seasons. Summertime is the time to work on fish and drying corn; falltime is finishing the late fish and getting cedar roots, getting huckleberries; wintertime is working on baskets, doing bead work; springtime is getting bitterroots, wild carrots. If I can follow the seasons in this order, it feels good to know that I am carrying on my culture, that in this land I am a sovereign person who can still use the things that the creator gave to my ancestors so that I may survive.

With the times changing so fast, it is hard to follow our customs. I do know that education is the key for everyone, but there is a real desire in my children to want to be Indians and to be respected as such. For me and my daughter to learn this art of basketry is fulfilling.

Making baskets has been important to our family for generations. I first watched my grandmother make baskets when I was small. I grew up around her near the Klikitat River, just north of the Columbia. She worked very hard at traditional life; she tanned buckskins to support herself—a very hard thing to do. And when the day was over and she could no longer work outside, she would light the oil lamp and work on her baskets. She used to weave her baskets in the evening just before bedtime. To keep our attention she would tell us stories about life. These were the golden times of my life. Today I feel very sad for my children and other children because we have lost this part of our culture. My grandmother made baskets for all of us grandchildren. She also made baskets to sell and for her trading—all sizes, from little, cupsize for the children to big, seven-gallon baskets you see in the old pictures.

"When you want to learn something, don't always talk and ask questions, just watch and do it," my mother and grandmother told us when we were children. "If it is in you, you will do it. Even if it seems as if you can't learn, it will come to you when you are ready." I did not learn to make baskets when I was a child watching my grandmother work. I did not want to learn. It was not until 1975 that it seemed important to me that I learn this part of my own family tradition.

That year Elsie Thomas started teaching basketmaking to our people along the river. It was hard. There were times when she showed me how to do something and, yet, I could not do it. There were times when I gave up. Then I decided to try again and was able to do it. I find it is a lot easier for my daughter to learn because she sees me work on baskets almost every day when I am home.

There are things I do not know but am trying to learn, such as how to dye my material the natural way of my grandmothers. This is something that has changed because of the times—I use commercial dyes. I do know that my grandmother liked to try new things. My aunt had a basket that my grandmother decorated with dyed cornhusk—unusual for a cedar root basket. A bag she made had a printed bread wrapper woven in.

We have lost the cultural value in many of our traditions because of the need for money to get by. Every basket I make, I can sell. There are times when I want to make a basket for the sake of the idea in a certain design or for someone I really care about. But I need money for the telephone bill, or the rent, or for fishing nets, and I hurry to finish the basket, making the traditional designs that a collector will buy, so I can pay that bill.

A problem to me is my desire to express my own idea in the designs. There are times when I think about a person and a design will come to me—or I have dreamed of certain baskets that I hope to make someday. But it is not often I have time to carry out those ideas. This is a change from my grandmothers' times. They relied on their religion and tradition for the inspiration for their designs.

I mostly design my baskets from feelings people express about baskets. I hear their thoughts, then I keep them in my mind until I am ready to start another basket. Then I run through the ideas and decide on what I want to make and the colors I will use. Sometimes my relatives criticize me for my baskets when they are really different. I made a big basket with a thunderbird in rainbow colors. Some laughed at that, but a woman liked it right away and bought it. I liked the colors, coral, turquoise, deep green, black—very non-traditional. I find that Indian people love the bright colors when I use them. It is the collectors who usually ask for the old colors.

Making baskets for my people is fulfilling for me, not only as a way of passing on a tradition, but also to provide baskets for those who no longer have the old ones in their families. Many have had to sell their old things just to get by.

I find that my standards are high for myself now, for workmanship and for design. I had to learn to please myself—to learn to recognize when I was not satisfied with my own work, and to finish every basket to the best of my ability, no compromise. This is good in that my baskets are finer and finer, but it is bad in that it takes more time and more materials, making it a hardship for some who want baskets but find them hard to pay for.

When I first thought about this, I felt my ancestors' traditions prevented me from expressing my own ideas in my basketry. But I now feel that the basketmakers' concerns since time began have been the need to support ourselves and our families; higher and higher standards for our own workmanship; and the lack of time to carry out all the ideas that we have.

Whatever the problems, I am grateful for my gift and I hope to be here for many years making baskets.

*White Swan, Washington*

# Notes

Epigraph: Yakima Indian Nation Cultural Center.

## 1. WAP'AT. *The Art of Basket Weaving*

Epigraph: From Major J. W. MacMurray's report in Mooney (1896, 722) of a visit in 1884 to the Wanapum religious leader Smohalla. MacMurray was sent into the Columbia River country by General Nelson A. Miles to assist the people in acquiring permanent homes before settlers had taken over the land (Relander 1956, 135). MacMurray described Kotai'aqan as "Smohalla's chief supporter and assistant at the ceremonies." See also Erdoes and Ortiz 1985, 118; Clark 1953, 142.

1. Ray's description of the uses of basketry among the native people to the north (1932) also applies to life along the Mid-Columbia.

2. The Middle Oregon Indian Historical Society has prepared an excellent one-page explanation of the Root Feast Ceremony.

3. Jacobson n.d., 16. LaRea D. Johnston, Oregon State University Herbarium, personal communication 1988.

4. For more information on the calendar ball, see Yakima Nation Museum 1984; French 1955, 51; J. D. Leechman and M. R. Harrington, "String Records of the Northwest" in *Indian Notes and Monographs No. 15,* ed. F. W. Hodge, New York: Museum of the American Indian, Heye Foundation, 1921; *The Montana Salish,* U.S. Department of the Interior Indian Arts and Crafts Board, Museum of the Plains Indian and Crafts Center, n.d.; Garrick Mallery, *Picture-writing of the American Indians.* Vol. 1 of unabridged republication. New York: Dover Publications, Inc. 1972.

5. Townsend was a scientist with Nathaniel J. Wyeth's 1984 Oregon expedition.

6. See Selam 1974 and Hymes 1984 for discussions of the sacramental importance of water and food in Native American life.

## 2. PATL'AAPA. *The Twined Basket Hat*

Epigraph: From the myth of Warm Man and Cold Man, in "The Wy-a-kin" (Fletcher 1891, 8). *Wy-a-kin* means "spirit helper" in Nez Perce.

1. Ramsey (1977, xxiv) explains that the narratives of the Columbia River people appear to be set in one or another of three loosely defined periods. Earliest was the age of the animal-people, the Myth Age. Next he describes the Age of Transformation when Coyote appears and goes about turning animal-people into animals, forming landmarks, and forecasting the coming of the People. The legends gradually move into tales of the third or "historical" period, when the world is more or less as we know it today.

2. See Ramsey (1977, 58) and Beavert (1974, 116, 194) for longer versions of this myth, and Spier and Sapir (1930, 279) for a shorter version.

3. See French 1955 for a discussion of cultural change among a group of Mid-Columbia native people.

4. In Irving's Astoria (1836, 2:64), men who were camped on the bank of the Umatilla River noted that "Women wore caps of willow neatly worked and figured." See also Ray 1942, 167, and Spier and Sapir 1930, 207. Geraldine Jim of Warm Springs suggests that the twined hats were worn only for special occasions. The explorers may have assumed they were part of everyday dress when seeing women dressed to meet strangers.

5. University of Oregon Museum of Anthropology. Data sheet for no. 1-5648 in Photograph and Inventory Documentation: Basketry Exhibit file. Eugene, n.d.

6. For a discussion of the Waashat religion, see Schuster 1975.

7. I am indebted to Barbara Hail for suggesting this idea in "Beaded Bibles and Visiting Pouches: Twentieth Century Lakota Honoring Gifts," *American Indian Art,* Summer 1988, 41.

8. Joane Duncan of Damascus Pioneer Craft School helped me understand and master this difficult technique. For detailed instructions for knee-spinning, see Samuel 1982, 58–60.

9. The spelling *yai* is commonly accepted among Yakima tribal members although it varies from *yaay* given in Beavert 1975. Bear grass is also referred to as squaw grass and elk grass in early writings.

10. Leona Schuster held up her cupped hands, "It grows in three parts, like this," she said. "On the hills below Maryhill . . . a red bloom in May." She described smashing the roots and cooking them with the basket materials for a bright yellow color (personal communication 1984). See also Hunn 1978, 7; Taylor and Valum 1974, 37.

11. Stroud or strouding was named for the town in Gloucestershire, England, where the mills were located (Montgomery 1984, 353; Dr. Jane Farrell, Iowa State University Department of Textiles and Clothing, personal communication 1987).

12. See Fraser 1989 for a full discussion of twining techniques and their distribution.

13. See chapter 5 for a description of false embroidery. It appears that full-turn twining became a lost art among all but a few weavers before the turn of the century. In the nineteenth century most of the people of the Mid-Columbia used full-turn twining solely for weaving hats. Weavers made their round and flat twined bags using a different technique—either simple twining or the more complicated false embroidery technique, a technique known to the people of the Mid-Columbia since ancient times. Only the Wasco/Wishxam and a few of their nearest neighbors made bags in full-turn twining. This weaving of hats and Wasco/Wishxam-style bags in full-turn twining appears to have declined in the late 1800s, long before most of the other Columbia River weavers stopped simple twining.

14. At least one unusual and very old Wasco/Wishxam hat is beaded but is not formed of canvas (Gogol 1985b, 22). Instead, its maker constructed this hat using the traditional loose-warp technique on a foundation of buckskin strips, sinew, and horsehair. Interestingly, many of the distinctive "loomed" beaded bags of the Wasco/Wishxam people, made in this same loose-warp technique, are worked in a circular manner and are bound off at the edge in a technique similar to that employed by the hat weavers of the Mid-Columbia. Patricia Atkins, a contemporary Wishxam/Wenatchee beadworker and basketmaker, made this discovery (personal communication 1988). Another unusual beaded hat has a basketry foundation. The hat, now in the Thomas Burke Memorial Washington State Museum at the University of Washington, was collected by Mary L. Goodrich on the Yakima Reservation.

15. See chapter 5 for discussion and diagram of this technique.

16. Confederated Tribes of the Warm Springs Reservation of Oregon 1984, 57. Considered of highest value among the people of the Mid-Columbia, the tusk-shaped dentalia shells were obtained from the people of the Northwest Coast in trade. Although generally reported to originate in the waters off Vancouver Island, dentalia also came from farther north. One story tells of the early people of the Sitka area who obtained the precious shells by sinking a dog to the ocean floor and leaving it until dentalia had attached themselves to every hair.

### 3. WAPAAS. *The Twined Root-Digging Bag*

Epigraph: Mary Eyley, an elderly Cowlitz woman, described some of the traditions of her people for anthropologist Melville Jacobs in 1927 (1934, 227). Here she is telling of sending young girls to the mountains to find their personal spirit power. The Cowlitz were close neighbors and linguistic relatives of the Klikitats in the Cascade Mountains.

1. The Klikitats, close neighbors of the Wishxam, may also have used these designs (Spier and Sapir 1930, 195).

2. Laurence Tyler, personal communication 1970. Goldendale is a small town north of the Columbia River on U.S. Highway 97 that has served the Mid-Columbia native population for many years. The Rock Creek settlement of Georgeville is nearby.

3. The bags were purchased by a Kansas City collector and, to my great pleasure, surfaced in 1986 in *Masterpieces of Native American Basketry,* the catalogue of an exhibition at Panhandle-Plains Historical Museum, Canyon, Texas. I am grateful to Bruce Hartman, curator of the Texas museum at the time of the exhibition and later curator of art at Cranbook Academy of Art in Bloomfield Hills, Michigan, for his description of bag details that escaped my notice in Seattle long ago (personal communication 1988).

4. Adapted from Ramsey 1977, 18. A digging bag is mentioned in another tale, "The Deserted Boy" (Spier and Sapir 1930, 274–75). A mother makes a little basket and digging stick for her daughter before taking her to visit her grandmother.

5. From a caption at the Oregon Historical Society, Portland, 1981. Catlin reportedly obtained a number of Indian specimens from the Columbia River region from William Clark while in St. Louis about 1830 (Cutright 1969, 165). If these specimens included a "sally" bag, or if Catlin returned to the east with such a bag from his own journey to the Columbia River about 1850 (Ross 1959, 181), it has not survived. Some Catlin material came to the Smithsonian Institution in 1881 after many years of storage. A portion of the collection was destroyed in a fire, and part of the remainder deteriorated from moths and moisture. (Letter from T. W. Donaldson to Spencer F. Baird, Sept. 25, 1881, in file for Accession no. 10638, Processing Laboratory, Smithsonian Institution.) The remaining Catlin material includes two sturdy digging sticks from the Columbia River that would have been intimately associated with the round twined bags in use (no. 73334).

The hardwood blades of the Catlin specimens are hand carved and are wider than the blacksmith-made digging tools used today. Their wooden handles are shaped in a graceful curve. Although deer or elk antlers also were used, a man could make a digger of wood strong enough to work the rocky soil. To do this, he cut and peeled a piece of hardwood shrub or tree about two feet long. Sharpening one end into a chisel shape, he hardened the blade in the fire over a period of hours. The maker had to watch that the green wood was charred enough to remove all the sap but did not burn (Weddle 1978).

6. Catalogue information with Smithsonian Institution no. 328074, gift of Miss E. F. Hubby; Frohman 1902.

7. This probably refers to the Rev. W. C. Curtis, pastor of the First Congregational Church in The Dalles from 1888 to 1898. Curtis and his son, Winterton C. Curtis, purchased baskets from the Columbia River people at The Dalles and at the ancient fishing village of Celilo, about twelve miles upriver. Many of these baskets are in the remarkable collection of Maryhill Museum of Art, on the north bank of the Columbia near Goldendale, Washington.

8. Housely 1984; Nancy Russell, personal communication 1989. For a description of Lewis's herbarium, see Cutright 1969, 359–64.

9. For quantitative data on root harvests, see Hunn and French 1981 and Hunn 1981.

10. Verbena Green in talk to Oregon Home Economics Association at Kahneetah, 1975.

11. Eugene Hunn, personal communication 1991, and Oregon State University 1972. According to OSU research, the Vitamin C value of the young wild celery plant is high, a cup providing more than an adult needs each day. This unique publication includes methods of cooking and preservation as well as the nutritive value of the following native foods: bitterroot, coush, luksh, camas, wild carrot, black lichen, wild celery, sweet corn, mint, huckleberries, chokecherries, wild cherries, salmon, pacific lamprey ("eels"), and venison.

Although the study confirmed that fresh roots contributed significant levels of vitamin C and iron to the diet, Indians already knew the roots were nutritionally sound. Mothers once taught their daughters to eat bitterroot while breastfeeding infants (Stowell 1980). When she has the flu or a bad cold, a Klikitat woman said of bitterroot, "It's about the only thing that makes me feel better . . . that I crave" (Sharon Dick, in Azzouz, Farnum and Kuneki 1989).

12. Nathan Jim mentioned this in a talk to the Oregon Home Economics Association in 1975; Sherry Kaseberg, personal communication 1987.

13. Their care of the digging areas through the years is supported by archaeologists who have found that root-digging and hunting rarely resulted in sufficient alteration of the landscape to produce identifiable sites for study (Osborne 1957, 7).

14. Eugene Hunn attended a first root bag ceremony held by the Toppenish Waashat congregation in 1990 (personal communication 1991).

15. Although generous in sharing these special foods with non-Indians, the people consider the roots sacred. This is one reason many tribal elders resist the showing of the tops of the plants in photos or museum displays. They are concerned about over-harvesting that might cause the roots to disappear forever.

16. Eugene Hunn (personal communication 1991) suggests that these dried salmon bags were made of cattail leaves (*Typha latifolia*). In the 1940s long after large cans such as those lard came in replaced the handwoven bags for fish storage, Columbia River native women continued to line the cans with salmon skin which helped preserve the contents (Nettie Jackson, personal communication 1988). A Yakima woman remembers her parents preparing the *ch'lay* each spring by cooking red salmon or steelhead around an open fire on sharp sticks, removing the bones from the nearly cooked fish and grinding it, then drying the ground fish in the sun and breeze. They pounded it to the consistency of fine powder and added the melted fat from steelhead entrails as an oil preservative. A very concentrated food, the powder can be eaten

plain with potatoes or fried bread or in various mixtures (*Toppenish Review* 1977).

17. In the Janice and Lew Merz collection.

18. Spier and Sapir (1930, 193) suggest that the making of bags in pairs is a transfer from the custom of making the rawhide "Indian suitcases" known as parfleches in pairs. However, the parfleche was made to carry on a horse where a balanced load may have been important.

19. Maryhill Museum of Art no 44-97B; Denver Art Museum no. 1951.401 in Conn 1979, 252.

20. Nelson Wallulatum, personal communication 1987; Osborne 1957, 113. Dr. Mary Lou Florian of the Royal British Columbia Museum, Victoria, identified cattail and cornhusk (and cotton) in two turn-of-the-century, Wasco-style bags.

21. Minnie Marie Slockish, personal communication 1982. Violet Carpenter, personal communication 1981. Alice Florendo remembers her grandmother "unraveling gunny sacks to make tump line," personal communication 1984.

22. Watson Totus, personal communication 1987; Viola Kalama, personal communication 1985; Leona Schuster, personal communication 1984; Spier and Sapir 1930, 193.

23. Smithsonian Institution no. 206408 (basket) and no. 206409 (material).

24. Eugene Hunn, personal communication 1988; Miller 1986, 122; Paul Harvey, agronomist with the US Department of Agriculture, Beltsville, MD, personal communication 1978.

25. Information about hop ranching in the Yakima Valley came from Violet Carpenter of Granger, WA, personal communication 1981. Carpenter's husband, Thomas D., is the grandson of Charles Carpenter who planted the first hops in that region.

26. Alice Florendo remembers helping her mother, Martha Sidwalter, gather hop twine at Independence, Oregon in 1928 to 1930 (personal communication 1984).

27. At about the same time, growers turned to less expensive rough hemp twine imported from India (Violet Carpenter, personal communication 1981).

28. Sally Buck, of Dallesport, Washington, was seven years old when her grandmother, Sally Wahkiacus, taught her to make bags. She didn't have time for twining after that until 1974 when an injury forced her to stop working on a farm. It was then that she "brought out" the skill from her memory and began to weave the traditional root-digging bags she is known for today (personal communication 1984).

Nora Kahclamet, who also lives along the Mid-Columbia, spoke about Louise Spino: "I didn't pay attention—I used to think I had forever to learn from Aunt Louise" (personal communication 1979).

Susie Walsey of Rock Creek taught her grandsons to make the round twined bags in the 1930s. The boys also learned to coil cedar root huckleberry baskets and to make grinding bowls from tree knots. Daisy Ike, personal communication 1984.

29. False embroidery technique is described in detail in chapter 5. Examples of bags with overlay: Lobb 1978, 24, and Lowie Museum of Anthropology, no. 2-18263.

30. The Pishquitpah, or Pishquilpah—the words are in the explorers' handwriting, not always easy to decipher—have been identified as a group of native people who lived part of the year along the Columbia in close proximity to the Wishxam, and who wintered in the Yakima Valley along Satus Creek (Mooney 1896, 739; Johnson Meninick and Watson Totus, personal communication 1974). For the story of the search for the twined bags collected by Lewis and Clark, see Schlick 1979.

31. The dogs were appropriate decoration for the Lewis and Clark bag, for the explorers found many of the pets in native settlements along the Columbia and purchased them as a welcome change in diet from the "pore" elk and dried fish. One tribal elder from the Satus area on the Yakima Reservation told of his great grandfather trading a dog to Lewis and Clark for a shirt (Watson Totus, personal communication 1983).

32. Comments about the fish motif were made by James Selam in 1981 and confirmed by Delores George and Hazel Umtuch in 1986. Nelson Wallulatum made the reference to the giant condors in 1989, referring to Thwaites 1905, 3:232—33, and 4:79–80. Wallulatum, the Wasco chief, said that his people kept a condor chick in camp to keep away thunder and lightning. By the 1850s, condor sightings were rare in the gorge (Gabrielson and Jewett 1970, 180–81).

33. Krieger Papers, "Material Concerning Columbia River Region," Box 9, 1927-40. From notes of H. T. Harding of Walla Walla, 1926.

34. In a letter in the 1902 catalogue of the Frohman Trading Company in Portland, Oregon, Otis Mason, curator of ethnology for the Smithsonian Institution, writes: "Do not fail to gather any stories that you may come across about the figures on these baskets. There is said to be a great deal of delightful folk-lore in them."

35. Chinook Jargon was a trade language of the Northwest, primarily Nootkan and enriched by the languages of others who used it. For more on native trade jargons, see Ruby and Brown 1976, 112–13.

36. Eliade 1972, 160; Paul Tacon, in speech at Native American Art Studies Association conference in Seattle, September 1983.

37. For more information on Columbia River beadwork, see Gogol 1985b, 4-28.

38. Alice Florendo was looking at photos of no. 1820.25-19 in the collection of the Los Angeles County Museum of Natural History and no. 9041 in the Smithsonian Institution Museum of Natural History.

39. Southwest Museum no. 964–G-90.

40. Lowie Museum of Anthropology, no. 2-18263.

41. Ruth Jackson Estebrook, personal communication 1983; Mrs. Willard Cloud, personal communication 1984; Tallulah Pinkham, personal communication 1983; Sally Slockish Buck, personal communication 1987.

42. Son of Louise Spino, Eddie Sconowah said, "I have a little bag she made. The sewing is crooked. I thought I should straighten it, then thought 'why should I, she was 74 years old when she made it, just before she died. This is her work!' " (personal communication 1985).

43. For examples of diagonal twining in Wasco-style bags, see Maryhill Museum of Art no. 1980.04-34; British Museum bag illustrated in *Man* I, 1901, 23–24; Spier and Sapir 1930, 292; Dockstader 1973, 203; Lobb 1978, 67; Conn 1979, 252. In the Lewis and Clark bag, Peabody Museum, Harvard University, no. 99-12-10/53160, the entire top band is worked in close diagonal twining.

### 4. XLAAM. *The Coiled Cedar Root Basket*

Epigraph: Shackelford 1900.

1. Oregon Historical Society Press in 1982 published Nettie Jackson's *The Heritage of Klickitat Basketry* (Kuneki, Thomas, and Slockish).

2. See Gogol 1979, 18–29, for a detailed description of Elsie Thomas making a basket in the classroom.

3. For stories of the *T'at'atɫya,* see Spier and Sapir 1930, 274; Beavert 1974, 78; and Ramsey 1977, 75. A similar mythical being is the cannibal woman who appears in Inuit myth as "the *amautalik,* an ogress who steals children and even adults . . . hiding her captives in the *amout,* a pouch in the back of her parka." (From Bernadette Driscoll's *Inuit Myths, Legends, and Songs,* Winnipeg Art Gallery, 1982, 6.)

4. Gibbs (1978, 405) in his report, dated March 4, 1854, to Capt. George B. McClelland, Commander, Western Division for the Northern Pacific Railroad Explorations: "They use for the most part the . . . utensils of the whites. The pails and baskets, constructed from the bark of cedars, saddles and fishing apparatus are their principle [*sic*] articles of domestic manufacture, and even of (these) it is common to find imported substitutes."

5. See Warm Springs Reservation Committee 1977, Book 12, for the story of Grandmother Squirrel storing food for the winter.

6. The Sargood collection is now in the Otago Museum, Dunedin, New Zealand, and includes sixteen coiled baskets attributed to the Klikitat and Yakima. With few exceptions they have imbricated decoration.

7. The Inuit of Northern Quebec have a word that describes works of art or utility—often the same works—which make sense, have logic, have an axis and an order in their proportions. The word is *tukilik.* The best of the Klikitat baskets fit this description. They show a spontaneity and directness that can only be created by a weaver with perfect control of her medium, control that must be maintained over a period of weeks.

8. From Kimberly Craven's article "Huckleberry harvest begins on Mount Adams," *The Portland Oregonian,* August 9, 1986.

9. In the early years of the twentieth century huckleberry pickers were paid 50 cents a gallon. By 1952, a gallon brought $2.50 to $3 (Filloon 1952, 4). In 1986, a gallon was worth about $10. See Filloon 1952 for an account of the huckleberry camps near Mount Adams over half a century.

10. Leona Smartlowit, "Food from land Indian tradition." *Head Start Messenger,* Wapato/Toppenish Head Start, Spring 1973, 5.

11. See Warm Springs Reservation Committee 1977, Book 10, for the story of Sucker winning all of Eel's best baskets. Indian Race Track is in the Mount Adams District of the Gifford Pinchot National Forest (Washington). White Swan is a community west of Toppenish, Washington, on the Yakima Indian Reservation.

12. Mary Eyley, a Cowlitz woman with Yakima and Klikitat relatives, told this mythlike story of a girl seeking her guardian spirit in the Cascade Mountains near the Columbia River in the late 1920s. *Yai* or bear grass (*Xerophyllum tenax*) is from the lily family and is the only material other than cedar root used in the coiled Klikitat-style baskets. "The leaves were a common item of commerce at the Columbia Rapids, the centre of the Chinook salmon trade" (Turner 1979, 132). The gift of basketmaking in the story, as well as in the legend of the first cedar root basket in Shackelford and others, is a gift from the materials themselves, a gift of the earth.

13. The Rock Creek grandmother of cedar bark basketmaker Warner Jim traded with the Klikitat for huckleberry baskets (personal communication 1987).

14. Grace Nicholson Papers, Box 9.

15. See also Gogol 1979, 31; Kuneki, Thomas, and Slockish, 1982, 17. Shackelford's (1900) brief version follows: "The Shade told the first weaver to weave a basket, so she repaired to the forest and pondered long over her mission. At last, gathering beargrass and red cedar roots, she began to weave. After many days a basket was produced. She carried it to the lake and dipped it full of water, but her heart was stricken with grief when it leaked. Shade said to her, 'It will not do, weave again . . . a tight basket with a pattern on it.'

"She sat by the waterside in despair, and as she looked down in the clear depths of the beautiful lake, the pattern of *Patu* [Mt. Adams] was revealed to her. With new courage she went into the depths of the forest alone and worked until she made a perfect basket."

16. Sally George, age eighty-four, in "Collected Reminiscences," Yakima Indian Nation, ca. 1978.

17. Nettie Jackson usually imbricates three stitches on the base of her baskets as a signature. See Kuneki, Thomas, and Slockish 1982; and Gogol 1979, 18–29, for further explanation and photographs of the weaving process.

18. Professor Mason received this information from Velina Nesmith [Mrs. W. M.] Molson, then living in Rickreall, Oregon. Molson's fine collection of Klikitat and other baskets is in the McCord Museum at McGill University, Montreal.

19. Nettie Jackson, in a demonstration at Oregon School of Arts and Crafts, Portland, 1987.

20. Speaking of the Wishxam, Sally Buck (Klikitat weaver), said, "They were close to us, would come and stay a week or so with us" (personal communication 1987).

21. *Yakima Nation Review,* February 1977; Cynthia Mesplie, personal communication 1981.

22. A great granddaughter of the basketmaker was Cecelia Totus, a well-known Yakima beadworker.

## 5. LAP'UY. *The Folded Cedar Bark Basket*

Epigraph: Jacobs 1929, 220. The stories in this volume were told to Professor Jacobs in March 1928 by Joe Hunt, an elderly Klikitat medicine man living a few miles north of the Columbia River at Husum, Washington. J. J. Spencer was the translator.

1. "Wishham Basket Worker" (Curtis 1911b, 112) and "Wishham Handicraft" (Curtis 1911b, 172); photo of Sally Wahkiacus taken in 1906; Filloon 1952, 7.

2. Barbara Hollenbeck, personal communication 1982; Michael Allen, personal communication 1982; Bella 1983; Marden 1987.

3. In 1855, the Yakima Indian Nation ceded to the United States lands outside the reservation boundaries that had been the Yakimas' land to use freely "since time began." However, the Yakima treaty specifies that "the exclusive right of taking fish in all the streams, where running through or bordering said reservation, is further secured to said confederated tribes and bands of Indians, . . . together with the privilege of hunting, gathering roots and berries . . ." on these ceded lands (Relander 1955, 22).

In 1923, recognizing these rights and the traditional significance of the area, the U.S. Forest Service set aside certain berry fields on the southern slopes of Mount Adams for the exclusive use of the Indian people. (The people, of course, have the same privilege of picking in other berry fields of the national forest enjoyed by all non-Indians.)

The ancient berry fields where the Jim family camps are in this special area. Every year the huckleberry feast is an important time for the families, but the feast held on 21 August in 1983 was especially important. On that Sunday, the families descended from those who negotiated the continued use of this area in the Yakima treaty invited state and federal officials to join them in commemorating sixty years since the Indian berry fields were established.

4. Anthropologist James Teit visited the Yakima and Klikitat in 1909 and was told of the bark baskets but did not see any because they "were seldom kept around the home" (1928, 353).

5. A toxic substance that resists rot in mature cedar trees may account for the reported preservative properties of the baskets according to Mack and Hollenbeck (1985, 7).

6. Molson [Mrs. William Markland], notes in 1928 catalogue file for no. 1645.3.

7. The Upper Cowlitz speak a dialect of the Sahaptin language and have close ties with the Sahaptin people of the Mid-Columbia.

8. Bella 1983; U.S. Forest Service publication, "Picking Huckleberries in the Gifford Pinchot National Forest," n.d.

9. Exhibit caption in Cheney Cowles Museum, Spokane, Washington, 1981.

10. Warner Jim's advice to take time for the work reminded me of the words of a Japanese builder of shrines in Kim Stafford's *Having Everything Right* (New York: Penguin Books, 1987, 105). " 'Life is for doing things slow,' Makoto said, 'like trees.' "

11. Louise Billy's photograph with her fine handiwork was included in Eduardo Calderon's exhibition of photographs, "Indian Artists of the Pacific Northwest," at the Burke Museum, University of Washington, Seattle, 1982.

12. Wallalukes Papkawammi, Warner Jim's grandmother (Warner Jim, personal communication 1983).

## 6. WAWXPA. *The Flat Twined Bag*

Epigraph: Kalaasya's grandmother, quoted in Beavert 1974, 116.

1. The story of this trade on the marriage of Melvern Sweowat and Casey Barney was reported in *The Toppenish Review,* December 31, 1970, 12. Kate C. McBeth, a missionary to the Nez Perce, wrote Alice Fletcher that sacks woven by hand were exchanged in a "marriage ceremony" about 1891 (in Fletcher Papers, manuscript no. 4558-63).

2. Processing the raw material required at least half of the labor involved in making a flat twined bag (Miller 1986, 113). The estimate of time necessary to make a root storage bag was made by Pauline Aleck (personal communication 1987). Lewis and Clark's attempt to trade for bags is recorded in Thwaites 1905 (5), 114. At this point in their journey, the explorers and their men had little to offer in trade.

3. Cecelia Bearchub, personal communication 1987; Shawley 1974, 273; French 1955, 75.

In 1976, a Yakima friend sent a beautiful fringed shawl in return for a handbag I had made for her. In 1973 my husband and I were honored with Indian names by a family that had been leaders in the Wapato Longhouse for many years. In return for this generous gift, we presented shawls and blankets to the family members. Looking for a special gift for the family elder who was responsible for the honor, I obtained a cornhusk bag, and, knowing that it should not be given empty, filled it with the only bulbs I could think of—gladioli bulbs. Now, from this perspective, I realize what an amusing and probably puzzling gift these inedible flower bulbs must have been. When the value of the cornhusk bag is in the food it contains, this must have seemed a very strange gift indeed.

4. From Ted J. Brasser note on no. II-X-7 (V-B-214) and twelve other bags collected by H. E. Smith in 1929.

5. Wanapum Dam display, and personal communication with Buck family, 1976.

6. Of more than two hundred examples of cornhusk work displayed in "Wap'ashash," a 1987 exhibition at Maryhill Museum of Art near Goldendale, Washington, only one bag was identified as having been decorated with bear grass.

7. Paul H. Harvey, agronomist with United States Department of Agriculture, Beltsville, MD, personal communication 1978. Corn (*Zea mays*) was domesticated in Central or Southern Mexico from *Zea mexicana* (Eugene Hunn, personal communication 1991).

8. Niron Hawley wrote in his memoirs of the trip to Oregon in 1852 that they saw corn and potatoes growing at a Umatilla village near the Oregon Trail (in McFarland and Clark 1960).

9. National Museum of Natural History, Smithsonian Institution, Cat. No. 378524.

10. A few weavers on the Yakima Reservation today are reviving the skill of spinning Indian hemp for use in their bags.

11. Flat twined bags made with an S-stitch are rare. It is assumed that the left-handed weavers learned to weave by observing another weaver and adapted the right-handed technique.

12. A photograph in Miller (1986, 89) shows a flat piece of wood being used as a template to maintain straight edges on the bag. Although this would be a logical use for the wood, weavers have described the purpose of such devices as "to keep the bag from twisting" (personal communication Karen Umtuch, 1980, and Sally Buck, 1987).

13. Virginia Canapo, Yakima, a Nez Perce woman living on the Yakima Reservation, and Esther Goodluck, a Rock Creek woman, make handbags using plain and full-turn twining. In 1975, Julia Sohappy and Mrs. Kelly George were making handbags in close plain twining and worked the designs in false embroidery. These bags have cotton or jute warps and wool yarn wefts.

14. Examples are Thomas Burke Memorial Washington State Museum no. 2-1982 and Nez Perce National Historic Park no. 141 in Miller 1986, 107.

15. The twined openwork is unusual among the Plateau flat twined bags and is similar to the compact plain and spaced, alternate-pair weft twining seen in Great Lakes area weaving (Whiteford 1977, 45). On a bag examined in 1980 in Portland, Oregon, that was constructed in this manner, the cornhusk or grass false embroidery was observed only in the design units, an early decorative technique on the Plateau.

16. In 1973, Patricia Umtuch of Toppenish used the horizontal banded design on a flat twined handbag that was a family heirloom as the inspiration for the beaded designs on the ceremonial outfit she wore as Miss Yakima Nation. The young beadworker repeated variations of the traditional design on moccasins, leggings, belt, fan handle, and braid ties as well as on the yoke of her buckskin dress.

17. An apparent exception to Teit's finding were the designs on a Plateau bag reported by Livingston Farrand as representing "lakes connected by streams" (Farrand 1900, pl. XXIII, fig. 1); and repeated in Ann Wyman's *Cornhusk Bags* (Southwest Museum Leaflet No. 1, 1935, 6). James Teit wrote that he could obtain no explanation of any of the designs given in Farrand's book. Franz Boaz (1955 [1927], 124) explains that the name was not given to the design by the maker, but rather came from a British Columbia woman who had purchased the bag and thought the designs looked like a series of lakes connected by a river.

18. Although it frequently is suggested that the introduction of trade goods caused a decline in native art, the new materials appear instead to have stimulated artistic production and improved quality in many cases. The decline in North American native art did not come until much later when other pressures came to the native people (Burnham 1981, 2).

19. Unless otherwise noted, information on design in this section is from studies reported in Schlick 1977 and Miller 1986.

20. Shawley (1975, 27) mentions two sources for black-brown among the Nez Perce: wild carrot root (*Perideridia gairdneri*) and tree moss (probably a lichen, *Alectoria jubata*). Other groups report using only alkaline mud which produces a grayed black. It is possible that black was a favored color among the Nez Perce before aniline dyed yarn was available.

21. For further discussion of the chronological framework for the changes in Plateau flat bag weaving, see Miller 1986, 186–98.

22. Collier (1934, 35–41) lists Nez Perce weavers as: Sophia Red Duck, Elsie Armstrong, Lucy Allen Hayes, Lily Lindsley, Hattie Carl Jackson, Rena McCormack Allen, Myra Samuels, Annie Miller, and Ida Allen of Lapwai; Jeanette Wilson of Spalding; Elizabeth Tawatoy of Julietta; Mary Phinney, Cecelia SunDown, Beatrice Samuels, and Almetia Stephens of Culdesac; Annie Hill, Rachel Henry Miles, Cecelia Guthrie, and Rachel Compo of Sweetwater; Rose Johnson, Rose McConville Hayes, Helen Lookingglass, Lizzie Powers, Lizzie Hayes Moody, Elizabeth Wilson, Jeanette Ezekiel, Celia Moffett, Mary Kipp, Elsie Spencer, Lydia Corbett, Hattie Enos, Alice Hayes Harsche, Daisy Parsons, Elizabeth F. Green, Lucy Oatman, Annie Little, and Ida Blackeagle of Kamiah; Dorcas Miller, Mary Spencer, Mabel Lowry, Madeline Lowry, Mabel Sky Nicodemus, Julia Scott Wheeler, Martha Morris, and Phoebe Lawrence of Kooskia; Agnes John, Hattie Axtell George, Julia James, Martha Nesbit, Carrie Brown, and Kesiah Samuel of Stites; Mary Moody Harrison, Louise Poweke, Mrs. Harry Wheeler, Lucy Marks, Lucy Corbett, Margaret Bronche Corbett, and Mary Marks Whitman of Ahsahka; Mancy Lawrence of Tensed; Mrs. Sam Friedlander of Tekoa; and Mrs. John Robillard of Plummer.

Umatilla weavers listed were: Mrs. Ernest Johnley, Lucy Pete, and Susie Pete, all of Pendleton.

In addition to this 1934 listing, we have the names of a few basketmakers from photographic records, from other written reports, and from word of mouth. They include Nez Perce weavers Ida Corbett Blackeagle, Annett Burke, Audrey Redheart, Nellie Broncheau Stanfield, Rose Frank, Bernice Moffett, Sam Jackson, Stella Amera Penney, and Katherine Ramsey; Spokane weavers Ella McCarty and Nancy Flett; Yakima weavers Julia Pimms Sohappy, Elsie Pistolhead, Minnie Wesley, Sarah Quaempts, Lena Barney, Mrs. Kelly George, Mary Jim Chapman, Helen Jim, Lena Jim, and Valerie Jim Calac; Colville weavers Elizabeth Davis, Ida Disautel, the grandmother of Cecelia Sherman, Mrs. Cleveland Kamiakin (Nez

Perce) and Mary Ann Wapato (Wenatchi); Rock Creek weavers Louise Billy, Susie Walsey Billy, and Esther Goodluck; Cayuse weaver *Petowya* or *Sechowa,* and Susan Williams; Cayuse/ Nez Perce weaver Maynard White Owl Lavadour; Umatilla weaver Thomas Morning Owl; Umatilla/Yakima/Nez Perce weaver Renee Katherine Ramsey; Warm Springs weavers Kathleen Moses, Lorena Suppah Bill, Geraldine Jim, Neda Van Pelt Wesley, Isabel Keo, and Sallie Swan.

This is an incomplete list. Of these, many are no longer living and many others have given up practicing their art.

Epilogue

Epigraph: Albert Buell Lewis, "Tribes of the Columbia Valley and the Coast of Washington and Oregon," *Memoirs of the American Anthropological Association* 1 (1906):147–209.

1. Special thanks to another gifted teacher, Georgia Rae Delaney, for sharing this book.

2. "Gift 'Good Collection' Museum Director Says." *Toppenish* (Washington) *Review,* 23 June 1971.

3. A Plateau-style basketry hat collected in 1792 on the lower Columbia by a member of the Vancouver expedition is in the British Museum, no. VAN197 (Wright 1989, 68).

4. See Cole 1985 and Gogol 1985a for more detailed discussions of the history of collecting.

5. Dr. Jane Walsh, Smithsonian Institution, personal communication 1987.

6. Smithsonian Institution Cat. No. 214455.

7. Smithsonian Institution Cat. Nos. 9040 (hat) and 9041 (bag).

8. Smithsonian Institution Cat. No. 23872 (Mason 1976, 431).

9. Smithsonian Institution Accession No. 35837, papers.

10. Pictured in O.M. Dalton, "California: Basket-Work." *Man,* vol. 1 (1901), 23–24. The bag also is mentioned in Mason 1976, 439.

11. Maryhill Museum of Art stands alone on a high bluff overlooking the Columbia River near Goldendale, Washington. Here, one hundred miles from the nearest major city, is one of the country's most eclectic collections, from works by the French sculptor Auguste Rodin to fashion designs in miniature by the foremost French couturiers of the 1940s, and furniture, clothing, and other mementos from Queen Marie of Romania who dedicated the museum in 1926.

12. Smithsonian Institution Accession No. 39,904 and No. 40,383. Lt. Emmons also was responsible for a major collection of Alaskan basketry in the American Museum of Natural History of New York (Mason 1976, 541).

13. Two examples of such piles of baskets were in old photographs discovered by American Indian artist Glenn LaFontaine at a house sale in Portland, Oregon. Nancy Blomberg, assistant curator of anthropology at the Los Angeles County Museum of Natural History, identified twelve of the baskets in the photograph as part of a collection that came to the museum from C. M. O'Leary of Los Angeles in 1925 (personal communication 1988). One of the baskets (Cat. No. A.1820.25-19) is a large and very early Wasco-style bag decorated with many internally elaborated human figures as well as abstracted face motifs.

14. Smithsonian Institution National Anthropological Archives, Baskets: Miscellane-

ous—Northwest Coast (unidentified). Photograph No. 74-11863 and No. 74-11864.

15. Strangely, Mason identified this important figure in the collecting world as "Florence" Nicholson (1976, 543). Grace Nicholson was well known to him as a correspondent over a period of several years (Grace Nicholson Collection).

16. Grace Nicholson Collection. Among baskets bequeathed to the Smithsonian Institution by Ella Hubby in 1925 is a Wasco-style bag, Cat. No. 328074, identified as having been collected by Shackelford "before 1899."

17. Smithsonian Institution Accession Nos. 37002, 37147, and 38636.

18. Lowie Museum Cat. No. 2-10308; Grace Nicholson Collection.

19. Smithsonian Institution Cat. No. 360,944. Grace Nicholson Collection Papers, ledger, 252.

20. Grace Nicholson Collection, correspondence with Joseph Henry Sharp, 1918; and Forrest Fenn's *Beat of the Drum and Whoop of the War Dance,* Santa Fe: Fenn Publishing Co., 1983, 145.

21. Grace Nicholson Collection, diary entry for 5 July 1911.

22. Kuneki, Thomas, and Slockish, 1982, 38 and 50. Both of these baskets were identified by Nettie Jackson and Elsie Thomas as possibly having been made by Elsie's mother, Lucy Cayuse Thomas of Husum, Washington.

23. Papers with Accession No. MR-103, Maryhill Museum of Art; Grace Nicholson Collection, Album I.

24. Further information from Collections Assistant Elaine T. B. Sullivan, personal communication 1988.

25. Mark Stevens in "Embraces of Nature," *Newsweek,* Sept. 12, 1977, 82–83.

26. Paul Pintarich in "Basketry and Preservation of Culture," *Northwest Magazine* (*The Portland Oregonian*), 19 June 1983, 17.

27. Dan Monroe, director, Oregon Art Institute, in a speech before the institute's Native American Art Council on 19 November 1985.

28. *A Special Gift: The Kutchin Beadwork Tradition,* by Kate C. Duncan with Eunice Carney (Seattle: University of Washington Press, 1988), resulted from one such project in which the research scholar and a Kutchin (a Northern Athapaskan group) beadworker carried color photographs of beadwork in museum collections to the people of several Athapaskan communities in Alaska and Yukon Territory for comment.

# Glossary

Terminology and spelling of native words vary among the people of the Mid-Columbia River. For consistency, the spelling of most of the native terms used in this book is taken from the only comprehensive reference available, the *Yakima Language Practical Dictionary* (Beavert 1975), or from Yakima language teachers, and reflects the dialect of the Sahaptin language spoken on the Yakima Reservation of Washington State.

*akw'alkt* (Wasco/Wishxam). Round bag for root-digging. See also *wapaas*.

*ala*. Grandmother on father's side; woman's son's child.

*anpsh*. Large basket for storing berries.

*At'at'atlia* (*At'at'ałia*). Wasco word for the legendary witch who liked to eat children, known also as T'at'ałya by Yakima people.

*Awl*. A pointed tool used to open a channel for the sewing element to enter on a coiled basket. Originally, the people of the Mid-Columbia used split and sharpened bones for this purpose.

*Basketry*. A manual weaving technique that, without the use of a frame or loom, employs semirigid materials to create a self-supporting object.

*Bast*. A strong, woody fiber from a plant used in cordage, matting, and fabrics.

*Bear grass* (*Xerophyllum tenax*). A perennial herb that grows in dense clumps of upright leaves in open woods and meadows at moderate to high elevations (3,000 to 6,000 feet). The strength and gloss of the leaves make them desirable as a decorative basket material. Known as *yai* to the people of the Mid-Columbia, the grass is used for the imbrication on Klikitat-style baskets. Also known as squaw grass and elk grass.

*Chinookan*. Language family that includes the Upper Chinook language spoken by the Cathlamet, Clackamas, Cascade, Wasco, and Wishxam people. On the Mid-Columbia the language is known as *Kiksht* or "Columbia River."

*Chinook Jargon*. A conglomerate language of American Indian, English, Spanish, French, and combination words that evolved during the fur trade era on the Columbia River (Ruby and Brown 1976, 112–13).

*ch'lay*. Dried and pounded salmon, also known as "salmon sugar" or "salmon flour."

*chmukli* (*chmaakli*). Black person.

*chuush* (*chiish* in Yakima dialects). Water.

*Coiling*. A basketry technique in which a stationary horizontal element or set of elements, the foundation, is sewn with moving vertical elements, the stitches, to form a continuous coil from start to rim. In Klikitat-style coiled baskets, the foundation is a bundle of split strands of cedar root; the stitching materials are the smoother outside portions of the cedar root. Close coiling occurs when the stitches are bound closely together, as in Klikitat baskets.

*Cornhusk bags.* A common name for the flat twined bags decorated in false embroidery by the weavers of the Columbia River and the plateau above.

*culla-culla.* Chinook Jargon for duck. Another version was *kweh-kweh.*

*Diagonal twining. See* Twining.

*False embroidery.* Also called "external weft wrap," this is a method of decorating a plain twined fabric with a third element (grass, cornhusk, or yarn in Columbia River twining) that is wrapped around the outside weft strand. The third element cannot be seen on the inner surface, except where the color begins and ends. The decorative element completely covers the twining stitch and can be identified by the stitch slant, which is in the opposite direction from the plain twining beneath. The name comes from the process of adding decoration during the weaving process rather than afterward, as in embroidery.

*Full-turn twining. See* Twining.

*Hard basket.* Term used by Cowlitz and other native people on the west side of the Cascades to describe a coiled basket.

*Hazel rope.* Shoots from hazelnut (*Corylus cornuta*) twisted until pliable, then used by hunters to tie bundles.

*Hop string.* Cotton twine strung in hop yards to support vines.

*Indian trading.* Exchange of goods of equal value.

*Imbrication.* A method of decorating the surface of a coiled basket with a third, flat, element that is caught under a sewing stitch, then folded forward over the stitch to conceal it. This is repeated over the entire basket in much Klikitat-style coiling. The name comes from the Latin *imbrex,* meaning a tile, for the tilelike appearance of the surface.

*Indian hemp (Apocynum cannabinum).* A dogbane known to Sahaptin-speakers as *taxos* or *taxus.* Tough fibers of the inner bark are spun to form a strong cordage.

*ititamat.* Calendar ball. A hemp string with knots and beads marking the days of a woman's life, rolled into a ball.

*Kalaasya.* The myth character Little Raccoon.

*kapin.* Stick for digging roots.

*katla (kała).* Grandmother on mother's side; also woman's daughter's child.

*Klamath/Modoc.* Related groups of native people from south central Oregon and northern California.

*kw'ınch.* Black lichen (*Alectoria* sp.) baked in the ground, stored, cooked in water to make a dessert. High in iron.

*lap'uy.* Folded cedar bark basket.

*luksh* (*sikáywa* in Yakima dialects). Canby's desert parsley (*Lomatium canbyi*), edible root species.

*Mid-Columbia.* As used in this book, the term refers to the region extending along the Columbia River and its tributaries roughly from the Priest Rapids in Washington State (the present site of Priest Rapids Dam) downstream to the Cascades (the present site of Bonneville Dam) where the river cuts through the Cascade Mountains.

*Mordant.* A chemical substance that combines with dye to enhance absorption of the color.

*mowitch.* Deer or venison in Chinook Jargon.

*Myth age.* The earliest of the time periods in which the ancient stories are set, when, according to Jarold Ramsey, "the great primal beginnings took place; there were no human beings yet; the world was peopled with animal-spirits in more or less human form . . ." (1977, xxiv).

*na'iɬas.* "My mother."

*naknuwisha.* "Caring for something precious."

*nakts ispalq.* Literally, "one bag" in Nez Perce.

*nusux.* Salmon.

*Olla.* Spanish for pot (esp. a jar), used to describe a container with rounded sides and a neck like a pottery vessel.

*pashxash.* Balsamroot (*Balsamorhiza* sp.), an Indian celery; *xasya* in Yakima dialect form.

*patu.* Snow peak, also spelled *pahtu.* The Yakima people refer to Mount Adams as *pahtu.*

*patl'aapa.* Woman's basket hat.

*pawap'asha.* "They are weaving."

*pish.* Fish, in Chinook Jargon.

*Plain twining. See* "Simple twining" under Twining.

*Plain weave.* Fabric in which one warp yarn interlaces with one weft yarn.

*Ply.* Two or more strands twisted together.

*pyaxi.* Bitterroot (*Lewisia rediviva*), edible root species. A long slender root dug in the spring. The outside skin is slipped off and the root dried in the sun, then stored to be boiled in water as needed.

*quadudk.* A word for frog in Chinook Jargon. Another form is *shwahkuk.*

*Sahaptian.* The language family which includes Nez Perce and Sahaptin languages.

*Sahaptin language.* A division of the Sahaptian language family. Various dialects of the Sahaptin language are spoken by the groups now enrolled on the Yakima and Warm Springs reservations with the exception of the Paiute, Wasco, and Wishxam people.

*Sally bags.* A common name for the round twined root-digging bags of the Mid-Columbia.

*sapk'ukt.* Woman's handbag.

*schklup.* A large coiled cedar root basket holding about ten gallons.

*Self-edge.* Finishing method on most full-turn twined hats and bags in which the warps are interlaced forming a braidlike finish above the final weft row.

*Served twined overlay.* A three-strand twining technique in which a decorative third strand lies over the external weft, twisting a full turn around the pair of wefts between each pair of warps. The third strand appears as a nearly vertical stitch between the warps on the inner face of the decorated portion of the weaving.

*shaptakay.* Folded container made of rawhide, a parfleche; known locally as Indian suitcase or trunk.

*shuyapu.* White man.

*Sisal.* Strong fiber grown in the West Indies and used for cordage.

*skolkol (shkúl kul).* Edible root species.

*Soft basket.* Term used by the Cowlitz and other native people on the west side of the Cascade Mountains to refer to a basket made by twining.

*Stitch slant.* The pitch or lean of the wefts. When viewed horizontally, in the normal orientation, a stitch that slants up to the right is described as S (the paired wefts in the twining stitch resemble the curve of an S on its side). A stitch that slants down to the right is described as Z (the twining stitch resembles a Z on its side).

*String.* A continuous strand of material spun from twisted fibers, usually of Indian hemp, cotton or other plant material when used in Mid-Columbia basketry.

*T'at'atlya (T'at'ałya) (Yakima).* Legendary witch woman who ate children. Known as *At'at'atlia* among the Wasco and Wishxam.

*taxos (taxus). See* Indian hemp.

*tillacum.* Chinook Jargon word for people, man, or person.

*tmaanit.* Berries, fruit.

*Tule. Scirpus acutus,* a stout perennial plant that grows in marshes and swampy ground at the edge of lakes and streams. Used for mats and bags by many native people of the Northwest.

*Tumpline.* A strap that goes across forehead or chest to support a basket carried on the back. The tumplines made by the people of the Mid-Columbia were twined and decorated with geometric designs on the wide band that crossed the forehead.

*Twill twining. See* "diagonal twining" under Twining.

*Twine.* To twist together.

*Twining.* A basket weaving method in which horizontal elements called wefts are twisted around one another as they interlace with vertical elements called warps. The wefts are active while the warps are passive. In Mid-Columbia twining, the warps are flexible and the technique creates a soft, textilelike basket.

In *simple twining* (also known as plain twining), two wefts are used and are crossed only once to engage each warp in turn. In Columbia River twining, wefts are usually twined in a **Z** stitch. The back weft is brought forward over the front, resulting in a stitch that slants down to the right.

In *full-turn twining* (also known as wrapped twining or full-twist twining), two wefts in different colors are used. The weaver crosses the wefts once or twice before engaging the next warp, to bring forward the desired color, making it possible to weave designs into the fabric of the basket. On the inner surface, the moving weft forms a series of vertical stitches, as opposed to the diagonal appearance of the stitch on the outside surface.

In *diagonal twining,* a basic weave characterized by raised diagonal lines across the "fabric" of the basket (also known as twill twining), a pair of warps is engaged alternately at each weft crossing. Each successive weft row separates the preceding pair of warps, creating a new pair and producing a diagonal effect on the surface.

*Twining off.* The finishing method on most flat twined bags, in which the warp ends are looped back into the final weft row.

*Umatilla Indian Reservation.* In northeastern Oregon, near the city of Pendleton. The reservation was established by treaty between the United States and the Umatilla, Cayuse, and Walla Walla people in 1855. Aboriginal territory at the time of the treaty was 6,400,000 acres. Remaining reservation lands in 1989 are about 85,500 acres.

*waashat.* A worship dance; also the name of a religion practiced by many native people in the Mid-Columbia region.

*wapaas.* Small basket. The term generally is used for a small round bag or basket worn around the waist while digging roots or picking berries. Wasco/Wishxam word for round bag is *akw'alkt.*

*wap'ani supk'ukt.* Woman's twined handbag.

*wap'asha.* To twine; literally, to touch, to lay one's hand on.

*wap'at* (noun). The art of weaving a basket.

*Warm Springs Reservation.* Established by treaty with the United States in 1855 on the eastern slopes of Cascade Mountains in north central Oregon. People enrolled on the Warm Springs Reservation are of Wasco, Warm Springs (Tygh, Tenino, Wyam, and John Day), and Paiute descent. Of these, the Wasco and Warm Springs ancestors considered the Mid-Columbia their homeland. Aboriginal territory included 6,500,000 acres, of which about 660,000 acres are in the reservation today.

*Warp.* The vertical element in a woven construction.

*Wasco.* The Chinookan-speaking people who lived along the Columbia on the south (now Oregon) side at The Dalles. Today their descendants are members of the Confederated Tribes of the Warm Springs Reservation of Oregon. The term often is used generically to describe all of the Chinookan-speaking bands of the Mid-Columbia region and to refer to their Upper Chinook language.

*wawxpa.* Flat bag for storing roots and other treasures.

*Weft.* The horizontal element in a woven construction, sometimes referred to as the "serving element."

*Wishxam.* The Chinookan-speaking people who lived along the Columbia River on the north (now Washington) side just upriver from The Dalles. Their descendants are enrolled on the Yakima Reservation in Washington. Variously spelled Wishram, Wishham, Wisham, this spelling was chosen to reflect the "back x" sound, similar to the sound of the Greek chi. Lt. Charles Wilkes (1845, 388) wrote that the name came from "a chief, long dead."

*xamsi.* Desert parsley (*Lomatium nudicaule*). One of several varieties of plants known as Indian celery.

*xaslu.* Star.

*xawsh.* Biscuit root or bread root (*Lomatium cous*). Dug in the spring and cooked fresh as a vegetable, or dried and ground to be used as thickening in soups or broth.

*xlaam.* Coiled basket made of cedar root.

*yai. See* Bear grass.

*Yakima Indian Reservation.* On the eastern slopes of the Cascade Mountains in south central Washington State. The 1,200,000-acre reservation was established by treaty with the United States in 1855. Fourteen bands and tribes who occupied about 12 million acres formed the Confederated Tribes of the Yakima Indian Nation at the time of the treaty. The bands—their names as spelled in the treaty—were the Kah-milt-pah, Klikitat, Klinquit, Kow-was-sayee, Li-ay-was, Ochechotes, Palouse, Pisquouse, Se-ap-cat, Shyiks, Skin-pah, Wenatshapam, Wish-Ham, and the Yakima.

*Yarn.* A continuous strand of material spun from twisted fibers. In Mid-Columbia basketry, the term usually is used for strands spun from wool. Strands spun from Indian hemp or other plant fibers are usually referred to as string or twine.

# Sources

Adovasio, J. M. *Basketry Technology: A Guide to Identification and Analysis*. Chicago: Aldine Publishing, 1977.

Aikens, C. Melvin. *Archaeology of Oregon*. U.S. Dept. of the Interior, Bureau of Land Management, Oregon State Office, 1984.

Anastasio, Angelo. *The Southern Plateau: An Ecological Analysis of Intergroup Relations*. Moscow: University of Idaho Laboratory of Anthropology, 1975.

Apostol, Jane. "Saving Grace," *Westways Magazine,* October 1976.

Azzouz, Bushra; Marlene Farnum; and Nettie Jackson Kuneki. "And Women Wove It in a Basket." Documentary film on Nettie Jackson. Portland, OR, 1989.

Beavert, Virginia (project director). *The Way It Was*. Toppenish, WA: Consortium of Johnson O'Malley Committees, Region IV, 1974.

———— (project coordinator). *Yakima Language Practical Dictionary*. Toppenish, WA: Consortium of Johnson O'Malley Committees, Region IV, 1975.

Beer, James M. "The First Congregational Church in The Dalles," *Senior Highlights,* p. 2, December 1984.

Bella, Rick. "The Culture That Cedar Made," *Oregonian* 30, October 1983.

Bergland, Eric O. "Evidence for Native American Bark Containers from the Western Cascades of Oregon." Paper presented at the Northwest Anthropological Conference, Eugene, OR, March 1990.

Bernstein, Bruce. "Native Explanatory Principles." Paper presented at the Native American Art Studies Conference, Seattle, WA, September 1983.

Boas, Franz. *Primitive Art*. New York: Dover Publications, 1955. (Originally pub. 1927.)

Brasser, Ted J. *A Basketful of Indian Culture Change*. Canadian Ethnology Service Paper, no. 22. Ottawa: National Museums of Canada, 1975.

Burnham, Dorothy K. *The Comfortable Arts: Traditional Spinning and Weaving in Canada*. Ottawa: National Museums of Canada, 1981.

Cahodas, Marvin. "Two and Three Dimensional Approach to Basket Design in Northern and Central California." Paper presented at conference, "Native American Basketry of Western North America: An Overview," Seattle Art Museum, 15 March 1981.

Cheney Cowles Memorial Museum. *Cornhusk Bags of the Plateau Indians*. Cheney: Eastern Washington State Historical Society, 1974.

Clark, Ella E. *Indian Legends of the Pacific Northwest*. Berkeley: University of California Press, 1953.

Coe, Ralph T. *Sacred Circles: Two Thousand Years of North American Indian Art*. Kansas City, MO: Nelson Gallery Foundation, 1977.

————. *Lost and Found Traditions*. New York: American Federation of the Arts; Seattle: University of Washington Press, 1986.

Cole, Douglas. *Captured Heritage: The Scramble for Northwest Coast Artifacts*. Seattle: University of Washington Press; Vancouver, B.C.: Douglas and McIntyre, 1985.

Collier, Mrs. Chas. "Survey of Indian Arts and Crafts, April 1934." Bureau of Indian Affairs, Washington, D.C., 1934.

Collings, Jerold. "American Indian Basketry," *Southwest Art,* pp. 102–13, June 1982.

Confederated Tribes of the Warm Springs Reservation of Oregon. *The People of Warm Springs.* 1984.

Conn, Richard. "Indian Arts of the Intermontane Region," *American Indian Art: Form and Tradition,* pp. 71–75. Minneapolis: Walker Art Center, 1972.

———. *Native American Art in the Denver Art Museum.* Denver: Denver Art Museum, 1975.

Connette, Ann. "Nez Perce Indian Arts and Crafts Revival," *Handweaver and Craftsman* 21, Fall 1970.

Cressman, Luther S.; David L. Cole; Wilbur A. Davis; Thomas M. Newman; and Daniel J. Scheans. "Cultural Sequences at The Dalles, Oregon," *American Philosophical Society Transactions* 50, pt. 10, 1960.

Currens, Gerald E. "The Festive Gathering Among the Yakima." Manuscript, Dept. of Anthropology, University of Oregon, 1970.

Curtis, Edward S. "The Yakima, the Klickitat, Salishan Tribes of the Interior, the Kutenai," *The North American Indian.* Vol. 7. Norwood, MA: Plimpton Press, 1911a. (Reprinted 1970; New York: Johnson.)

———. "The Nez Perces, Wallawalla, Umatilla, Cayuse, the Chinookan Tribes," *The North American Indian.* Vol. 8. Norwood, MA: Plimpton Press, 1911b. (Reprinted 1970; New York: Johnson.)

Curtis, Winterton C. *A Yankee Boy on Oregon Trails.* 1956. (Reprinted from *The Dalles Chronicle,* November and December 1955.)

Cutright, Paul R. *Lewis and Clark: Pioneering Naturalists.* Urbana: University of Illinois Press, 1969.

———. *Contributions of Philadelphia to Lewis and Clark History.* WPO Publication no. 6, July 1982. Lewis and Clark Trail Heritage Foundation.

Dalton, O. M. "California: Basketwork," *Man* 1, pp. 23–24, 1901.

DeVoto, Bernard, ed. *The Journals of Lewis and Clark.* Boston: Houghton Mifflin, 1953.

Dockstader, Frederick J. *Indian Art in North America: Arts and Crafts.* Greenwich, CT: New York Graphic Society, 1961.

———. *Indian Art of the Americas.* New York: Museum of the American Indian, Heye Foundation, 1973.

———. *Weaving Arts of the North American Indian.* New York: Thomas Y. Crowell, 1978.

Doubleday, Mrs. F. N. "Discouraging Basketry Arts: Two Ways to Help the Indians," *The Indian's Friend* (monthly pub. of the Women's National Indian Assn.) 8, January 1901.

Douglas, David. *Douglas's Journals.* Published under direction of the Royal Horticultural Society. New York: Antiquarian Press, 1959.

Douglas, Frederic H., and René d'Harnoncourt. *Indian Art of the United States.* New York: Museum of Modern Art, 1941.

Drucker, Philip. *Cultures of the North Pacific Coast.* Scranton, PA: Chandler Publishing Co., 1965.

DuBois, Cora. *The Feather Cult of the Middle Columbia.* General Series in Anthropology, no. 7. Menasha, WN: George Banta, 1938.

Eliade, Mircea. *Shamanism: Archaic Techniques of Ecstasy.* Bollingen Series, no. 76. Princeton, NJ: Princeton University Press, 1972.

Erdoes, Richard, and Alfonso Ortiz, eds. *American Indian Myths and Legends*. New York: Pantheon, 1985.

Evans, Glen L., and T. N. Campbell. *Indian Baskets of the Paul T. Seashore Collection*. Museum Notes, no. 11, Texas Memorial Museum, Austin, 1970.

Everette, Will E., MD. "Indian Languages of North America, Yakima, Vol. 2, 1883." Manuscript no. 698, National Anthropological Archives, Smithsonian Institution, Washington, D.C.

Farrand, Livingston. "Basketry Designs of the Salish Indians," *Memoirs of the American Museum of Natural History* 2, no. 5, pp. 391–99, 1900.

Ferrier, Chester M. "The Native American Basket Cap of the Eastern United States: A Study of Woven Headgear and Its Supporting Technology." Master's thesis, University of Washington, 1978.

Filloon, Ray M. "Huckleberry Pilgrimage." *Pacific Discovery* 5, pp. 4–13, May–June 1952.

Fletcher, Alice C. "Ethnologic Gleanings Among the Nez Percés." Manuscript no. 4558 (57), National Anthropological Archives, Smithsonian Institution, Washington, D.C., 1891.

————. Papers. Miscellaneous notes—general, *Askilwesh*. Manuscript no. 4558 (63), National Anthropological Archives, Smithsonian Institution, Washington, D.C., ca. 1891.

Fraser, David W. *A Guide to Weft Twining and Related Structures with Interacting Wefts*. Philadelphia: University of Pennsylvania Press, 1989.

French, Kathrine Story. "Culture Segments and Variations in Contemporary Social Ceremonialism on the Warm Springs Reservation." Ph.D. dissertation, Columbia University, 1955.

Frohman Trading Co. *Alaska, California and Northern Indian Baskets and Curios*. Portland, OR: Crocker Press, 1902. (Reprinted 1977; Portland: Binfords & Mort.)

Gabrielson, Ira N., and Stanley G. Jewett. *Birds of the Pacific Northwest*. New York: Dover Pub., 1970.

Gibbs, George. *Indian Tribes of Washington Territory*. 1855. Reprint of sections from U.S. War Department Report of Explorations and Surveys. Fairfield, WA: Ye Galleon Press, 1978.

Gibson, James R. *Farming the Frontier: The Agricultural Opening of the Oregon Country, 1786–1846*. Seattle, WA: University of Washington Press; Vancouver, B.C.: University of British Columbia Press, 1985.

Gogol, John M. "Basketry of the Columbia River Indians," *American Indian Basketry Magazine* 1, no. 1, 1979.

————. "Rose Frank Shows How to Make a Nez Perce Cornhusk Bag," *American Indian Basketry Magazine* 1, no. 2, pp. 22–30, 1980.

————. "Klamath, Modoc, and Shasta Basketry," *American Indian Basketry Magazine* 3, no. 2, pp. 4–15, 1983.

————. "American Indian Art: Values and Aesthetics," *American Indian Basketry Magazine* 4, no. 4, pp. 4–30, 1984.

————. "The Golden Decade of Collecting Indian Basketry," *American Indian Basketry Magazine* 5, no. 1, pp. 12–29, 1985a.

————. "Columbia River/Plateau Indian Beadwork," *American Indian Basketry Magazine* 5, no. 2, pp. 4–28, 1985b.

————. "Cowlitz Indian Basketry," *American Indian Basketry Magazine* 5, no. 4, pp. 4–20, 1985c.

Grace Nicholson Collection. Albums and ledger. Robert H. Lowie Museum of Anthropology, University of California, Berkeley.

———. Papers, and Summary Report. Henry E. Huntington Library, San Marino, California.

Guppy, Ruth. "Bon Ton Closure Ends Old Era," *Hood River New,* 13 April 1988.

Haeberlin, H. K.; James A. Teit; and Helen H. Roberts. "Coiled Basketry in British Columbia and Surrounding Region," *Forty-first Annual Report of the Bureau of American Ethnology, 1919–1924.* Washington, D.C.: Government Printing Office, 1928.

Harsant, Wendy J. "The Otago Museum, Dunedin, New Zealand: The North American Indian Collection," *American Indian Art* 13, pp. 38–45, Spring 1988.

Held, Shirley E. *Weaving: A Handbook of the Fiber Arts.* New York: Holt, Rinehart and Winston, 1978.

Hicks, Russell. "Culturally Altered Trees: A Data Source," *Northwest Anthropological Research Notes* 19, pp. 100–18, Spring 1985.

Housely, Lucille. "Lithosols: Grocery Stores in the Plateau and Great Basin." Paper presented at the Thirty-seventh Annual Northwest Anthropological Conference, Spokane, WA, March 1984.

Hunn, Eugene. "Sahaptin Plant Terms." Manuscript for Consortium of Johnson O'Malley Committees, Region IV, 1978.

———. "On the Relative Contribution of Men and Women to Subsistence Among Hunter-Gatherers of the Columbia Plateau: A Comparison with *Ethnographic Atlas* Summaries," *Journal of Ethnobiology* 1, pp. 124–34, 1981.

Hunn, Eugene, and David H. French. "Lomatium: A Key Resource for Columbia Plateau Subsistence," *Northwest Science* 55, pp. 87–94, 1981.

Hymes, Dell. "Bungling Host, Benevolent Host: Louis Simpson's 'Deer and Coyote,' " *American Indian Quarterly,* pp. 171–98, Summer 1984.

Irving, Washington. *Astoria: Anecdotes of an Enterprise Beyond the Rocky Mountains.* Vols. 1 and 2. Philadelphia, PA: Carey, Lea and Blanchard, 1836.

Jackson, Donald, ed. *Letters of the Lewis and Clark Expedition with Related Documents, 1783–1854.* Urbana: University of Illinois Press, 1962.

Jacobs, Melville. *Northwest Sahaptin Texts.* University of Washington Publications in Anthropology, no. 2, pp. 175–244, 1929.

———. *Northwest Sahaptin Texts, Part 1.* Columbia University Contributions to Anthropology, no. 19. New York: Columbia University Press, 1934.

Jacobson, Martin. *Insecticides from Plants: A Review of the Literature.* U.S. Department of Agriculture, n.d.

James, George Wharton. *Indian Basketry.* New York: Dover Publications, 1972. (Originally published 1909.)

Kahlenberg, Mary Hunt, and Anthony Berlant. *The Navajo Blanket.* Los Angeles, CA: Praeger Publishers, 1972.

Kent, Kate Peck. *The Story of Navaho Weaving.* Phoenix, AR: Heard Museum, 1961.

Kiefer, Kathy. "Captions for Wanapum Dam Tour Center." Typescript. Public Utility District of Grant County, Washington, 1988.

Krieger, Herbert W. "Aspects of Aboriginal Decorative Art in America Based on Specimens in the U.S. National Museum." *Smithsonian Institution Report for 1930,* Publication 3102, pp. 519–56. Washington, D.C.: Government Printing Office, 1931.

Krieger Papers. "Report of Federal Project 418–Indians." National Anthropological Archives, Smithsonian Institution, Washington, D.C., 1934.

Kuhlken, Robert. "Selected Factors Affecting Rangeland Use on the Warm Springs Indian Reservation." Unpublished research paper, Dept. of Geography, Oregon State University, 1982.

Kuneki, Nettie J.; Elsie Thomas; and Marie Slockish. *The Heritage of Klickitat Basketry*. Portland: Oregon Historical Society Press, 1982.

Lester, Joan. "The American Indian: A Museum's Eye View," *Indian Historian* 5, no. 2, pp. 25–31, 1972.

Lewis, Albert Buell. "Tribes of the Columbia Valley and the Coast of Washington and Oregon," *Memoirs of the American Anthropological Association* 1, pp. 147–209, 1906.

Libhart, Myles. "To Dress with Great Care," *American Indian Art* 14, pp. 38–51, Spring 1989.

Lobb, Allan. *Indian Baskets of the Northwest Coast*. Portland, OR: Graphic Arts Center Publishing, 1978.

Lubell, Cecil, ed. *Textile Collections of the World*. Vol. 1: United States and Canada. New York: Van Nostrand, Reinhold, 1976.

McArthur, Harriet. "Basketry of the Northwest." In *Basketry of the Coast and Islands of the Pacific*. Portland, OR: Portland Library, 1896.

———. "Flax Culture in Early Days," *Oregon Historical Quarterly* 12, pp. 118–19, 1911.

McFarland, Lena, and Wanda Clark. "The Family of Ira Hawley." Manuscript in family collection, Redmond, OR, 1960.

McKelvey, Susan D. *Botanical Explorations of the TransMississippi West, 1790–1850*. Cambridge, MA: Harvard University Press, 1955.

McLendon, Sally. "Preparing Museum Collections for Use as Primary Data in Ethnographic Research." In *The Research Potential of Anthropological Museum Collections,* ed. Anne M. Cantwell, Annals of New York Academy of Science, 1981.

McLendon, Sally, and Brenda Shears Holland. "The Basketmaker: The Pomoans of California." In *The Ancestors: Native Artisans of the Americas,* ed. A. C. Roosevelt and J. G. E. Roosevelt. New York: Museum of the American Indian, Heye Foundation, 1979.

Mack, Cheryl A., and Barbara J. Hollenbeck. "Peeled Cedar Management Plan." Gifford Pinchot National Forest, Vancouver, WA, December 1985.

Malin, Edward. "Folklore. Art of the American Indian and Eskimo," *Smoke Signals* 46, pp. 3–12, Autumn 1965.

Marden, Guy. "Cultural Resource Surveys in the Southern Washington Cascade Mountains, 1980." Paper presented at 40th Northwest Anthropological Conference, Gleneden Beach, OR, March 1987.

Marr, Carolyn J. "Wrapped Twined Baskets of the Southern Northwest Coast: A New Form with an Ancient Past," *American Indian Art* 13, pp. 54–63, Summer 1988.

Mason, Otis T. "Directions for Collectors of American Basketry." Part P of *Bulletin of the United States National Museum,* no. 39. Washington, D.C.: Government Printing Office, 1902.

———. *Aboriginal American Indian Basketry*. Santa Barbara and Salt Lake City: Peregrine Smith, 1976. (Originally published 1904.)

Maurer, Evan M. *The Native American Heritage: A Survey of North American Indian Art*. Chicago: University of Chicago Press, 1977.

Meany, Edmond S., ed. *Mount Rainier: A Record of Exploration*. Portland, OR: Binfords and Mort, 1916.

Middle Oregon Indian Historical Society. "The Root Feast Ceremony." Confederated Tribes of the Warm Springs Reservation of Oregon, 1987.

Miller, Christopher L. *Prophetic Worlds: Indians and Whites on the Columbia Plateau*. New Brunswick, NJ: Rutgers University Press, 1985.

Miller, G. Lynette. "Flat Twined Bags of the Plateau." Master's thesis, University of Washington, 1986.

Minor, Rick. "Lower Columbia Study Unit," *The Thunderbird* 7, no. 3, pp. 4–5, 1986.

Molson, Mrs. William Markland. Papers. McCord Museum, McGill University, Montreal.

Molson, Velina P. "The Basket of the Klickitat." In *Basketry of the Coast and Islands of the Pacific*. Portland, OR: Portland Library, 1896.

Montgomery, Florence N. *Textiles in America: 1650–1870*. New York: W. W. Norton, 1984.

Mooney, James. *The Ghost Dance Religion and the Sioux Outbreak of 1890*. Fourteenth Annual Report of the Bureau of Ethnology. Washington, D.C.: Government Printing Office, 1896. (Reprinted 1965. Chicago: University of Chicago Press.)

Moulton, Gary E., ed. *Atlas of the Lewis and Clark Expedition*. Lincoln: University of Nebraska Press, 1983.

Murphey, Edith V. A. *Indian Uses of Native Plants*. Fort Bragg, CA: Mendocino County Historical Society, 1959.

Neils, Selma M. *So This Is Klickitat*. Klickitat, WA: Klickitat Women's Club, 1967.

Nicholson, Grace. *See* Grace Nicholson Collection.

Osborne, Douglas. "Excavations in the McNary Reservoir Basin Near Umatilla, Oregon." *River Basin Survey Papers,* no. 8, Smithsonian Institution, Bureau of American Ethnology Bulletin 166. Washington, D.C.: Government Printing Office, 1957.

Phillips, Ruth B. "Like a Star I Shine: Northern Woodlands Artistic Traditions." In *The Spirit Sings,* Calgary: Glenbow-Alberta Institute, 1987.

Portland Library. *Basketry of the Coast and Islands of the Pacific*. Portland, OR, 1896.

Ramsey, Jarold. *Coyote Was Going There*. Seattle: University of Washington Press, 1977.

Ray, Verne F. "The Sanpoil and Nespelem: Salishan Peoples of Northeastern Washington." *University of Washington Publications in Anthropology* 5. Seattle: University of Washington Press, 1932.

Ray, Verne F., et al. "Tribal Distribution in Eastern Oregon and Adjacent Regions." *American Anthropologist* 40, pp. 384–415, 1938.

———. "Culture Element Distribution." *University of California Anthropological Records* 8, no. 2, 1942.

Relander, Click, ed. *1855–1955: The Yakimas*. Toppenish, WA: Yakima Indian Nation, 1955.

———. *Drummers and Dreamers*. Caldwell, ID: Caxton Printers, 1956.

———. *Strangers on the Land*. Toppenish, WA: Yakima Indian Nation, 1962.

Ross, Marvin C., ed. *George Catlin: Episodes from Life Among the Indians and Last Rambles*. Norman: University of Oklahoma Press, 1959.

Rossbach, Ed. *Baskets As Textile Art*. New York: Van Nostrand Reinhold, 1973.

Ruby, Robert H., and John A. Brown. *The Chinook Indians*. Norman: University of Oklahoma Press, 1976.

Samuel, Cheryl. *The Chilkat Dancing Blanket*. Seattle, WA: Pacific Search Press, 1982.

Schlick, Mary D. *Design Elements in Yakima Weaving: A Source for Learning Materials*. Kamiakin Research Institute, Toppenish, WA, 1977.

———. "Strongheart Chronology." Paper prepared for Washington Press Women, Toppenish, WA, 1979a.

———. "A Columbia River Indian Basket Collected by Lewis and Clark," *American Indian Basketry Magazine* 1, no. 1, pp. 10–13, 1979b.

———. "Art Treasures of the Columbia Plateau," *American Indian Basketry Magazine* 1, no. 2 pp. 12–20, 1980.

———. "Cedar Bark Baskets," *American Indian Basketry Magazine* 4, no. 3, pp. 26–29, 1984a.

———. "Klickitat Weavers Continue Tradition," *Hood River* (Oregon) *News* (25 April), 1984b.

———. "Wasco Wishxam Basketry: Who Were the Weavers?" *American Indian Basketry Magazine* 5, no. 4, pp. 21–27, 1985.

Schlick, Mary D., and Kate C. Duncan. "Wasco-Style Woven Beadwork: Merging Artistic Traditions," *American Indian Art* 16, no. 3, pp. 36–45, Summer 1991.

Schuster, Helen H. *Yakima Indian Traditionalism: A Study in Continuity and Change*. Ph.D. dissertation, University of Washington. Ann Arbor: University Microfilms, 1975.

———. *The Yakimas: A Critical Bibliography*. Bloomington: Indiana University Press, 1982.

Scott, Leslie M. "Indian Women as Food Providers and Tribal Counselors." *Oregon Historical Quarterly* 42, pp. 208–19, 1941.

Seaman, N. G. *Indian Relics of the Northwest*. Portland, OR: Binfords and Mort, 1967.

Selam, Leroy B. "Cultural Position of the Yakima People in Relation to Water." Photocopy. Yakima Indian Agency, Toppenish, WA, 1974.

Sellers, Charles Coleman. *Mr. Peale's Museum*. New York: W. W. Norton, 1980.

Seymour, Flora Warren. "Report on the Warm Springs Indian Reservation, Oregon." Manuscript no. 4525, Box 6, National Anthropological Archives, Washington, D.C., 1931.

Shackelford, R. S. "Legend of the Klickitat Basket," *American Anthropologist* 2, pp. 779–80, 1900.

———. "The Wasco Sally Bag," *Sunset*, pp. 258–59, January 1904.

Shane, Ralph M. "Early Explorations Through the Warm Springs Reservation Area." Reprint from *Oregon Historical Quarterly*, December 1950.

Shawley, Stephen D. "Nez Perce Dress: A Study in Culture Change." *University of Idaho Anthropological Research Manuscript Series* 44, 1974.

———. "Hemp and Cornhusk Bags of the Plateau Indians," *Indian America* 9, pp. 25–30, Spring 1975.

Smith, Marian W. *The Puyallup-Nisqually*. New York: Columbia University Press, 1940.

Spier, Leslie, and Edward Sapir. "Wishram Ethnography." *Publications in Anthropology* 3, p. 3, 1930.

Spinden, Herbert J. "The Nez Perce Indians." *Memoirs of the American Anthropological Association* 2, no. 3, pp. 165–274, 1908.

Splawn, Andrew Jackson. *Ka-mi-akin, Last Hero of the Yakimas*. Yakima, WA: Caxton Printers, 1958. (Originally published 1917.)

Stafford, Kim R. *Having Everything Right*. New York: Penguin Books, 1987.

Stowell, Cynthia. "Indians Dig Roots for Spring Ritual," *The Oregonian,* 17 April 1980.

Strong, Emory. *Stone Age on the Columbia River*. Portland, OR: Binfords and Mort, 1967.

Strong, W. Duncan; W. Egbert Schenck; and Julian H. Steward. "Archaeology of The Dalles–Deschutes Region." *University of California Publications in American Archaeology and Ethnology* 29, no. 1, 1930.

Taylor, Ronald J., and Rolf W. Valum. *Wildflowers, 2: Sagebrush Country*. Beaverton: Touchstone Press, 1974.

Teit, James A. "Basketry of Neighbors of the Thompson." *Forty-first Annual Report of the Bureau of American Ethnology,* 1919–1924. Washington, D.C.: Government Printing Office, 1928.

———. "The Salish Tribes of the Western Plateaus." *Forty-fifth Annual Report of the Bureau of American Ethnology*. Washington, D.C.: Government Printing Office, 1930.

Thompson, David. *David Thompson's Narrative of His Explorations in Western America, 1784–1814*. Ed. by Joseph Burr Tyrell. Toronto: The Champlain Society, 1916.

Thompson, Nile, and Carolyn Marr. *Crow's Shells: Artistic Basketry of Puget Sound*. Seattle, WA: Dushuyay Publications, 1983.

Thwaites, Rueben Gold, ed. *The Original Journals of Lewis and Clark*. New York: Dodd, Mead and Company, 1905.

Toelken, Barre. "The Basket Imperative." In *Pacific Basket Makers: A Living Tradition,* ed. Suzi Jones. Fairbanks: University of Alaska Museum, 1983.

Toepel, Kathryn Anne; William F. Willingham; and Rick Minor. "Cultural Resource Overview of Bureau of Land Management Lands in North Central Oregon: Ethnography, Archaeology, History." *University of Oregon Anthropology Papers,* no. 17, 1980.

*Toppenish* (Washington) *Review*. "Powdered Salmon Traditional Fare," 21 November 1977.

Townsend, John K. "Narrative of a Journey Across the Rocky Mountains to the Columbia River," in *Early Western Travels: 1784–1846,* ed. R. G. Thwaites, vol. 21. Cleveland, OH: Arthur H. Clarke Co., 1905.

Turner, Nancy J. *Plants in British Columbian Indian Technology*. Handbook, no. 38. Victoria: British Columbia Provincial Museum, 1979.

Tyrell, Joseph Burr. *See* Thompson, David.

U.S. Army, Medical Dept. Register, Jan. 1862. Portland: Oregon Historical Society.

U.S. Forest Service. "Picking Huckleberries in the Gifford Pinchot National Forest." Leaflet available from Forest Supervisor, 500 W. 12th St., Vancouver, Washington. n.d.

Warm Springs Reservation Committee. "The Sucker and the Eel," *Tales of Coyote and Other Legends,* Book 10; *Chipmunk Meets Old Witch,* Book 12. The Indian Reading Series, Level I. Portland, OR: Northwest Regional Educational Laboratory, 1977.

Washington State Arts Commission. *Workbook: Beyond Blue Mountains*. Art in Public Places Program, 1988.

Weber, Ronald L. "Tsimshian Twined Basketry: Stylistic and Cultural Relationships," *American Indian Basketry Magazine* 2, no. 2, pp. 26–30, 1982.

Weddle, Ferris. "A Primitive but Better Tool," *Sunday Oregonian,* 23 April 1978.

Weltfish, Gene. "Prehistoric Native American Basketry Techniques and Modern Distribution," *American Anthropologist* 32, no. 3, pt. 1, pp. 454–95, 1930.

Wheat, Margaret M. *Survival Arts of the Primitive Paiutes*. Reno: University of Nevada Press, 1967.

Whiteford, Andrew Hunter. "Fiber Bags of the Great Lakes Indians," *American Indian Art* 2, Winter 1977.

Wilkes, Charles. *Narrative of the United States Exploring Expedition*. Vol. 4. Philadelphia: Lea and Blanchard, 1845. (Reprinted 1970. Upper Saddle River, NJ: Gregg Press.)

Williams, Lewis D. "Nez Perce Vocabulary." Manuscript no. 685, Smithsonian Institution National Anthropological Archives, 14 July 1896.

Wright, Robin K. "The Collection of Native Art in Washington: New Georgia Through Statehood," *American Indian Art* 14, Summer 1989.

———. "A Collection History: Washington Native Art." In *A Time of Gathering: Native Heritage in Washington State* Seattle, WA: Burke Museum, 1991.

Yakima Nation Museum. "The Yakima Time Ball." Toppenish, WA: Yakima Nation Media Program, 1984.

Zucker, Jeff; Kay Hummer; and Bob Høgfoss. *Oregon Indians: Culture, History and Current Affairs, An Atlas and Introduction*. Portland: Oregon Historical Society Press, 1983.

# Index